THE ROMANCE OF TUSCANY, ITALY

The Romance of Tuscany, Italy

RAFEAL MECHLORE

WSM Publisher

Contents

INDEX	1
INTRODUCTION	3
Chapter 1	16
Chapter 2	36
Chapter 3	55
Chapter 4	75
Chapter 5	93
Chapter 6	111
Chapter 7	127
Chapter 8	143
Chapter 9	163
Chapter 10	184

INDEX

Introduction

1. Setting the Stage: Tuscany's Timeless Allure
2. The Power of Place: Tuscany's Romantic Charm
3. Purpose of the Book

Chapter 1: Tuscany's Enchanting Landscapes
1.1 The Rolling Hills of Chianti
1.2 The Olive Groves and Vineyards
1.3 Cypress-Lined Roads
1.4 Picturesque Villages and Towns
1.5 The Mystical Beauty of Tuscany's Coastline

Chapter 2: A Journey Through Tuscany's Rich History
2.1 Etruscans: The First Inhabitants
2.2 The Renaissance: Tuscany's Golden Age
2.3 Medici Legacy and Florence
2.4 The Artistic and Architectural Wonders of Tuscany
2.5 Tuscan Traditions and Culture

Chapter 3: Culinary Delights of Tuscany
3.1 Tuscan Cuisine: Simple, Fresh, and Flavorful
3.2 Tasting the Chianti Wines
3.3 Olive Oil and Truffle Delights
3.4 Dining in Charming Tuscan Trattorias
3.5 Preparing Tuscan Dishes: Recipes and Cooking Classes

Chapter 4: The Language of Love in Tuscany

4.1 The Musicality of the Italian Language
4.2 Love and Romance in Italian Culture
4.3 Romantic Phrases and Expressions
4.4 Love Stories and Legends from Tuscany

Chapter 5: Tuscan Villas and Retreats
5.1 A Romantic Stay in a Tuscan Villa
5.2 Exploring Tuscany's Luxury Retreats
5.3 Honeymooning in Tuscany
5.4 Spa and Wellness Escapes

Chapter 6: Tuscany's Festivals and Celebrations
6.1 The Palio di Siena: A Horse Race like no other
6.2 Tuscany's Festivals of Love
6.3 Witnessing Traditional Tuscan Celebrations
6.4 Creating Your Own Celebration in Tuscany

Chapter 7: Exploring Tuscany's Art and Architecture
7.1 The Uffizi Gallery and the Art of Florence
7.2 The Leaning Tower of Pisa
7.3 Siena Piazza del Campo
7.4 The Artistic Legacy of Tuscany

Chapter 8: Love and Romance in Tuscan Literature
8.1 Dante Alighieri's Divine Comedy
8.2 Petrarch's Sonnets to Laura
8.3 Boccaccio's The Decameron
8.4 Modern Tuscan Writers and Poets

Chapter 9: Tuscany's Hidden Romantic Gems
9.1 Exploring Lesser-Known Tuscan Destinations
9.2 Secret Gardens and Hidden Courtyards
9.3 Romantic Strolls and Off-the-Beaten-Path Adventures

Chapter 10: Practical Tips for a Romantic Getaway
10.1 Planning Your Romantic Tuscany Trip
10.2 Traveling in Tuscany: Transportation and Accommodation
10.3 Romantic Gestures and Activities
10.4 Packing for Tuscany: Essentials and Wardrobe Tips

INTRODUCTION

Tuscany, in Italy, is known for being a location that expertly combines love, beauty, and enduring allure. The very name conjures up visions of rolling hills blanketed with vineyards and olive groves, medieval villages nestled amid cypress trees, and art and architecture that have inspired people all over the world for hundreds of years. The allure of Tuscany is one that is elevated above the mundane and compels lovers, dreamers, and wanderers to make their way to its very center.

We set sail on a magical adventure in "The Romance of Tuscany, Italy: A Journey Through Love and Beauty," which takes us deep into the heart of one of the most enthralling regions in all of Italy: Tuscany. This book is a celebration of all things romantic and beautiful. It is an ode to the vistas that appear to have been ripped from a dream. It is a trip through the annals of history and culture. And it is a toast to the gastronomic and cultural treasures that make Tuscany an unparalleled destination.

Tuscany is a visual symphony that incorporates all of the colors that nature has to offer as a result of its stunning landscapes, which range from the rolling hills of Chianti to the rough coastline. You will find roads lined with cypress trees that call you to discover gorgeous towns and villages, each of which has a story to tell. These landscapes, which are illuminated by a warm golden light, are a canvas for an artist, and the fascination they exude is ingrained in the memories of anybody who visits them.

However, Tuscany is much more than a gorgeous scene to look at. Since it has been inhabited ever since the time of the mysterious Etruscans, it is considered to be the cradle of history. Tuscany first made its influence on the rest of the world during the Renaissance, which is considered the region's golden period. The Italian Renaissance, a period of artistic, cultural, and intellectual awakening that continues to have an influence on the globe even today, began in Florence, a city that is considered to be the crown gem of Tuscany.

The legacy of the Medici family is intertwined with the history and culture of Tuscany. The Medici were a prominent family that not only supported some of the most renowned artists and intellectuals but also had a significant impact on the direction that Florence's history would take. Their legacy lives on in the palaces, museums, and libraries that are located throughout the city.

Tuscany is where you'll find the most authentic examples of Italian cuisine, which is famous across the world for its delicacy and ease of preparation.

In this town, eating is considered an art form, and masterpieces of cuisine are created using seasonal, locally sourced ingredients. Dining in Tuscany is an experience that goes beyond the palate and penetrates the soul. Whether you are relishing a bowl of traditional ribollita or indulging in a juicy bistecca alla fiorentina, dining in Tuscany is a memorable event.

Tuscany is a place where love is embedded into the very fabric of the region. The musicality of the Italian language, combined with its expressions of affection that generate a sense of yearning and passion, makes the language a seductive one. We investigate the language of love in "The Romance of Tuscany," unearthing beautiful phrases and sentiments that have enthralled lovers for generations. Tuscany is the setting for this investigation.

The scenery, history, and culture of Tuscany are the perfect ingredients for a love story that goes well beyond words. Couples are able to choose the ideal setting for their own love tale at the classic villas and retreats that are located across the region. Honeymooners find places that are like something out of a dream, and people who frequent spas can feel their spirits being revived by the natural environment.

Joy and affection may be felt throughout the year thanks to all of Tuscany's festivals and celebrations. Participate in the exhilarating Palio di Siena, lose yourself in the celebrations of love that are held throughout Tuscany, and plan your own party while drawing inspiration from the region's extensive cultural heritage.

The art and architecture of Tuscany are rich with tales of passion and inventiveness. The region is home to some of the world's most famous works of art and architecture, such as the Leaning Tower of Pisa and the masterpieces on display at Florence's Uffizi Gallery.

And love isn't simply a motif in Tuscany; it's also a significant component of the literary tradition of the region. The writers of the "Divine Comedy" by Dante Alighieri, "The Decameron" by Boccaccio, and the sonnets of Petrarch were all influenced by the love and beauty that they observed in their surroundings in Tuscany. Tuscan poets and novelists of the modern day continue to draw inspiration from the region.

THE ROMANCE OF TUSCANY, ITALY ~ 5

This book reveals hidden romantic jewels and off-the-beaten-path excursions in Tuscany, including secret gardens, hidden courtyards, and delightful strolls that allow moments of intimacy and connection. While Tuscany's well-known locations are adored, this book also reveals hidden romantic gems in the region.

You will also have access to helpful suggestions for the logistical aspects of organizing your

romantic trip to Tuscany, such as recommendations for modes of transportation, accommodations, romantic gestures, and basics for packing. If you want to write your own love story set in Tuscany, "The Romance of Tuscany" is the reliable guide you need.

This book is a riveting tour of one of the most romantic destinations in the world. It is also an invitation to immerse yourself in the ageless appeal of Tuscany, as well as a chance to discover the various dimensions of love and beauty that this region has to offer. This book is your passport to a world of love and beauty in the very center of Italy. Whether you're planning a romantic getaway, daydreaming about Tuscany, or simply wishing to be transported to a place of unrivaled charm, this book is your ticket to a world of love and beauty in Italy.

1. Setting the Stage: Tuscany's Timeless Allure

   Tuscany, with its ageless fascination, is a region that unfailingly grabs the hearts of those who journey into its breathtaking landscapes and immerse themselves in its rich cultural tapestry. Tuscany is home to some of Italy's most famous art and architecture, as well as some of the country's most famous wineries. This picturesque location, which can be found in the middle of Italy, has been luring tourists and people looking for romantic opportunities for many years. In order to get a complete understanding of the allure that is Tuscany, it is necessary to investigate the factors that contribute to the region's enduring allure. Tuscany's attractiveness is a tribute to the peaceful coexistence of nature and culture. From the undulating hills and rolling vineyards to the charming villages and the ever-present perfume of blooming flowers in the air, the allure of Tuscany is a testament to the coexistence of nature and culture.
   The Scenery of One's Nightmares
   The landscapes of Tuscany, which are known for their breathtaking beauty, are possibly the most obvious and impressive feature of the region's charm. It is a spot where nature paints its own portrait, and the canvas is an undulating expanse of hills, fields, vineyards, and olive groves. This place is known as "The Land of Olives and Vineyards." These hills become a living postcard in the spring when they

are covered with colorful wildflowers and vivid greenery, transforming the region into a picture-perfect setting. The golden tones of summer give the environment an almost dreamlike character, while the huge cypress trees, which stand in the warm Mediterranean sun, produce long shadows.

The countryside of Tuscany is where some of Italy's best wines and olive oils come from, making it the region's beating heart. Tuscany's vineyards and olive groves create some of the most exquisite wines and oils in the country. The famed Chianti region of Tuscany, known for its sun-kissed vineyards and undulating hills, exemplifies the pastoral allure that is synonymous with the region. The environment, which has been caressed by the sun, is not only a treat for the eyes but also a sandbox for the other senses to play in.

As you navigate the meandering roads, the earthy scent of the countryside and the gentle rustle of leaves in the breeze surround you, providing an immersive experience that feels like a timelessly passionate relationship with the land itself.

The Symbolic Significance of Roads Lined with Cypress Trees

When discussing the sceneries of Tuscany, it is impossible to avoid mentioning the famous cypress-lined roads that run all throughout the region. This striking visual spectacle that wonderfully defines Tuscany's charm is created by the tall, slender trees that stand sentry along the twisting roads. These trees, which are ever-present over the landscape of Tuscany, exemplify a sense of grace and elegance, and the symbolism associated with them is profound.

The cypress trees of Tuscany, also called the "sentinels of Tuscany," are notable not just for their aesthetic appeal but also for the cultural value they have. They frequently appear in association with cemeteries, which serves as a visual representation of the connection between life and death. On the other hand, the fact that they are still there along the roadsides in Tuscany is evidence of the region's continued connection to the land. It feels as if you are beginning a voyage through time as you drive along these cypress-lined lanes. You are guided by the knowledge of the past while advancing toward a future that is infused with optimism, beauty, and, inevitably, romance.

Stunningly Charming Towns and Villages

The allure of Tuscany is not restricted to the region's landscapes alone. The region's quaint little towns and villages are like something out of a dream; each one has its own distinct personality and history to share with visitors. Due to the fact that the architecture of these villages dates back to the Middle Ages and the Renaissance, tourists are given the opportunity to travel through time and become fully immersed in the history of the area.

San Gimignano is renowned for its skyline of medieval towers and its beautiful panoramic views of the surrounding Tuscan countryside. It is also known as the "Manhattan of the Middle Ages," which is a nickname given to the city because of its similarities to Manhattan. The exciting Palio di Siena, a historic horse race that epitomizes the competitive energy and deeply ingrained traditions of the region, is held in Siena's Piazza del Campo, which is shaped like an iconic shell. The event takes place in the heart of the city. The ancient splendor of Monteriggioni may be experienced in its walled town center, which features walls and towers that have been immaculately preserved.

On the other hand, it is possible that you will find the heart and soul of Tuscany in one of the region's smaller, less well-known communities.

Montalcino, with its picturesque hilltop setting and world-famous Brunello wine, and Pienza, which was intended by Pope Pius II as a utopian Renaissance town, are examples of places that encourage tourists to get lost in the maze-like streets, find hidden courtyards, and experience the warmth of the local culture.

The Tuscan Coastline's Mysterious and Stunning Beauty

As you travel through the gorgeous landscapes of Tuscany, you shouldn't forget to make your way to the seaside at some point. The coastline of Tuscany is renowned for its breathtaking scenery and peaceful atmosphere. The land and the sea collide at this point, producing a singular concoction that is equal parts magic and romance. The coastline of Tuscany is caressed by the Tyrrhenian Sea, which features sandy beaches, rocky coves, and azure waters that are crystal clear. The unspoiled coastline of Maremma, which is located in southern Tuscany, is a well-preserved jewel that features isolated beaches and thick pine trees. The island of Elba, which can be found in the Tyrrhenian Sea, is well-known for the breathtaking bays and underwater treasures that can be found there, making it a paradise for scuba divers and others who enjoy the outdoors.

This otherworldly beauty is brought out even further by the islands that make up the Tuscan Archipelago, each of which has its own unique personality and appeal. Discover a more personal side of Tuscany, indulging in the region's best seafood, finding your own little cove, and doing all of these things here.

The everlasting fascination of Tuscany is not only based on the beauty of its landscapes, but also on its capacity to inspire feelings of awe and passion in its visitors. Travelers, artists, and lovers from all over the world have been drawn to this region for centuries due to its quaint villages, winding roads lined with cypress trees, and breathtaking coastline. This region's undeniable charm is what has kept them coming back for more. This is where the tale of Tuscany is told, and it is an open invitation to anybody who visits to become a part of the region's enduring romance.

2. The Power of Place: Tuscany's Romantic Charm

The power of place, which is a force that reverberates with all those who are fortunate enough to experience it, lies at the heart of Tuscany's fascination, which extends far beyond the region's breathtaking landscapes and fascinating history. The powerful effect that Tuscany's natural and cultural surroundings have on the human spirit is evidenced by the region's well-known reputation as a haven for lovers of all things romantic. It's a place where every ancient village, every vineyard, and every cobblestone street all seem to be whispering love stories to each other, tempting tourists to immerse themselves in the region's enchanted atmosphere.

Chianti, and the Enchantment of Its Vineyards

The world-famous Chianti area is one of the most emblematic features that contribute to Tuscany's allure as a romantic destination. The term "Tuscan beauty" has come to be synonymous with this expansive landscape of rolling hills, vineyards, and ancient villages. Chianti's capacity to whisk visitors away to a world where time seems to stand still, where the embrace of nature is palpable, and where love and beauty are celebrated through the cultivation of the land is the source of the region's charm is what makes Chianti such an attractive destination.

The vineyards of Tuscany, known for their orderly rows of grapevines, are responsible for the production of some of Italy's most acclaimed wines. The very act of taking a leisurely stroll through these vineyards is in and of itself a romantic experience. An atmosphere that is at once calming and stimulating is created when the aroma of grapes reaching full maturity combines with the soft rustling of leaves caused by the movement of air. Couples frequently find themselves mesmerized by the breathtaking scenery and the enticing scent of grapes and earth as the sun sets over the vineyards, giving them a golden glow and bathing them in its warm light.

You can taste the passion and dedication of the winemakers who have honed their trade for generations in every bottle of Chianti wine, which is famous for its deep red wines. Chianti is noted in particular for its dark red wines. A traditional activity in Tuscany is to sit down with someone you care about and enjoy a bottle of Chianti, whether you're at a quaint country inn or a sultry restaurant in the middle of a vineyard. In that instant, time seems to stand still, and the strength of the setting envelops you in a comforting embrace.

Cypress Trees are known as the Keepers of Romance

The cypress tree, with its tall, slender form that reaches into the heavens, is one of the characteristics that gives Tuscany's landscapes their most recognizable look. Travelers might feel a visual and emotional connection to the area through the presence of these recognizable trees, which stand sentinel along roads and driveways. The value of the cypress tree extends far beyond its function as a decorative component; in fact, it encapsulates the very heart of the alluring allure that Tuscany is known for.

Cypress trees, which are frequently referred to as the "sentinels of Tuscany," are more than just visually appealing; in addition, they carry significant cultural and symbolic importance. The presence of these trees in cemeteries is sometimes seen as a symbolic representation of the unbreakable bond that exists between life and death. In Tuscany, on the other hand, you'll find them standing tall along the highways, transforming ordinary thoroughfares into avenues of incomparable beauty and mystery. They are a sign of perseverance and resiliency as well as the protectors of the land.

The evergreen aspect of the cypress tree, which stands towering and dark against the constantly shifting sky, is symbolic of consistency as well as the everlasting spirit of love. As two people in a relationship take a stroll hand in hand along one of these cypress-lined roads, they become a part of an enduring story, one in which love and romance have been cherished for generations. The juxtaposition of the slender trees against the vivid environment is a reminder that while love may be ephemeral, the essence of romance is evergreen and endures through the centuries. While love may be fleeting, the essence of romance is everlasting.

The Villages of Tuscany: Snapshots of Romance in Time

The picture-perfect towns and villages that dot the landscape of Tuscany are like romantic time capsules. They provide a peek into a world that appears to have been unaffected by the passage of time, in which ancient districts are traversed by cobblestone streets, and the architecture resounds with the echoes of ages gone by. The towns and villages that make up Tuscany each have their own distinct personalities, which contribute to the region's overall allure.

Take for instance the city of San Gimignano, which is so prosperous that it has been nicknamed the "Manhattan of the Middle Ages."

Visitors are taken back in time to an era of prosperous trade and artistic innovation when they visit this settlement, which features medieval towers dotting its landscape. A romantic competition of a different kind, the competition between noble families to build larger and grander structures can be seen in each tower as it stands as a witness to the competition. Because the picturesque lanes of San Gimignano are lined with artisan stores where you can purchase regional handicrafts and souvenirs of your trip, the town is an excellent place to stroll hand in hand with the person you care about.

Piazza del Campo in Siena, on the other hand, is a masterpiece in the shape of a shell. It is surrounded by structures that date back hundreds of years, and it is where the famous Palio di Siena takes place. This classic horse race perfectly encapsulates both the spirit of fierce competition as well as the time-honored customs of the area. It is a display of color and excitement that pulls the people of Siena together, and it is a striking reminder that the power of location is not confined to landscapes but also extends to cultural events and traditions. It is a celebration of the Palio di Siena, which is an annual horse race held in Siena, Italy.

The concept of a medieval stronghold is exemplified most clearly by the city of Monteriggioni, which boasts walls and towers that have been immaculately preserved. You can walk around on the circular walls and picture a time when knights and nobility roamed the countryside if you come here. Couples are encouraged to go on adventures together and make their own sweet romantic memories in the stone alleyways and small stores.

As you make your way through these hamlets and cities, it is not difficult to become engulfed in the palpable sense of history and the enduring spirit of love that permeates the atmosphere. The natural beauty of Tuscany is only one component of the region's alluring allure; the region's buildings and the stories they tell also contribute significantly to this allure.

Treasures Concealed Within: Intimacy and Thrill Seeking

A number of people have a soft spot in their hearts for the well-known villages and towns of Tuscany, but the region's undiscovered treasures provide a different kind of romantic experience. Intimacy and excitement may be found in equal measure at these off-the-beaten-path spots, which are typically only known by residents of the area and seasoned travelers.

By venturing to some of Tuscany's less well-known nooks and crannies, you can avoid the crowds and find spots that have the air of being secrets just waiting to be divulged. You can take a leisurely stroll through Montalcino's meandering lanes and treat yourself to a glass of the region's renowned Brunello wine. It's a gathering spot for those who share a passion for wine, culture, and the arts. Another well-kept secret is the Renaissance town of Pienza, which was laid out by Pope Pius II. Lovers of architecture and the scenic splendor of Tuscany will find this location to be a haven due to the harmonious design of the structure as well as the stunning views of the Val d'Orcia.

These little-known treasures bring to light a more sedate and personal aspect of Tuscany. It is an opportunity to make intimate relationships with the place and the people who live there, as well as to create moments that are uniquely your own. You can become a part of the tale of Tuscany by relishing a peaceful time in a local café or having a leisurely walk through a tiny village. Either way, the force of location will wrap you and make you feel like you're a part of it.

The Coastline of Tuscany: A Scenic and Romantic Embrace of Nature

The allure of Tuscany's inland landscape can't be denied, but the region's coast also captivates in its own unique way and is beautiful in its own right. The sandy beaches, rocky coves, and clear seas of the Tyrrhenian Sea may be found along the coast of Tuscany, which is kissed by the Tyrrhenian Sea. It is a spot where the land and water come together to produce a one-of-a-kind ambiance that is characterized by enchantment and passion.

Every traveler who comes to Tuscany is mesmerized by the undisturbed and untouched natural beauty of the region's shoreline. Those who are looking for a more personal experience by the water will find the Maremma coastline in the southern part of Tuscany to be a well-preserved treasure. Here, hidden beaches and verdant pine trees provide a haven for visitors.

Couples can have a romantic stroll down the shoreline here, holding hands while listening to the soothing sound of the waves and experiencing the warmth of the ocean and the sky.

Elba Island, which is located in the Tyrrhenian Sea, is well-known for the breathtaking bays that surround it as well as the undersea treasures that can be found there. It is a destination frequented by scuba divers and nature lovers who like to investigate the depths of the sea and take pleasure in the natural splendor of the Mediterranean region. The crystal-clear waters show an underwater world of wonders where colorful fish and coral reefs lend a touch of magic to the romantic beauty of the coastline. The pristine waters also reveal an underwater world of wonders.

The islands that make up the Tuscan Archipelago, such as Giglio and Capraia, each have their own distinct personality and charm to offer visitors. Every island has a unique history to share as well as secluded bays and inlets that beg to be explored. The Mediterranean way of life, with its emphasis on unhurried meals and enjoyment of environment, is the common thread that connects these islands to the core of the romantic appeal that is found in Tuscany.

The ever-present allure and charming antiquity of Tuscany's romantic atmosphere

The power of place lies at the heart of Tuscany's irresistible romantic allure, which is a symphony of the region's sensory sensations as well as its cultural wealth. From the undulating vineyards of Chianti to the cypress-lined roads that evoke a sense of timeless love, from the picturesque villages that preserve the spirit of the past to the hidden gems that offer intimate adventures, and from the coastline's natural embrace to the bustling urban squares that come alive with tradition and festivity, Tuscany offers an enchantment that transcends the ordinary in every way possible.

The power of location in Tuscany is not simply about aesthetics; rather, it is about the tremendous mental, emotional, and spiritual influence that this region has on those who come to visit it. It is a location where couples discover that they are drawn closer together, where the beauty of the surroundings intensifies the love that they share with one another, and where time appears to slow down to allow for moments that may be spent connecting with one another and reflecting on life.

When the sun goes down over the vineyards and the cypress trees create long shadows down the roads, when you walk hand in hand through historic villages and relish calm moments on secluded beaches, you become a part of the everlasting love tale that is Tuscany. Tuscany's fascination as a romantic destination goes much beyond its surface beauty; rather, it lies dormant inside the very core of the region, where it patiently waits to be uncovered and embraced by anybody who is fortunate enough to fall under its spell.

3. **Purpose of the Book**

The book "The Romance of Tuscany, Italy" is more than just a travel guide; rather, it is an invitation to go on a life-changing adventure through one of the most beguiling places in the world. This book has a purpose that goes far beyond giving practical information for tourists; it seeks to fire a deep appreciation for the rich tapestry of Tuscany's culture, history, landscapes, and the continuing force of love and passion that define the region. The purpose of this book is to provide a deep appreciation for the rich tapestry of Tuscany's culture, history, landscapes, and the enduring strength of love and romance that define the region.

A Letter of Affection to the Tuscan Region

This book, at its core, functions as a love letter to the region of Tuscany. This is a clear indication of the profound love and respect that a large number of people from different parts of the world have for this particular place. Tuscany, with its enduring attraction and enchantment, possesses the capacity to enliven the human soul and serve as a source of inspiration. The book endeavors to portray the great sensation of amazement and adoration that Tuscany inspires in its guests by way of captivating storytelling and detailed descriptions. This is one of the book's primary goals.

This objective is not restricted to those individuals who have previously directly experienced the wonder that Tuscany has to offer. It is also for those who enjoy daydreaming and traveling virtually, people who wish to have a stronger connection to the allure of the location being discussed. The book enables readers to mentally transport themselves to the region of Tuscany by vividly presenting the landscapes, history, culture, and romance that define Tuscany. This fosters a sense of desire and anticipation in the reader as they look forward to visiting the region.

The Hidden Treasures of Tuscany's Rich Tapestry

Tuscany is like a gem with many facets; each one reveals a different and distinctive feature of the region's appeal. The goal of the book is to provide readers with a holistic perspective of the beauty that Tuscany has to offer by revealing the underlying layers of the tapestry. It explores the undulating vineyards of Chianti, as well as the roads lined with cypress trees, the attractive villages and cities, the jewels along the shore, and the hidden gems that dot the landscape of the region. In doing so, the book assists readers in comprehending the breadth and depth of the romantic charm that Tuscany possesses.

This book treats Tuscany's long and illustrious history with the respect it deserves as it delves into yet another layer of this intricate fabric. Since the time of the mysterious Etruscans and continuing through the splendor of the Italian Renaissance, Tuscany has been an essential contributor to the growth of artistic expression, cultural expression, and intellectual thought.

Dante Alighieri and the Medici family are only two of the historically significant personalities that have called this location home at some point. The purpose of this book is to portray Tuscany's everlasting relevance as well as its influence on the rest of the globe by diving into its historical wealth.

An Invitation to Indulge in the Feelings of Romance

To put it simply, Tuscany deserves its reputation as a romantic destination. The goal of the book is to convey to readers an invitation to lose themselves in the ethereal atmosphere of the location described in the book. The sceneries of Tuscany, with its undulating hills, vineyards, and cypress trees, provide the ideal environment for the development of romantic feelings. The goal of the book is to encourage readers to visualize themselves taking a romantic stroll through vineyards as the sun sets, drinking a bottle of Chianti with the person they care about most, or going hand in hand through the winding alleyways of a medieval village. These adventures, which are brought to life via vivid descriptions and captivating storytelling, stoke the fire of romance that already exists inside the hearts of the book's readers.

Another major focus of the book is on the way in which people in Tuscany express their affection for one another. The romantic allure of Tuscany is largely due, in large part, to the melodious tones and ardent emotions of the Italian language. The goal of the book is to give readers a taste of the language by providing them with romantic phrases and expressions that they may adopt and use in their own lives in order to strengthen connections with the people they care about. This way, the book functions as a bridge between the romantic culture of Tuscany and the individual experiences of love and affection that its readers have had.

Instructions for a Magical Adventure in Everyday Life

In addition to being filled with lyrical descriptions and storylines that come from the heart, the book also has a function that should not be overlooked. It provides readers with a detailed guide that they may use to organize their very own enchanting vacation in Tuscany. This includes recommendations on how to get around, where to stay, what to eat, and what activities are best suited to a romantic atmosphere. The book offers suggestions for experiencing some of Tuscany's most well-known tourist spots, as well as directions for finding some of the region's lesser-known treasures, which are ideal for having more private and in-depth adventures.

In addition to that, the book provides a variety of resources as well as suggestions for more research. This includes websites and travel resources for practical planning, as well as suggested readings and films that allow readers to delve further into the history and culture of Tuscany. The readings and films may be found on this page. In addition to that, it provides a selection of dishes from the Tuscan cuisine, enabling readers to bring the tastes of Tuscany into their own homes.

Encouragement to Concoct One's Own Romantic Adventures

In addition to acting as a travel guide and a demonstration of Tuscany's charm, the book inspires readers to imagine and write their own romantic adventures in the region. It highlights the fact that the romance that can be found in Tuscany is not confined to the pages of a book or the frames of a painting; rather, it is a real, breathing organism that encourages engagement on the part of its visitors.

Readers are encouraged to take a trip to Tuscany so that they can take in the region's breathtaking scenery, delectable cuisine, and vibrant culture. The goal of the book is to serve as a wellspring of ideas for those who are looking to reignite their passion for one another, whether they are on their honeymoon, celebrating their anniversary, or traveling. It encourages the notion that Tuscany is more than just a location; rather, it is a canvas upon which individuals can paint their own personal stories of love, beauty, and adventure.

Chapter 1

Tuscany's Enchanting Landscapes

Dreams can come true in Tuscany, which is located in the middle of Italy. Its picturesque landscapes, which are renowned for their picture-perfect attractiveness, provide a visual symphony that mesmerizes the hearts of anybody who has the privilege of stepping foot on the land there. During this voyage through Tuscany's entrancing landscapes, we will explore the rolling hills and vineyards of Chianti, the iconic cypress-lined roads, the gorgeous villages and towns, the otherworldly splendor of Tuscany's coastline, and the hidden jewels that provide private retreats from the everyday. Each of these components contributes to the creation of a story that is irreplaceably captivating and a testament to the strength of place. This story describes how the natural and cultural worlds merge to produce a landscape that has a timeless appeal.

Chianti: A Landscape of Gently Undulating Hills and Vineyards

The countryside of Tuscany is where the heart of the region's scenery lies; it is a place of astounding beauty and frequently serves as the very embodiment of the "Tuscan dream." This pastoral enchantment is personified in its purest form in the Tuscany region known as Chianti. Its undulating hills, which are adorned with vineyards and olive groves, form a distinctive panorama that appears to have been lifted straight from a picture.

The charm of Chianti is not only in its visual elegance but also in the feelings that it arouses in people. You become a part of the love story being told by the landscape as you stand among the vines, feeling the warmth of the Tuscan sun on your skin and smelling the aroma of ripe grapes filling the air around you. The warmth of nature and the connection to the land are palpable, and it feels as if the very ground that you stand on has a tale to tell.

The Grace and Beauty of Driveways Lined with Cypress Trees

The renowned cypress tree can be found in many different settings across Tuscany's landscapes. These trees, which are tall and slender with evergreen foliage, are a beautiful addition to the region's sceneries, particularly along the winding roads that take visitors to remote areas of the countryside. These winding lanes adorned with cypress trees are more than simply a pretty sight; they are a potent reminder of the enduring allure of Tuscany.

The presence of cypress trees, which are frequently referred to as the "sentinels of Tuscany," has a purpose beyond purely aesthetic considerations. It is significant from a cultural and symbolic standpoint. Cypress trees, which are frequently found in cemeteries, are thought to represent the unbreakable bond that exists between life and death. On the other hand, they are a common sight along the roadsides of Tuscany, where they help create stunning and mysterious alleyways. When tourists go down these roads, it seems as if they are treading a path that has been trodden by centuries before them, being guided by the knowledge of the past while simultaneously moving forward into a future that is beautiful, hopeful, and filled with love.

The tall, slender form of the cypress, which reaches upward toward the heavens, is symbolic of perseverance and the undying spirit of love. Although love may be transient, the essence of romance is eternal, a force that transcends through the years. The juxtaposition of these trees against the vivid landscape of Tuscany serves as a reminder of this fact, and while love itself may be ephemeral, the essence of romance is not.

Stunningly Charming Towns and Villages

Tuscany is filled with quaint little towns and villages that look like they were taken straight from a storybook. Each has a distinct personality, which is frequently reflected in the architectural styles of the Middle Ages and the Renaissance. These communities have done more than just preserve the past; they have incorporated it into the present, and the allure that they exude is contagious.

The skyline of medieval towers in San Gimignano has earned the town the nickname "Manhattan of the Middle Ages." San Gimignano is located in Italy. These towers, which reach for the clouds, each have a different tale to tell. Each one was constructed by a wealthy family in an effort to one-up their neighbors, resulting in a competition of grandeur that gives the town a dash of romantically charged competitiveness. The alleyways of San Gimignano are dotted with stores owned by local artisans, and the town's towers offer breathtaking panoramas of the surrounding Tuscan countryside.

The Piazza del Campo in Siena, which is known for its characteristic scalloped shape, might be considered the city's beating heart. The exciting Palio di Siena, a historic horse race that epitomizes the competitive spirit and deeply ingrained traditions of the region, is held in this area. The city is swept up in a frenzy of color, excitement, and pride twice a year as the many contrade (neighborhoods) battle for victory in this spectacular event. This event takes place in the streets of the city.

The idea of a medieval stronghold is encapsulated in Monteriggioni, which boasts walls and towers that have been immaculately preserved.

You can wander along the circular walls while visualizing a time when knights and nobility roamed the land at this location. Those who are looking to completely submerge themselves in the splendor of the past will find Monteriggioni to be an ideal location thanks to its quaint shops and cobblestone streets.

These villages not only provide a glimpse into the past but also a setting in which one may make memories that will last a lifetime. The landscapes of these cities are infused with a sense of love and history, and it doesn't matter if you're sipping a gelato in the shade of a medieval tower or wandering small, twisting streets hand in hand; you'll get the same feeling either way.

Intimate Retreats Are Some of These Hidden Gems

There are many people who have a soft spot in their hearts for the well-known cities and villages of Tuscany, but the region also has numerous hidden jewels that provide a more private and individualized experience. These lesser-known places frequently avoid the attention of the large-scale tourist crowds, and as a result, they offer visitors a tranquil and more intimate connection to the heart of Tuscany.

A perfect illustration of a hidden gem is the town of Montalcino, which may be found in the Val d'Orcia. This picturesque village perched on a hill is well-known around the world for producing the revered Tuscan classic, Brunello wine. Because of its picturesque landscape and world-famous wine, Montalcino is a paradise for those who are passionate about both culture and aesthetics. A romantic experience that is seductive in its simplicity is wandering its meandering alleyways and having a glass of Brunello wine in the shade of the town's old citadel. Both of these activities may be done in the town of Montalcino.

Another well-kept secret is the town of Pienza, which was envisioned as a Renaissance utopia

by Pope Pius the Second. It is a striking example of Renaissance urban planning and design, and it has produced a space that is at once harmonious and captivating to the viewer. Pienza is a wonderful location for those individuals who are looking for architectural beauty as well as natural grandeur due to the fact that it offers stunning views of the Val d'Orcia.

Travelers can get away from the crowds and experience moments of intimacy and a personal connection with the landscapes of Tuscany by visiting these well-kept secrets. They are locations in which one can take pleasure in the friendliness of the native culture and produce memories that are distinctively their own.

The Tuscan Coastline's Mysterious and Stunning Beauty

Where the land meets the water along the coast of Tuscany is a magical area, providing a one-of-a-kind blend of beauty, romance, and natural wonders. This place is known as the Tuscan coast. A trip to the coast of the Tyrrhenian Sea, with its sandy beaches, rocky coves, and gin-clear waters, may be both relaxing and stimulating, depending on how you choose to spend your time there.

The stretch of coastline known as the Maremma in southern Tuscany is a beautiful jewel that has been carefully protected. It features isolated beaches and dense pine forests. Couples can have a romantic stroll down the shoreline here, holding hands while listening to the soothing sound of the waves and experiencing the warmth of the ocean and the sky. A location where nature still reigns and the human impact is limited, the Maremma is a region in Tuscany, Italy, that offers the opportunity for a profound connection to the elemental forces of the soil and water.

Elba Island, which can be found in the Tyrrhenian Sea, is well-known for the breathtaking bays and underwater treasures that can be found there. For scuba divers and other nature lovers with an interest in exploring the depths of the water, this location is a paradise. The crystal-clear waters show an underwater world of wonders where brilliant coral reefs and colorful fish lend a touch of magic to the romantic beauty of the coastline. The pristine waters also reveal an underwater world of wonders.

Each of the islands that make up the Tuscan Archipelago, such as Giglio and Capraia, possesses a personality and appeal that are entirely their own. They provide tourists with a more private and intimate seaside experience, one in which they may explore hidden coves, dine in the finest seafood, and immerse themselves in the natural beauty of the Mediterranean region.

The coastline of Tuscany is a site of natural beauty, where the elements of earth, water, and air join together to produce an atmosphere that is simultaneously calming and exhilarating. It is a place to find peace in the embrace of the sea, a place to investigate the mysteries of the deep, and a place to taste the bounty of the ocean. All of these things can be done here.

The Enchanting Landscapes of Tuscany: A Perfect Harmony of Beauty and Romance

The sceneries of Tuscany, with their undulating hills, vineyards, attractive villages and towns, cypress-lined highways, and magical shoreline, form a visual symphony of nature and culture that captivates the hearts of all those who visit the region. These vistas are more than just pretty backdrops; they are living testaments to the power of love, beauty, and history.

The persistent appeal of Tuscany can be attributed to a number of factors, including the stately cypress trees, the quaint medieval villages, and the breathtakingly beautiful coastline.

The power of place in Tuscany is not restricted to its visual qualities; rather, its significance lies in the psychological and metaphysical effect it produces on individuals who visit the region. It is a location where travelers feel that they are drawn closer to each other, where the beauty of the surroundings magnifies the love that they have with one another, and where time seems to slow down to allow for moments of connection and introspection.

In this symphony of beauty and romance, the landscapes of Tuscany serve not only as the

backdrop but also as the inspiration for artistic works, cherished memories, and stories of love and longing. They are a living monument to the everlasting fascination of a place that, for generations, has been captivating the hearts and souls of everybody who is fortunate enough to come into its embrace. They serve as a living testament since they are still around today.

1.1 The Rolling Hills of Chianti

The undulating landscape of Chianti in Tuscany is a perfect example of the breathtaking natural splendor that has come to be synonymous with this area. For countless years, travelers and artists have been inspired to create beautiful works of art by the gentle rise and fall of these hills, which are reminiscent of nature's own verses. They are a visual symphony in which every contour, every vineyard, and every cypress tree plays a part in producing a panorama that inspires feelings of magic, romance, and the enduring appeal of Tuscany. Each of these elements contributes to the overall effect of the landscape.

A Plaid Comprised of Shades of Green and Gold

The undulating and symmetrical forms that the hills of Chianti have to offer make them a sight to behold. In the spring, they explode into a tapestry of emerald green, and wildflowers dot the landscape like bright punctuation points, turning the whole thing into a beautiful kaleidoscope. It is almost as if the earth itself is enjoying the approach of warmer days as the hills begin to spring to life with their own unique brand of pyrotechnics.

As the summer draws closer, the color of the grass on the hills becomes more vibrant and takes on a yellowish tint. The slopes that are covered with vineyards, which are responsible for producing grapes used in some of the best wines in Italy, become the most prominent feature of the landscape. The grapevines are arranged in straight rows that create designs that are aesthetically pleasing as well as orderly, and their golden leaves enjoy the warmth of the Mediterranean sun. This scene is an homage to the everlasting link that exists between the land and the people who live on it, and it reeks of both warmth and romance.

The Chianti Region's World-Famous Vineyards

The Chianti region, which stretches between Florence and Siena, is famous the world over for the quality of its red wines. Some of the most renowned vineyards in all of Italy may be found in the rolling hills of Chianti, which are also the birthplace of these excellent wines. These hills also provide an iconic background for these vineyards.

The Chianti Classico wine region, considered to be among the most prestigious in all of Chianti, is known for producing wines that are more than just a product of the soil; rather, they are an embodiment of the soul of the place. Vineyards, which have been cultivated with affection and care for many generations, can be found nestled among the rolling hills, which are caressed by the sun and cradled by the gentle breezes of night. As a direct consequence of this, the wines that are made here capture the exact spirit of the surrounding environment; they are robust, rich, and packed to the brim with personality.

A trip to a Chianti vineyard is more than simply an opportunity to sample the region's wines; it's an adventure for the senses. The perfume of the earthy vineyard, the sound of the leaves rustling in the breeze, and the sound of glasses clinking together all contribute to the creation of an atmosphere that is at once engrossing and inviting. It's an adventure that makes you feel like you're in a never-ending love affair with the land itself.

The Mystifying Sequence of Cypress Trees

As you make your way across the undulating terrain of Chianti, you will notice that the cypress tree is one of the most distinctive features of the surrounding environment. Along the twisting roads is where you'll find this striking visual spectacle created by these tall, slender trees standing guard. They are more than simply a pretty sight; they have profound cultural significance and carry with them a wealth of symbolic meaning.

The cypress trees of Tuscany, which are commonly referred to as the "sentinels of Tuscany," serve a purpose that goes beyond the mere attractiveness of their appearance. They frequently appear in the vicinity of graves, which serves as a visual representation of the unbreakable bond that exists between life and death. However, their continued existence along the roadsides of Tuscany is evidence of the region's long-standing relationship to the land in that area.

These trees, because of their evergreen nature, maintain a tall and dark presence in contrast to the sky's constant transformation. They are a symbol of steadfastness as well as the love that lasts forever. It feels as if you are beginning a voyage through time as you drive along these cypress-lined lanes. You are guided by the knowledge of the past while advancing toward a future that is infused with optimism, beauty, and, inevitably, romance.

A Satisfying Experience for the Senses

The landscape of Chianti, with its undulating hills, is a treat for the eyes and the ears. The tourists are captivated not only by the breathtaking aesthetic value of the terrain, but also by the multisensory adventure that it provides. An immersive experience is something that feels like a love affair with the land itself, and the earthy scent of the countryside, the gentle rustle of leaves in the breeze, and the warm embrace of the sun all contribute to creating this feeling.

The beauty of Chianti is not limited to the rolling hills; it also encompasses the quaint little towns that are scattered across the terrain. Travelers are encouraged to wander the cobblestone streets of towns like Greve, Radda, and Castellina in Chianti, sample the cuisine of the region, and find secret nooks and crannies where history and culture come to life. These settlements, with their preserved medieval architecture and friendly locals, provide opportunities for moments of introspection and connection with the surrounding environment.

Love that has stood the test of time in the scenery

The undulating landscape of Chianti is more than just a picture perfect scene for a postcard; it is also a blank slate onto which countless couples have written their love stories. It is a place where couples discover that they are brought closer together, and the beauty of the surroundings accentuates the love that they share with one another. It is possible for lovers to have a life-changing experience by doing something as simple as basking in the golden light of the hills, sharing a bottle of Chianti, or going for a stroll through vineyards while the sun is setting.

Chianti is more than just a place to visit; rather, it is a setting where individual love stories can be written. It is a location in which the very essence of romance is woven into the terrain, and it beckons couples to become a part of the story that will continue to be told there.

1.2 The Olive Groves and Vineyards

The lush olive orchards and vineyards that cover the rolling hills of Tuscany are responsible for a significant amount of the region's visual poetry, which is one of the reasons Tuscany is so well-known for its lovely scenery. These well-known vineyards and groves are not only a source of agricultural prosperity, but they also serve as a living illustration of the profound relationship that exists between the people and the land. During this excursion, we dig into the world of Tuscany's olive orchards and vineyards, discovering their cultural significance, their role in Tuscan food, and the ageless romance that they add to the region's natural beauty.

A Tradition That Has Stood the Test of Time: Olive Growing

Olive trees, which are considered to be a sign of both peace and wealth, have been farmed in Tuscany for many years. This time-honored custom is evident in the form of living testimony provided by the olive orchards that dot the landscape of Tuscany. These ancient trees have been lovingly cultivated by countless generations of farmers, as seen by the gnarled trunks and silvery leaves that cover their branches.

Olives have a significant cultural significance in the Tuscan region. In addition to its importance in the production of some of the best olive oil in the world, Tuscan olives are also an essential component of the regional cuisine. The golden elixir that is olive oil from Tuscany is an essential component of many different recipes, lending those foods a flavor that is both delicious and hearty. Olive oil is a fundamental component of the cuisine of Tuscany and is utilized in a variety of ways, including drizzling it over salads, incorporating it into meals, and serving it over freshly baked bread.

Olive picking is a customary activity in Tuscany, and around this time of year, the community comes together to celebrate. The air is filled with the sound of people laughing and chatting as they get together to pluck olives from their branches once they have reached maturity. The olives are then subjected to a pressing process, which results in the production of a luxurious, green-gold liquid that is highly esteemed in Tuscany and beyond.

The Stunning Beauty of Tuscan Wine Country

Another distinguishing feature of Tuscany's agricultural environment is the presence of vineyards, which are characterized by their ordered rows of grapevines. These vineyards are a source of regional pride because they are responsible for the production of some of the most acclaimed wines in Italy. Winemaking in Tuscany is an age-old tradition that is rich in history and has a long-standing romantic association with the region.

As far as the eye can see, vineyards stretch out in every direction in Chianti, which is one of the most famous wine areas in all of Tuscany. The grape-bearing vines transform from green to scarlet as the harvest nears, transforming the landscape into a bright patchwork that is decorated with colorful designs. The hillsides are a magnificent symphony of color.

The wines of Tuscany, and particularly Chianti Classico, are renowned for having a distinct personality and a high level of complexity. They are a representation of the one-of-a-kind terroir that the region possesses, with the terrain playing a vital role in the function that it plays in developing the taste profiles of the wines. Strong, aromatic, and profound wines are produced in Tuscany as a result of the influence of the region's mineral-rich soil, the warm sun, and the gentle winds.

A trip to a Tuscan vineyard is more than simply a treat for the taste buds; it's an adventure for all of the senses. The earthy scent of the vineyard, the gentle rustling of the leaves in the breeze, and the sound of glasses being clinked together all work together to produce an atmosphere that is at once engrossing and inviting. It is a time when guests can not only appreciate the taste of the wine, but also feel a connection to the very soul of the place.

The Cultural Significance and the Gastronomic Abundance

Olive groves and vineyards are more than simply a source of nutrition in Tuscany; they are profoundly ingrained in the culture and identity of the region as a whole. Olive oil, sometimes known as "liquid gold," is not only put to use in the kitchen, but it also carries significant cultural connotations. It is a symbol of holiness, tranquility, and the dissemination of light. Olive oil is often utilized in religious rituals and has even been known to be used to anoint kings and other prominent figures.

The cultural value of Tuscany's wine is comparable to that of the region itself. It is a sign of getting together with others and having a good time. It is something that is passed around at parties, celebrations, and meals with the family. The custom of breaking bread with one another and drinking wine together is one that serves to bring people together and strengthen the ties that bind them to their community.

The cuisine of Tuscany, which is famous for its uncomplicated nature and focus on locally sourced, high-quality ingredients, is inextricably linked to the goods produced by the land. Olive oil and wine are two of the most important ingredients in traditional Tuscan cuisine. These two ingredients are essential to the preparation of meals such as bruschetta, ribollita, and pappa al pomodoro. Not only do these components contribute to an enhanced flavor profile, but they also help to forge a connection between the food and the local culture and history.

The Eternal Charm of Italy's Vineyards and Olive Groves

The natural splendor of Tuscany is complemented by an air of enchantment provided by the region's olive trees and vineyards. They are more than just agricultural fields; rather, they are landscapes that tell stories of love, toil, and legacy. An olive grove, with its silvery leaves glimmering in the sunlight, or a vineyard, with its variegated grapevines, is a charming setting in and of itself, and either one can be explored on foot.

When couples travel to Tuscany, the region's surroundings transform into a setting for moments of intimacy and connection between them. Memories that are infused with the essence of romance are created when two people share an experience such as dining in a vineyard restaurant as the sun sets over the vines or drinking a bottle of Chianti under the shade of an olive tree. The ageless beauty of these places has a way of pulling people together and fostering a sense of wonder and magic in those who experience it.

1.3 Cypress-Lined Roads

Tuscany is renowned for numerous iconic aspects that define its attractiveness, and cypress-lined roads are among the most scenic of these elements. Tuscany is known for its beautiful landscapes, which are among the reasons it is so beautiful. Not only do these slender and evergreen sentinels contribute to the aesthetics of the region, but they also contribute to the cultural and symbolic value that the area possesses. They stand tall and proud along the meandering thoroughfares. During this excursion, we go along the cypress-lined roads of Tuscany in order to discover their significance, as well as the part they play in the beauty of the region and the ageless charm they provide to this entrancing land.

Cypress Trees are known as the "Sentinels of Tuscany"

The Tuscan countryside is characterized by the presence of cypress trees in almost every area. They provide a striking contrast to the undulating hills and the ever-changing skies of Tuscany due to their height, slenderness, and ever-present green coloration. These famous trees are more than just ornamental features; they are living symbols that perfectly capture the character of the area.

Cypress trees are not native to Tuscany but were brought there over the course of several centuries. Because of their unusual shape and color, they are an essential component of the panorama of Tuscany. These trees are frequently connected with concepts such as infinity, tenacity, and recall. Their evergreen foliage is a representation of steadfastness as well as the love that lasts forever. The cypress trees of Tuscany have come to be seen as a visual depiction of the region's alluring allure since Tuscany is a place where beauty, history, and romance all come together.

Elegance in terms of aesthetics and contrast in terms of appearance

Travelers and artists alike are drawn to Tuscany's cypress-lined roadways because they are a visual marvel that evokes a sense of enchantment. These slender trees are like punctuation marks over the landscape; they guide the eye and the imagination along the winding roads that lead to attractive villages and hidden corners. Their angular shapes offer a striking contrast to the gentle, undulating hills and the brilliant colors of the landscape, resulting in a scene that is at once sophisticated and emotive.

The aesthetic value of roads bordered with cypress trees is not restricted to the daylight hours; rather, it is enhanced in the evening, when the sun is lower in the sky and produces long, slender shadows down the roads. The landscape takes on a more dramatic and mysterious air as a result of these shadows and the subtle interplay between the light and the darkness. As the sun sinks below the horizon, the silhouette of the cypress trees takes on a look that is both eerie and romantic; it is the perfect way to bring an eventful day filled with adventure and discovery to a close.

Importance from a Cultural and Symbolic Standpoint

In the Italian region of Tuscany, cypress trees have an extremely significant cultural and symbolic meaning. In addition to their reputation for aesthetic beauty, they also play an important part in tying the present landscape to its past and preserving its customs. It is common practice in Tuscany to decorate cemeteries with cypress trees, which represent an unbreakable connection between life and death. This symbolic association evokes feelings of profound awe and spirituality in the listener.

The presence of cypress trees along the roadways, on the other hand, is not a somber reminder but rather a celebration of life and the exquisiteness of nature. As they make their way across the Tuscan countryside, they serve as silent sentinels of the land, providing visitors with a sense of security and directing them in the right direction. It seems as if the knowledge of times gone by is woven into the very fabric of the landscape, pointing tourists in the direction of a future that is enlightened by the everlasting beauty of the area.

A Romantic Adventure Through Time and Space

It is almost as if one were to set out on a trip through time when driving along roads bordered with cypress trees. The terrain, which is led by these slender trees, encourages visitors to follow in the steps of previous generations, to investigate the history and culture of the area, and to look to the future with a sense of awe and optimism.

Tuscany, with its extensive past and creative legacy, has served as motivation for a great number of poets, writers, and artists throughout the centuries. The winding roads lined with cypress trees, with their stately appearance and profound significance to various cultures, have found a home in the works of these inventive minds. They have served as the setting for tales of love, the subject of artworks, and the motivation for writing that gets to the essence of the region's enduring fascination.

These pathways lined with cypress trees bring an extra dose of romanticism to the trip that couples take when they come to Tuscany. The thin trees produce an atmosphere of closeness and connection, which encourages couples in love to stroll hand in hand, to linger in the shade, and to take in the enduring beauty that is all about them. It is almost as if the cypress trees in Tuscany, which are known for their lengthy shadows, are bearing witness to the romantic adventures of tourists who have been won over by the region's eternal allure. The golden light of the Tuscan sunset illuminates the cypress trees in such a way that they cast long shadows.

The cypress trees that line the roadways in Tuscany are more than simply a pretty sight; they are also a cultural symbol and a demonstration of the region's enduring appeal. These thin evergreen sentinels serve as symbols of faithfulness and love as they direct travelers through the breathtaking landscapes of Tuscany.

They are a key component of the natural beauty of the area, and they serve as a wellspring of creativity for everyone who is fortunate enough to be able to travel along the charming pathways that they line because of their sophistication, visual contrast, cultural significance, and ageless romanticism.

1.4 Picturesque Villages and Towns

Tuscany is more than just a destination of natural beauty, despite the magnificent scenery that can be seen there. The scenic nature of its cities and villages contributes significantly, if not entirely, to the allure of the region. These communities, which may be found tucked away among the undulating hills and vineyards, provide a window into the cultural and historical core of the region. During this excursion, we will travel through the lovely villages and towns of Tuscany in order to discover the tales that they tell, the architectural treasures that they hold, and the personal, enduring beauty that they provide to this remarkable land.

San Gimignano is sometimes referred to be the "Manhattan" of the Middle Ages

San Gimignano is a sparkling gem that can be found in the Tuscan countryside. It is sometimes referred to as the "Manhattan of the Middle Ages." An amazing sight to behold is the city's skyline, which is characterized by fourteen towers from the middle ages that reach far into the air. These towers, which are relics of a time when wealthy families competed to see who could build the tallest structure, are symbolic of the city's grandiosity and its aspirational nature.

The alleys of San Gimignano are a winding maze of cobblestone pathways that snake through the town. On either side of these lanes are stone structures that have been embellished with exquisite arches and shuttered windows. You are taken back in time as you explore its scenic corners, and you can almost feel the presence of the noble families who used to rule the city and the artists who contributed to its artistic history.

The square della Cisterna is the primary square in San Gimignano. It is a popular gathering

place for both residents of the town and tourists. The medieval structures that surround the piazza have been preserved in excellent condition, and the landmark Torre Grossa provides breathtaking vistas of the natural scenery in the area. It is a place where the spirit of the Middle Ages mingles with the vibrancy of the present, producing an environment that is both historic and dynamic at the same time. It is a place where the spirit of the Middle Ages mingles with the vitality of the present.

Siena's Palio, a Race Steeped in History and Rivalry

Siena, with its majestic Piazza del Campo, is widely regarded as the city that best exemplifies the splendor of Tuscany.

The city's beating heart is a shell-shaped plaza that is famous for the unusual red-brick paving that it features. The Palio di Siena, regarded as one of the most exciting and well-known equestrian competitions in all of Italy, is held right here.

On July 2nd and August 16th of each year, the city of Siena is engulfed in a frenzy of color, enthusiasm, and pride. These dates occur twice yearly. This exciting competition pits the historic districts, often known as neighborhoods, of the city against one another. Each area in Siena is known as a contrada, and each contrada has its own set of colors, symbols, and customs. The Palio is a festival that honors Siena's long and illustrious history as well as the fierce competition between the contrada.

The horse race is a spectacular event that perfectly encapsulates the spirit of the customs and culture of Siena. The streets are decorated with vibrant banners, and members of the contrada, who are attired in traditional garb, take part in the processions and festivities. As the horses and jockeys make their way around the perilous course that circumnavigates the Piazza del Campo, the tension and excitement that can be felt in the air is overwhelming.

Siena is renowned not only for its fierce competition but also for its outstanding artistic and architectural achievements. A spectacular example of Italian Gothic architecture, the Cathedral of Siena in Siena, Italy, features elaborate facades embellished with statues as well as a breathtaking marble floor that depicts the story of creation. The frescoes, mosaics, and sculptures found inside the cathedral were created by some of Italy's most well-known painters, making its interior a veritable art treasure chest.

A Replica of a Medieval Stronghold in the Form of Monteriggioni

The little village of Monteriggioni, which is perched on top of a hill, exemplifies the concept of a medieval stronghold. The settlement has the appearance of a little medieval city due to the fact that it is surrounded by walls that have been meticulously maintained and fourteen towers that are rectangular in shape. You may imagine a time when knights and nobles roamed the countryside, utilizing Monteriggioni as a strategic fortress, as you make your way along the circular walls as you explore the town.

The cobblestone lanes of Monteriggioni, which are dotted with beautiful stores and boutiques run by local artisans, provide visitors with the opportunity to travel through time. It is a place where the history of Tuscany comes to life, where you can practically hear the echoes of the past and envision a time when this stronghold played an important role in the history of the region. It is a place where the history of Tuscany comes to life.

The town's medieval walls offer a breathtaking vantage point from which to take in the surrounding countryside and take in its history. You may get breathtaking views of the Tuscan landscape from atop the walls, which are characterized by undulating hills, vineyards, and winding lanes lined with cypress trees. It is a place where you may feel a connection with the timeless beauty of Tuscany and experience the spirit of the region's landscapes.

Montalcino Is Considered to Be the Core of the Brunello Wine Region

Montalcino is a picturesque hilltop town that is known for its Brunello wine, which is one of the most beloved varietals produced in Italy. Montalcino is located in the Val d'Orcia. Visitors are able to have a real Tuscan experience because to the town's picturesque surroundings and its well-preserved buildings from the medieval period.

As you make your way through Montalcino, the friendly and hospitable ambiance of the town is sure to catch your attention. The streets are made of stone, and they are lined with businesses owned by local artisans, enotecas (wine bars), and restaurants serving food typical of Tuscany. The aroma of the regional food, which may include roasted meats and wild mushrooms, permeates the air and beckons you to indulge in the delectable sensations that Tuscany has to offer.

The Rocca, a medieval fortification that overlooks the town, serves as a monument to both Montalcino's history and its present. The views of the Val d'Orcia and the vineyards that surround the stronghold are very breathtaking when viewed from the top of the fortress. Montalcino is an absolute must-see location for anybody who is interested in architectural beauty as well as the natural beauties of the surrounding area because the environment is a wonderful blend of history, nature, and culinary delights.

Utopia of the Renaissance, Pienza

Pienza is a town that exemplifies Renaissance urban planning and design, and as a result, it is frequently referred to as the "Ideal City." Pope Pius II was responsible for the town's transformation into an idealized Renaissance city, which resulted in the creation of an aesthetically pleasing and harmonious place. Pienza is a town in Tuscany, Italy, that is known for its beautiful architecture, as well as its rich artistic and natural traditions.

The Piazza Pio II, which is surrounded by several very fine structures, serves as the focal point of the town. The masterpiece of Renaissance architecture that is the Palazzo Piccolomini is a tribute to Pope Pius II's vision for the Renaissance. The Duomo, both outside and inside, is a spectacular example of the artistic prowess of the period it was built in and provides a space for people to contemplate and think deeply.

The UNESCO World Heritage site of Val d'Orcia may be seen from Pienza, which is famous for its stunning vistas of the valley. The town's perch on top of a hill affords residents a one-of-a-kind vantage point over the scenery in all directions. The perspectives are nothing short of stunning, inviting tourists to immerse themselves in the natural splendor of Tuscany and admire the ingenuity and foresight of the builders of the Renaissance period.

Volterra: An Enduring Relic of Etruscan Heritage

Volterra, which has Etruscan roots, is a town that successfully bridges the gap between the old world and the modern one. The history of the town can be traced back to the Etruscan period, and the town's ruins and antiquities, which have been kept remarkably well, provide a peek into the pre-Roman culture.

The heritage of the Etruscans is one of the most prominent aspects of Volterra, and the Guarnacci Etruscan Museum is home to one of the most comprehensive collections of Etruscan artifacts that can be found anywhere in Italy. The town's historical center is a maze of winding alleyways, secret courtyards, and medieval architecture that displays the many layers of history that have contributed to the development of the town.

Alabaster work is another thing that makes Volterra famous all over the world. These stunning sculptures and works of art have been crafted from this priceless material for generations in the town's alabaster studios, which have been in operation for millennia. Visitors are welcome to explore the workshops, where they may see skilled craftspeople at work and purchase one-of-a-kind mementos to remember their trip by.

Boccaccio was born at Certaldo, which is known as his birthplace

The little village of Certaldo in the Val d'Elsa is well-known for its connection to the famous Italian author Giovanni Boccaccio. Boccaccio, a famous writer and poet of the 14th century, was born in Certaldo, and the municipality of Certaldo celebrates his legacy to this day. Boccaccio was born in Certaldo.

The lovely medieval village of Certaldo Alto, which serves as the town's historical heart, has managed to keep much of its original architecture intact. It is a spot where tourists may stroll down stone lanes, appreciate the rustic structures, and immerse themselves in the environment that was influential to one of Italy's most famous authors.

The funicular train at Certaldo, which links the lower town with Certaldo Alto, is another reason why the town is so well-known.

The ride provides breathtaking views of the surrounding countryside and offers a fresh point of view on the town's unique dual personality, which combines aspects of both the past and the present.

Castiglione d'Orcia: A Shining Example of Medieval Brilliance

Castiglione d'Orcia is a picture-perfect medieval village that is located in the center of the Val d'Orcia and is well-known for the stunning architecture and peaceful atmosphere that it exudes. The village is situated on a hill, which provides mesmerizing views of the sceneries that are in the surrounding area.

The Rocca di Tentennano, which is located in Castiglione d'Orcia, is a medieval fortress that serves as a symbol of the town's medieval legacy. The fortress provides a setting that is ideal for discovery and introspection, with breathtaking vistas of both the Val d'Orcia and the Amiata Mountains in the distance. It is a location that encourages guests to engage with the natural and cultural history of the area they are visiting.

A Tale from Tuscany Called Poppi

Poppi, which can be found in the Casentino region, is a town that looks if it was taken straight from a storybook. The Castello dei Conti Guidi, a historic castle that dates back to the Guidi family and features a tower made of distinctive red bricks, is the primary tourist destination in this town. In addition to being a location of historical significance, the castle is also home to a public library that features an important collection of old manuscripts.

A feeling of enchantment and timelessness may be found in the historic heart of the town, which is distinguished by its medieval architecture that has been wonderfully conserved. The ambiance is both inviting and evocative thanks to the tiny lanes, stone houses, and artisan shops that are scattered throughout.

The village of Radda in Chianti is known as the "Heart of Chianti"

A charming town in the middle of the Chianti wine region, Radda in Chianti provides an insight into the culture and tradition of Tuscany. The village is characterized by its peaceful atmosphere and endearing allure as a result of its setting among olive orchards and vineyards.

In the historical heart of Radda, visitors will find ancient lanes and alleyways that they may wander through, shops selling local goods, and restaurants serving traditional Tuscan food. The Piazza IV Novembre, which serves as the town's major plaza, is a hive of activity and frequently plays host to local events and festivals that promote the region's culinary and winemaking heritage.

The magnificent towns and villages of Tuscany are not simply architectural masterpieces; rather, they are the custodians of the culture, history, and customs of the region. The architectural marvels, artistic legacies, and a sense of timelessness that characterize the region can be found in each town and village, and together they create a story that is one of a kind. Because of their everlasting charm, visitors to Tuscany are encouraged to trek over the region's varied landscapes and make personal connections with the people who call this magnificent place home. Each of these cities and villages contributes to the tapestry of Tuscany, making it a location of everlasting enchantment and cultural richness. Whether it is the medieval grandeur of San Gimignano, the traditions of the Palio in Siena, the Renaissance paradise of Pienza, or the fairytale charm of Poppi, each of these towns and villages adds to the beauty of the region.

1.5 The Mystical Beauty of Tuscany's Coastline

Even while Tuscany is most famous for its stunning landscapes, the region's shoreline is just as alluring and possesses its own special allure. There is a special kind of beauty that is shrouded in mystery that can be found along the Tuscan coastline. This beauty can be seen in the coastline's untouched beaches, craggy cliffs, and beautiful coastal towns. During this expedition, we dig into the mysterious appeal of the coastline of Tuscany, uncovering the hidden wonders, the fascinating scenery, and the romantic atmosphere that make it a destination unlike any other.

A Shining Star in the Tyrrhenian Sea is the Island of Elba.

One of the most coveted places to visit along the coast of Tuscany is Elba Island, which is located in the Tyrrhenian Sea. Divers and anyone who enjoy the outdoors will find paradise on this scenic island, which is famous for the beautiful bays, waters that are crystal clear, and riches that can be found underwater.

The natural splendor of the coastal districts of Tuscany is on full display along the coastline of Elba Island. The crystal clear seas reveal an underwater world of wonders, where vivid coral reefs and colorful fish lend a touch of magic to the idyllic allure of the shoreline. Divers and snorkelers have the opportunity to explore the depths of the water, where they may come upon secluded bays and fascinating marine species. Every type of beachgoer can find something to their liking on this island thanks to its varied shoreline, which includes sandy beaches, craggy cliffs, and hidden grottos.

The natural beauty of the island's coastline is intricately entwined with the island's history. The remains of Napoleon Bonaparte's home can still be seen in the town of Portoferraio, which is located on the seaside. This area is famously recognized as the location where he was forced into exile. The island of Elba is a symbol of both the bounties of nature and the importance of history; as such, it establishes a magical link between the two time periods.

The Islands of the Tuscan Archipelago: A Chorus of Beauty

The coastline beauty of Tuscany is enhanced by the presence of the Tuscan Archipelago, a group of islands that can be found off the region's coast and include Elba, Giglio, and Capraia. Each island has its own distinct personality and appeal, giving tourists a more isolated and personal experience of the shoreline.

Peace may be found on Giglio Island, which is famous for the clarity of its waters and the abundance of marine life that can be found there. Those in search of seclusion and breathtaking scenery can find both on this island's shoreline, which is replete with secluded coves and rocky cliffs. The coastal sceneries of Giglio, such as Cala delle Caldane and Cala degli Alberi, exude an air of romanticism and offer a sense of tranquility.

On the other side, Capraia Island is a dream destination for outdoor enthusiasts, particularly hikers and wildlife lovers. The wild beauty of the nature can be seen all across the island, thanks to its mountainous topography and rocky coastline. Discover hidden coves, swim in freshwater pools, and take in breathtaking vistas of the Mediterranean Sea when you hike along Capraia's coastal pathways.

The mystic allure of Tuscany's shore is highlighted by the Tuscan Archipelago, which is a collection of islands and coastal jewels that form a mosaic. It gives one the feeling of being able to get away from it all and go on an adventure, with each island having its own unique tale to tell about the natural beauty and cultural significance of the area.

Maremma is a Coastal Retreat Wrapped in the Arms of Mother Nature

The Maremma region of Tuscany's southern shore is a hidden gem that provides a more authentic and unspoiled coastal experience. This region is known as Maremma. In this area, there is less development along the shoreline, which makes it possible to have a closer connection to the elemental forces of the ground and the water.

The shoreline of Maremma is home to a number of stunning natural attractions. A sense of privacy and seclusion can be found on deserted beaches, while lush pine forests can act as a haven for those seeking shade and refuge. Walking hand in hand along the seashore while listening to the soothing lull of the waves and feeling the embrace of the sea and sky is a romantic activity that couples can enjoy. Maremma is a region in Tuscany, Italy, where nature still rules and the influence of humans is negligible; as a result, visitors can experience a profound oneness with the elemental energies of the land and water.

The landscapes of Maremma are a demonstration of the region's dedication to preserve the natural beauty of its surroundings. The protected region of Maremma, known as Parco Regionale della Maremma, is home to unspoiled coastal ecosystems such as wetland areas, dune systems, and lagoons. The coastal landscapes provide a sense of Tuscany's wild beauty, with migratory birds, rich flora, and native wildlife surviving in their natural habitats. These coastal landscapes offer a view of Tuscany's wild beauty.

The Cinque Terre: Five Fishing Villages on the Extreme Fringe of Romance

A spectacular site to witness is the Cinque Terre, which consists of a line of five colorful coastal settlements perched on steep cliffs. The communities that run along the Italian Riviera each have their own special brand of coastal enchantment to offer. The sight of their colorful homes clinging to the edge of the cliffs in such a perilous manner produces a scene that is at once dramatic and evocative.

The five villages that make up the Cinque Terre—Monterosso al Mare, Vernazza, Corniglia, Manarola, and Riomaggiore—are linked together by a series of breathtaking hiking paths that provide breathtaking vistas of the Mediterranean. These routes offer the chance to become one with the coastal sceneries by discovering the secluded coves and vineyard terraces that cling to the rocks.

The natural beauty of the Cinque Terre is simply one component of the region's allure; the

region's culinary and cultural traditions contribute significantly as well. Fresh seafood, regional wines, and authentic Italian cuisine can be enjoyed by tourists as they gaze out over the turquoise sea in any of the region's little villages, each of which has a personality all its own. The five villages of Cinque Terre are a stunning example of coastal romance because they are situated in an area where land and sea come together in a vibrant display of beauty and culture.

Known for its coastal elegance and secluded beauty, Monte Argentario

The promontory of Monte Argentario, which is located on the Tyrrhenian Sea, is well-known for the beauty and sophistication that it exudes along the coast. A sense of seclusion and awe-inspiring natural beauty can be found on the peninsula, which is distinguished by its rugged cliffs and the rich vegetation typical of the Mediterranean.

Travelers looking to get away from the rush and bustle of their daily lives can do so by escaping to the coast of Monte Argentario and losing themselves in the peaceful atmosphere of the sea. Exploration and relaxation are encouraged due to the presence of rocky coves, secret beaches, and clean waters. Sun, sea, and peace are just some of the basic joys that may be enjoyed by travelers at this destination.

A sense of coastal refinement may be found in the seaside communities of Porto Santo Stefano and Porto Ercole, both of which are positioned on a promontory. Visitors get the opportunity to observe the yachts and vessels that are anchored in the harbor while taking a leisurely stroll along the water's edge. Seafood dishes are also available. Monte Argentario is a destination that creates a feeling of seclusion and enchantment due to its combination of coastal elegance and hidden natural beauty.

The Coastline of Tuscany Is a Mystical Connection Between the Land and the Sea

The coast of Tuscany is a great example of the region's complex beauty because of the region's diverse landscapes and the cultural value of those regions. It gives tourists the opportunity to get in touch with the fundamental forces of the land and the water, to discover secluded coves and coastal trails, and to experience the allure and culture of the Italian Riviera. The mystical attractiveness of the coastline of Tuscany is not based solely on the scenery; rather, it is based on the psychological and metaphysical effect that it has on those who are able to experience it. It is a location where travelers feel that they are drawn closer to each other, where the beauty of the surroundings magnifies the love that they have with one another, and where time seems to slow down to allow for moments of connection and introspection. The coastline of Tuscany is a place that offers a one-of-a-kind combination of nature and culture, resulting in a mystical link between land and sea that cannot be found anywhere else.

Chapter 2

A Journey Through Tuscany's Rich History

Tuscany is a region of Italy that is recognized for its timeless beauty. It is known for its breathtaking landscapes, artistic treasures, and a rich history that spans millennia. Tuscany is located in the middle of Italy. This journey across Tuscany's history is a tribute to the enduring heritage of this region, where each cobblestone street, rolling vineyard, and Renaissance masterpiece tells a narrative of a lively past that has formed the cultural tapestry of not only Italy but also the entire Western world. This journey is a testament to the enduring legacy of this region because it is a testament to the enduring legacy of this region.

Traditional Origins:

The ancient Etruscans are credited with establishing prosperous city-states all across Tuscany about the 9th century BC. These city-states played a significant role in the development of Tuscany's history. These mysterious people, who are recognized for their high civilization, are said to have left behind a rich legacy consisting of art, architecture, and cultural practices that continue to fascinate historians and archaeologists to this very day. Sites such as the Etruscan tombs at Tarquinia, Volterra's Etruscan walls, and the archaeological museum in Florence offer a peek into the early foundations of Tuscan culture and can be visited to gain an understanding of their former splendor.

The Impact of Roman Culture:

Tuscany was an important contributor to the cultural, political, and economic development of the region before the establishment of the Roman Empire, when it became a component of the Roman Empire and became an integral part of the Roman Republic. The Roman influence may be seen in various places in Tuscany, notably Florence, where remnants of Roman amphitheaters, baths, and villas have been discovered.

These discoveries are a testament to the opulence and intricacy of Roman architecture and engineering. The Romans left an unmistakable stamp on the cultural development and urban design of Tuscany, which has played a significant role in the evolution of Tuscany's identity over the course of history. This heritage serves as a witness to the Romanss' persistent effect on these aspects of the region's development.

Glory of the Middle Ages:

The Middle Ages marked the beginning of a new period in the history of Tuscany. This period was distinguished by the establishment of powerful city-states, such as Florence, Siena, and Pisa, who competed with one another for political domination, economic prosperity, and cultural pre-eminence. During the middle ages, Tuscan art, literature, and architecture reached their pinnacle of excellence, thanks in large part to the proliferation of well-known religious and secular institutions that served as hubs of intellectual and artistic innovation. The towering grandeur of medieval cathedrals, such as the Duomo in Florence and the Siena Cathedral, is a tribute to the spiritual dedication and architectural prowess of this age. These cathedrals may be found in Florence and Siena, respectively.

The Emergence of the Modern Renaissance:

The Renaissance, which is considered to be the most important period in the history of Tuscany,

marked the beginning of an extraordinary period of creative, intellectual, and cultural revival that would leave an indelible impression on the entire continent of Europe. In particular, Florence became the hub of the Renaissance, as it was the city that was responsible for cultivating the creativity of illuminating figures like as Leonardo da Vinci, Michelangelo, and Botticelli. The Medici family, which was one of the most powerful families in Florence, was instrumental in subsidizing the arts and creating an environment that was favorable to the growth of humanist ideas, scientific investigation, and artistic quality. The Medicis played a vital role in both of these endeavors. The academic and cultural triumphs of this magnificent century are attested to by the opulent palaces, art-filled galleries, and ornate churches that grace the streets of Florence and other cities in Tuscany. This tangible legacy of the Renaissance is a tribute to the exceptional period's intellectual and cultural advancements.

Renaissance in Cultural Expression:

Tuscany's long and illustrious history comprises not only the domains of art and architecture, but also a deep cultural renaissance that extended beyond geographical limits and left an indelible mark on the artistic and intellectual consciousness of people all over the world. The intellectual fire and literary brilliance that marked the cultural landscape of Tuscany during the late Middle Ages and the early Renaissance may be seen exemplified in the works of significant characters in the Italian literary tradition such as Dante Alighieri, Petrarch, and Boccaccio. These authors were active in the region of Tuscany. Their contributions to poetry, prose, and philosophical thought continue to inspire academics, writers, and readers all over the world, which highlights the lasting value of Tuscany's cultural heritage in molding the development of Western literature and ideas.

Resilience in the Modern World:

The voyage through history that Tuscany has taken continues on into the modern era, which has been defined by times of political turmoil, social reform, and cultural revitalization. Tuscany was a testament to the resiliency and fortitude of its people, who persevered through misfortune and embraced the spirit of renewal and growth. From the trials of the Napoleonic Wars and the unification of Italy to the turbulent years of World War II, Tuscany was a region that was a witness to this resiliency and fortitude. In the decades following World War II, Tuscany established itself as a center for technological advancement, cultural revitalization, and international tourism. These developments attracted tourists from all over the world, who came to the region to take in its breathtaking landscapes, delectable cuisine, and priceless works of art. The region's capacity to adapt and thrive in the face of changing global dynamics and socio-economic challenges is demonstrated by the current vibrancy of Tuscany's cities, which, when combined with the region's preservation of old traditions and cultural legacy, is a monument to the region's ability to adjust to new circumstances.

Heritage in the Kitchen:

In addition to being represented in the region's architectural marvels and artistic masterpieces, Tuscany's rich history is also mirrored in the region's culinary tradition, which has received worldwide praise for its ease of preparation, its freshness, and its scrumptious flavors. Tuscan food, which is famous for its concentration on locally produced ingredients, powerful flavors, and rustic charm, encapsulates the very essence of the agricultural riches and culinary traditions of the Tuscan region. From the renowned Florentine steak, ribollita, and pappa al pomodoro to the exquisite wines produced in the Chianti and Montepulciano regions, Tuscan gastronomy offers a sensory journey that resonates with the cultural ethos and agrarian roots of the region, encapsulating the essence of Tuscan identity and hospitality. This sensory journey begins with the renowned Florentine steak and ends with the exquisite wines produced in the Chianti and Montepulciano regions.

Preserving and reclaiming natural resources:

There is a determined effort being made to preserve and safeguard Tuscany's rich historical and cultural legacy for the benefit of future generations as the region continues to develop in the modern day. The rigorous conservation efforts that are being conducted by local authorities, cultural institutions, and historical organizations are a prime example of the region's commitment to the repair and upkeep of its architectural landmarks, artistic treasures, and natural landscapes. This devotion has been exemplified by the region. Tuscany's commitment to preserving its heritage while fostering a sustainable and responsible approach to cultural stewardship and environmental conservation is demonstrated by a number of initiatives, including the protection of UNESCO World Heritage sites, the promotion of sustainable tourism practices, and the preservation of traditional craftsmanship. These initiatives serve as a testament to Tuscany's commitment to preserving its heritage.

The long and illustrious history of Tuscany is like a tapestry that has been sewn together with the threads of ancient civilizations, medieval splendor, Renaissance brilliance, and modern fortitude. From the enigmatic legacy of the Etruscans to the enduring cultural legacy of the Renaissance, Tuscany's historical journey is a tribute to the ongoing spirit of creativity, innovation, and cultural excellence that has defined the region's character over the course of the ages. From the Etruscan legacy to the cultural heritage of the Renaissance, Tuscany's historical journey is a testament to the enduring spirit of creativity, innovation, and cultural excellence. As Tuscany continues to embrace the difficulties and opportunities of the modern world, its dedication to the preservation of its historical and cultural legacy acts as a beacon of inspiration for the preservation of global cultural legacies and the promotion of sustainable cultural tourism. Tuscany is a region in central Italy. Visitors from all over the world continue to be inspired and captivated by Tuscany's rich history, which is not only a chronicle of the past but rather a living monument to the enduring legacy of human ingenuity, perseverance, and cultural transcendence.

2.1 Etruscans: The First Inhabitants

In Italy, the region that is today known as Tuscany was once inhabited by people who are commonly referred to as the Etruscans. The Etruscans were a mysterious and ancient culture. They flourished in the area a long time before the birth of the Roman Empire and left behind an enduring legacy that continues to fascinate historians, archaeologists, and everyone who are interested in history to this day. This article looks into the interesting world of the Etruscans, investigating their origins, culture, and contributions to the diverse fabric of Italy's historical past.

The First Settlers and Their Cultures:

Historians continue to disagree about where exactly the Etruscan people originated from to this day. It is impossible to deny the Etruscan people's cultural and artistic impact on the Italian peninsula, despite the fact that their language, Etruscan, is unrelated to any of the known groups of languages. Around the 9th century B.C., the Etruscan people most likely began settling in what is now known as Tuscany, where they went on to establish a civilization that thrived for several centuries. They formed a network of city-states, including as Cerveteri, Tarquinia, and Vulci, each of which had its own governance and cultural traits.

Society and Cultural Traditions:

The society of the Etruscans was renowned for its high level of development and complexity. They were accomplished in the fields of architecture, engineering, and craftsmanship. The beautiful craftsmanship of their jewelry, pottery, and sculptures demonstrates the high level of metallurgy and ceramic work that they have mastered. Particularly noteworthy is the fact that Etruscan art frequently featured scenes from everyday life, fantastical creatures, and elaborate designs for grave art.

Their society was organized in a hierarchical fashion, and at the very top was an elite governing class. The Banditaccia Necropolis near Cerveteri and the Tarquinia tombs are two examples of Etruscan burial sites that show a great deal about the Etruscans' ideas concerning the afterlife. The elaborate burial rooms and frescoes showed scenes of feasting and dance as well as the passage of the deceased to the underworld.

Religion and Political Power :

The religion of the Etruscans was very important to their culture and civilization. They shared a complex pantheon of gods with the early Romans, to whom they attributed their religious beliefs. Some of these gods, such as Tinia, who was the Etruscan equivalent of the Roman god Jupiter, had a significant role in the Etruscan religious community. Divination was an important part of the Etruscan religion, and the priests, who were called haruspices and were experts in the practice, strove to understand the intentions of the gods by performing rituals such as examining the intestines of animals.

The rituals and beliefs of the Etruscans, in addition to their one-of-a-kind writing system, had a significant impact on the development of the Roman culture. The Romans took many aspects of Etruscan religion, art, and architecture and incorporated them into their own, which was a significant contributor to the development of the Roman civilization.

The Fall and Complete Disappearance of:

In the fourth century B.C., the Etruscan civilization started to go into decline. Their demise was brought on by a number of circumstances, including civil unrest within their own society, wars with the civilizations that lived in close proximity, and the expansion of Rome. After originally adopting many aspects of Etruscan civilization, the Romans finally absorbed and integrated the Etruscans into their expanding empire. This occurred after the Romans initially acquired many features of Etruscan culture.

The Etruscan language, which was once widely used in the area, eventually died out, and now the only remnants of it are inscriptions, which offer intriguing insights into the culture of the people who once spoke it. Even though their written language was decoded in the 19th century, numerous Etruscan works have not been translated and are hence buried in mystery.

Discoveries in the Field of Archaeology and Their Legacy:

The Romans were instrumental in the development of Western civilization, and the Etruscans played a significant part in the creative, architectural, and theological inspirations they passed on to the Romans. As a result, the Etruscans' legacy goes on today.

The beautiful jewelry, ceramics, and sculptures created by the Etruscans are on exhibit at museums all around the world, including the National Archaeological Museum in Florence. Visitors to these museums are able to gaze in awe at these works of art.

The Italian region of Tuscany is the site of ongoing archaeological digs that have uncovered numerous Etruscan villages, tombs, and artifacts. Each new discovery elucidates previously unknown aspects of their history, including their culture, social organization, and technological accomplishments, so expanding our knowledge of this long-lost civilization.

The earliest people to live in the region that is now known as Tuscany, the Etruscans, made an unmistakable effect on the cultural and historical landscape of Italy and, by extension, the rest of the Western world. They continue to provide an important link to the past through their art, religion, and societal structure, all of which continue to interest historians and enthusiasts. Even though their civilization has been lost to the annals of time, the Etruscans have left behind a legacy that lives on as a tribute to human ingenuity, creativity, and the ever-present fascination with the secrets of the past.

2.2 The Renaissance: Tuscany's Golden Age

A tremendous rebirth of art, culture, and intellectual achievement was ushered in with the beginning of the Renaissance, which was a pivotal period in the history of Europe. It developed as a beacon of invention and enlightenment, and the Italian region of Tuscany was the site that personified the spirit of the Renaissance more than anywhere else in the world. During the Renaissance period, Tuscany experienced its Golden Age, which was characterized by a flourishing of art, literature, science, and philosophy that has left an indelible effect on the development of human civilization. In this investigation, we delve into the rich fabric of the Tuscan Renaissance and investigate the important individuals, creative masterpieces, and intellectual breakthroughs that distinguished this unique age.

The Initial Stages of the Renaissance:

The term "renaissance," which comes from the French word for "rebirth," refers to a period of time that saw a flourishing of cultural and creative expression roughly between the 14th and 17th centuries. It developed as a response to the medieval period that came before it, which was marked by religious dogma, feudalism, and a lack of emphasis on individualism and humanism. The Renaissance was a time when the human spirit was liberated from the restraints of tradition and religion, which enabled a flowering of human creativity and intellectual curiosity. This liberation occurred during the time period of the Renaissance.

Tuscany, with its wealthy and politically stable city-states, most notably Florence, was in a position unlike any other to become the hub of the Renaissance. It was during this time period that Florence came to be known as "the cradle of the Renaissance."

During this time period, the city became home to a plethora of talented artists, thinkers, and patrons who were responsible for transforming Florence into a center of cultural innovation.

Important People in the History of the Tuscan Renaissance:

He was a famous patron of the arts and a vital figure in the blooming of the Renaissance in Florence during the time of Lorenzo de' Medici (1449-1492), often known as Lorenzo the Magnificent. Lorenzo de' Medici lived from 1449 until 1492. Botticelli and Michelangelo were only two of the many artists and intellectuals who benefited from Lorenzo's patronage, and his impact was felt throughout the entire region, not just at Florence.

Leonardo da Vinci lived from 1452 to 1519 and is considered to be one of the most famous personalities associated with the Renaissance period. Leonardo was a polymath whose areas of expertise included anatomy, engineering, science, and art. His most famous paintings, including as "Mona Lisa" and "The Last Supper," are regarded as artistic masterpieces and continue to enthrall people all around the world.

Michelangelo Buonarroti was active from 1475 until 1564. Michelangelo was a gifted sculptor, painter, and architect who is known for producing iconic works such as the Statue of David, the ceiling of the Sistine Chapel, and the dome of St. Peter's Basilica in Rome. He was born in Italy in 1475 and died in 1564.

Sandro Botticelli, who lived from 1445 until 1510: Botticelli was a renowned painter of the Florentine School. His works, particularly "The Birth of Venus" and "Primavera," are typical of the Renaissance's emphasis on classical mythology and the beauty of human beings.

Dante Alighieri, who lived from 1265 to 1321: Even though Dante lived before the Renaissance was in full bloom, his "Divine Comedy" is nevertheless considered a key work of Italian literature. It had a significant impact on the evolution of the Tuscan language as well as Italian vernacular writing during its time.

Petrarch (1304–1374) was a poet, scholar, and philosopher. He is commonly referred to as the "Father of Humanism" since his works were so influential in the growth of humanist ideas and the resurgence of ancient literature. Petrarch lived from 1304 to 1374.

Accomplishments in the Arts:

The art of the Renaissance was characterized by an emphasis on classical ideals, a preoccupation with the human form, and an in-depth investigation of perspective and depth. Particularly important was the contribution that Tuscan artists made to expanding the parameters of artistic expression throughout this period.

Leonardo da Vinci: Leonardo's painting went much beyond merely representing the subject matter; rather, it explored scientific concepts and anatomical details. His "Vitruvian Man" depicts the human body in an ideal form that wonderfully reflects the Renaissance's preoccupation with the proportions of the human body.

Michelangelo: Michelangelo's sculptures, such as "David," demonstrated his ability in representing the human figure in all of its grandeur. Michelangelo was born in Florence, Italy, in 1475. His frescoes in the Sistine Chapel, such as the well-known "Creation of Adam," revealed a profound understanding of anatomy as well as a sense of being inspired by divine forces.

Sandro Botticelli: Botticelli's representations of mythical figures and allegorical themes, particularly in "The Birth of Venus" and "Primavera," represented the Renaissance's interest with ancient mythology and idealized beauty. Botticelli's paintings of mythological people and allegorical themes are ethereal and beautiful.

Amazing Works of Architecture:

Dome created by Filippo Brunelleschi The dome of the Florence Cathedral, which was created by Brunelleschi, is an architectural marvel that demonstrates the advancements in engineering and perspective that were developed throughout the Renaissance.

Perfect Cities by Leonardo Da Vinci Leonardo da Vinci's architectural drawings featured ideas for perfect cities that mirrored the Renaissance's concern with geometry, proportion, and harmony. These concepts were never constructed during da Vinci's lifetime, but they were included in his architectural drawings.

This palace in Florence, known as Palazzo Medici Riccardi, was designed by Michelozzo and is considered a great example of architecture from the Renaissance period due to its harmonious proportions and exquisite front.

Improvements in Intellectual Capability:

The artistic and architectural achievements of the Tuscan Renaissance are only part of the story. Additionally, it resulted in tremendous intellectual progress being made.

A defining characteristic of the Renaissance was the intellectual movement known as humanism, which placed an emphasis on the reading of classical writings as well as the cultivation of an individual's potential.

Petrarch is credited with being the founder of humanism, which advocated the quest of knowledge, the investigation of the human condition, and the revitalization of classical education. Pico della Mirandola and Marsilio Ficino were two of the prominent intellectuals who supported humanism. The cultivation of a humanistic outlook established the groundwork for the Enlightenment, which would emerge in the succeeding centuries.

Printing Press Johannes Gutenberg's creation of the printing press in the middle of the 15th century considerably facilitated the distribution of information. It made written works more widely available and accelerated the spread of ideas associated with the Renaissance.

The period known as the Renaissance in Tuscany was characterized by a remarkable flowering of intellectual and cultural life. It was a time when intellectual enlightenment was sought for with great zeal, architectural marvels were built, and works of art that are considered to be masterpieces were produced. The art galleries, museums, and architectural wonders of Tuscany are examples of the Renaissance's ongoing legacy, which can be observed throughout the region. It has made an everlasting imprint on the world, directing the development of Western civilization and serving as an inspiration to countless generations of creatives, intellectuals, and pioneers. The Tuscan Renaissance, with its celebration of the human spirit, the beauty of the natural world, and the pursuit of knowledge, continues to be an ongoing source of inspiration and admiration even in modern times.

2.3 Medici Legacy and Florence

The legacy that the Medici family has left behind in Florence is a tale of unmatched patronage, the development of culture, and political intrigue. Over the course of several centuries, members of the Medici family were instrumental in establishing Florence as the center of artistic and intellectual activity during the Renaissance period. Their impact, both as patrons of the arts and as rulers of Florence, left an unmistakable effect on the history of the city as well as its reputation as a global cultural and creative capital. Their legacy lives on in Florence.

Gaining Authority:

During the 15th century in Florence, the Medici family, which had its roots in the banking industry, rose to prominence as one of the most powerful and prominent families in the city. Cosimo de' Medici, also known as Cosimo the Elder, was the driving force behind the family's rise to prominence. He deftly navigated the complicated political landscape of the time, putting on the appearance of republicanism while quietly amassing power behind the scenes.

Support for the Arts: Patronage

Along with his descendants Lorenzo and Giuliano, Cosimo the Elder was a fervent supporter of the arts in Italy. They were aware of the culture's capacity to bring about change, and as a result, they made significant financial investments in artists, scholars, and architects. As a result of this assistance, the Renaissance was able to flourish in Florence, and the city was able to attract some of the most brilliant creative minds of the time.

Artists of Notable Reputation:

Sandro Botticelli was one of the most well-known artists to get financial support from the Medici family. Under the patronage of the Medici, he produced a number of his most famous works, including "The Birth of Venus" and "Primavera," both of which are recognized the world over as outstanding examples of Renaissance art. Lorenzo de' Medici, also known as Lorenzo the Magnificent, was not only a poet but also a patron of several writers during his reign. Through his patronage of individuals such as Angelo Poliziano and Luigi Pulci, he made a significant contribution to the growth of Italian literature as well as the revitalization of traditional forms of poetry.

Amazing Works of Architecture:

In addition, the Medici family made significant contributions to the field of architecture. The magnificent San Lorenzo Basilica in Florence, which was planned by Brunelleschi and funded by Cosimo the Elder, is a prime example of the stress placed on classical aesthetics and proportion throughout the early stages of the Renaissance. This architectural legacy was carried on by Lorenzo the Magnificent, who is known for commissioning the Palazzo Medici Riccardi, which is considered to be a prominent example of Renaissance architecture.

The Garden's Bequest to Future Generations:

The Medici family was famous for their love of gardening and the development of some of the most beautiful gardens in history during their time in power. Eleonora di Toledo, wife of Cosimo I de' Medici, is responsible for the construction of the Boboli Gardens in Florence. These gardens are a tribute to the couple's love of nature and landscaping. These gardens are a magnificent combination of formal Italian gardens and more relaxing, winding paths, and they give spectacular views of Florence from the hill on which they were built. These gardens are a stunning blend of formal Italian gardens and more relaxed, winding walkways.

Political Culpability:

In addition to the significant impact that they had on the artistic community, the Medici family held a great deal of political sway. They established a pseudo-dynasty in Florence by producing four popes and various rulers of the city over the course of their time there. Cosimo I de' Medici, who was elevated to the position of Grand Duke of Tuscany in 1569, is widely regarded as one of the most influential Medici rulers.

His administration was responsible for the fall of the Florentine Republic, but it was also responsible for establishing peace and a certain level of wealth in the area.

Banking Empire of the Medici:

The riches and power of the Medici family came from their extensive banking empire, which was spread all across Europe. They were shrewd financiers who controlled the accounts of the pope and several royal families and exerted sway over the economies of a number of different governments. Because of the interconnected nature of their riches and political influence, they were able to mold not only Florence but also the political and economic landscape of Europe.

The Fall and the Comeback:

During the Pazzi Conspiracy in 1478, which resulted in the assassination of Giuliano de' Medici and the attempted murder of Lorenzo, the Medici family went through periods of exile and internal warfare. This was most notable during the Pazzi Conspiracy in 1478. The Medici family was exiled from Florence for a short period of time, but they eventually came back and were even more powerful and cruel than before.

The end of the rule of the Medici:

In the 18th century, the authority of the Medici family in Florence was put to an end for good. The direct lineage of the Medici dynasty ended in 1737 with the passing of the last Medici king, Gian Gastone de' Medici, who did not leave any heirs. After that, Florence was under the dominion of the Habsburgs, and it wasn't until the 19th century that it was finally incorporated into a unified Italy.

Florence's Inheritance :

The influence that the Medici family had on Florence's art, culture, and politics ensures that their legacy will live on throughout the city. Their generosity is evidenced by the wonderful art galleries, museums, and architectural gems that are located throughout the city. The "David" by Michelangelo can be seen at the Accademia Gallery, "The Birth of Venus" by Botticelli can be found in the Uffizi Gallery, and the Medici Chapels can be found in the San Lorenzo Basilica. All of these works of art are considered to be masterpieces.

Although their political influence was not without its share of controversy, the Medici family was instrumental in Florence's development into a center of intellectual and artistic innovation. Their encouragement of humanism and the resurgence of classical learning were important factors in the emergence of the Renaissance, which in turn had a significant bearing on the development of Western civilization.

2.4 The Artistic and Architectural Wonders of Tuscany

Tuscany is a region in central Italy that is well-known for its exquisite artistic and architectural heritage, which spans centuries of human invention and innovation. This heritage has earned Tuscany a reputation for being one of the most beautiful in all of Italy. Tuscany is a place filled to the brim with awe-inspiring works of art and architecture, including the enduring masterpieces of the Renaissance, the beautiful villages of the middle ages, and the breathtaking vistas. In the course of this investigation, we delve into the most well-known and alluring examples of the creative and architectural beauty that can be found in Tuscany.

The Inheritance of the Renaissance:

A time of cultural and creative revival that began in the 14th century and continued into the 17th, the Renaissance left an unforgettable impression not just on Tuscany but also on the rest of the globe. The area became the hub of the Renaissance and was responsible for the development of some of the most brilliant artistic and architectural minds in the annals of human history. The city of Florence, in particular, was extremely important throughout this period of revolutionary change.

The city of Florence is known as the "cradle of the Renaissance"

Famous artists such as Leonardo da Vinci, Michelangelo, Botticelli, and Raphael all called Florence, which is commonly known as "the cradle of the Renaissance," home throughout their lifetimes. Their influence on art and architecture has retained its power to enthrall people all over the world.

The Art of Florence:

The Michelangelo sculpture known as David: The sculpture known as "David" by Michelangelo is widely regarded as one of the most recognizable works of art ever made. It is often interpreted as a representation of the aspirations of the Renaissance period. The Galleria dell'Accademia in Florence is where it is kept for public viewing.

Botticelli's masterpieces, "The Birth of Venus" and "Primavera," exemplify the Renaissance's preoccupation with classical mythology, idealized beauty, and a new approach to perspective. Both of these subjects are depicted in Botticelli's paintings. The Uffizi Gallery is where you may see them on display.

Both the "Mona Lisa" and Leonardo da Vinci's "Annunciation" are famous works of art. The "Mona Lisa" is housed in the Louvre in Paris, while Leonardo da Vinci's "Annunciation" is on display in the Uffizi Gallery in Florence. each works demonstrate Leonardo's skill of portraiture as well as his contributions to the art of sfumato, which can be seen in each of the aforementioned works.

Architecture in the Florentine Style:

The Florence Cathedral, also known as Santa Maria del Fiore, is a magnificent example of Gothic architecture. The dome of the Florence Cathedral was designed by Brunelleschi. The dome of the structure, which was constructed by Filippo Brunelleschi, is an architectural marvel that exemplifies the shift from the Gothic aesthetic to the Renaissance aesthetic.

The formidable Palazzo Vecchio, which dates back to the middle ages, currently functions as Florence's municipal hall. It has an elegant exterior and is home to an art museum that exhibits works by artists such as Michelangelo and Donatello.

Ponte Vecchio is a historic bridge in Florence, Italy, and is well-known for the one-of-a-kind shops that line both sides of the bridge. The establishments, which were once butcher shops, have since been converted into jewelry stores, creating a magnificent backdrop above the Arno River.

The Architectural Glory of Siena, a Conqueror's Rival:

Siena, located in Tuscany and with a picture-perfect medieval center, competed historically with Florence during the Renaissance. Its architecture, in particular its cathedral and the center square, which is known as the Piazza del Campo, shows an artistic and architectural legacy that is distinct from others but is just as intriguing.

Cathedral of Siena (also known as the Duomo di Siena): The Siena Cathedral, also known as the Duomo di Siena, is a Gothic masterpiece that is famous for its ornate front, breathtaking interior, and unique marble floor depicting biblical themes. It has been designated by UNESCO as a World Heritage Site.

Piazza del Campo: The Piazza del Campo is one of the most impressive medieval squares in all of Europe. It is home to the Palazzo Pubblico, which is known for housing the famous fresco "The Allegory of Good and Bad Government" by Ambrogio Lorenzetti.

The Tower of Pisa, Also Known as Pisa's Other Attractions:

Pisa is another city in Tuscany, and although it is best known around the world for its iconic Leaning Tower, the city of Pisa has much more to offer than simply this architectural marvel.

The Leaning Tower of Pisa is a bell tower that is a component of the Pisa Cathedral complex yet stands on its own as a separate structure. Its distinctive tilt, which is the result of unstable foundations, has become a symbol of the eccentricity that can be found in architectural design.

The Cathedral of Pisa, also known as the Duomo di Pisa, is a remarkable example of Pisan Romanesque architecture. The cathedral is known for its complex facade sculptures, striking interior, and gorgeous baptistery.

An Unspoiled Jewel of the Middle Ages: Lucca

Lucca is a medieval town that has been kept exceptionally well, and it is encircled by walls that date back to the Renaissance period. These walls offer tourists a glimpse of the town's rich history and architecture.

The walls of Lucca were constructed during the Renaissance period and currently serve as a tree-lined promenade that provides visitors with a fresh perspective on the city. Tourists frequently engage in the popular activities of walking or biking along these walls.

Cathedral of Lucca (San Martino church): Lucca's cathedral is a spectacular example of Pisan Romanesque architecture, notable for its exquisite marble facade and the Volto Santo, a revered wooden crucifix. The church is also known as "San Martino Cathedral."

Hill Towns of the Middle Ages:

San Gimignano is a town in Tuscany, Italy, that is famous for the many towers that date back to the middle ages. The town's cobblestone lanes and well-preserved architecture make for a picture-perfect trip back in time.

The Medicean Fortress and the Roman Theater are two of the architectural marvels that can be seen in the city of Volterra, which was founded by the Etruscans and features an old gate and walls.

This hill town, Cortona, is famous for its architecture from the Middle Ages as well as for breathtaking views over the Val di Chiana.

Villas and Farmhouses Situated in Rural Areas:

The rural landscape of Tuscany is peppered with picturesque farmhouses, villas, and estates all over the region. Numerous artists and photographers have found inspiration in the rustic elegance of these rural structures, which they have captured in their paintings and images. Some of them have been renovated into luxurious lodgings, providing guests with the opportunity to live a traditional Tuscan lifestyle while on their vacation.

Art in the Great Outdoors:

Beyond its museums and buildings, Tuscany is home to a wealth of cultural treasures. The picturesque scenery, rolling hills, vineyards, and olive groves of the region have been the source of creativity for a great number of artists, and they continue to enthrall visitors today.

Landscapes of Tuscany The rural landscapes of Tuscany are renowned for the scenic beauty

that they possess and have been depicted in a great number of artistic works. There are some of the world's most recognizable landscapes to be found in the Chianti area, the Val d'Orcia, and the Crete Senesi.

Vineyards and Olive Groves: The gentle hills of Tuscany are covered in vineyards and olive groves, which are responsible for the production of some of the best olive oils and wines in all of Italy. These vistas are stunning in addition to being abundant in all that they offer.

The artistic and architectural marvels that may be seen in Tuscany cover a broad and varied assortment of prizes. The region is a tribute to human creativity, innovation, and an ongoing commitment to preserving its rich legacy. From the masterpieces of the Renaissance in Florence to the medieval charm of Siena, the leaning tower of Pisa, and the serene beauty of rural Tuscany, the region is a testament to human creativity, innovation, and an ongoing dedication. The fascination of Tuscany resides not only in its artistic and architectural wonders but also in its capacity to transport tourists to a different period, where the past and the present coexist together in every cobblestone street, cathedral, and rolling vineyard. Tuscany's artistic and architectural treasures are only a small part of the region's overall appeal.

2.5 Tuscan Traditions and Culture

Tuscany, which is located in the middle of Italy, is well-known not only for the breathtaking scenery and artistic history that it possesses, but also for the many cultural practices and rich traditions that it upholds. The cultural fabric of the region is intertwined with centuries of history, art, and local customs, which makes Tuscany a riveting destination for people who are interested in discovering the heart of Italy. Within the scope of this investigation, we investigate the customs and the way of life that are characteristic of Tuscany.

This is the sweet life:

The joy of living well and relishing each moment is encapsulated in the Italian expression "la dolce vita," which translates to "the sweet life." This word perfectly encapsulates the spirit of life in Tuscany. The citizens of Tuscany take great satisfaction in their appreciation for the simple pleasures of life, such as taking their time over a leisurely dinner, savoring a glass of Chianti, or simply taking in the natural splendor of their surroundings. The Tuscan way of life is heavily influenced by its culinary traditions, wine culture, and the art of conversation.

Delectables for Your Mouth:

The ease, freshness, and depth of flavor that characterize Tuscan cooking have earned it acclaim all over the world. The culinary traditions of the area are strongly ingrained in the utilization of ingredients that are sourced regionally and the steadfast adherence to tried-and-true recipes. The culinary tradition of Tuscany is characterized by a wide variety of mouthwatering meals that celebrate the region's agricultural past and its commitment to the craft of leisurely food preparation.

Ribollita is a hearty vegetable soup that is a specialty of Tuscany. Its ingredients include bread, cannellini beans, kale, and a variety of other vegetables that are in season. This recipe exemplifies the Tuscan principle of reducing waste while boosting flavor, which is reflected in its name.

Pappa al Pomodoro is a dish that exemplifies Tuscan comfort cuisine because of its ease of preparation while still retaining its robust flavor. It is a thick tomato and bread soup. Basil and olive oil that has been pressed from its own fruit are the customary seasonings for this dish.

The Florentine Steak, also known as Bistecca alla Fiorentina, is a well-known meal from Tuscany that is made with a thick T-bone steak, typically sourced from Chianina cattle, that is seasoned with little more than salt, pepper, and olive oil and then grilled over a wood or charcoal fire.

Panzanella is a Tuscan salad that is created with stale bread, tomatoes, onions, and fresh basil. It is a food that is perfect for the warm summer months since it is both reviving and delectable.

Wine from Tuscany is world famous, and for good reason: the region's vineyards consistently produce world-class vintages. Chianti, Brunello di Montalcino, and Vino Nobile di Montepulciano are just a few examples of the world-class wines that are produced in this region's vineyards, which are located mostly in the Chianti, Montepulciano, and Montalcino districts.

Celebrations and Festivities that Burst with Life:

The region of Tuscany is well renowned for its vibrant festivals and celebrations, which offer a glimpse into the diverse cultural fabric of the region. These events, which range from pageants set in the middle ages to grape stomping, exhibit the heart and spirit of Tuscany.

The legendary horse race known as the Palio of Siena is held in the Piazza del Campo of the city of Siena. It is an exciting and intensely competitive festival that pits the neighborhoods, also known as contrade, of the city against one another for glory.

Viareggio Carnival: The Viareggio Carnival is one of the most famous carnivals in all of Italy. It is known for its grandiose parades, colorful floats, and beautiful papier-maché masks.

Lucca Summer Festival: This music festival is held in the picturesque town of Lucca, and because it features performances by well-known bands and musicians from all over the world, it is an event that music fans just must miss.

Festivals Celebrated During the Grape Harvest The vineyards of Tuscany come to life during the season of the grape harvest. Grape stomping, wine sampling, and other traditional forms of music and dancing are frequently included activities during these festivities.

Traditions of the People:

The region known as Tuscany is rich in folk traditions that have been handed down from generation to generation. The agricultural past of this area is reflected in these traditions through the use of song, dancing, and other forms of local ceremony.

Dance of the Tarantella The tarantella is a vibrant and rhythmic dance that is performed differently in different parts of Italy. It is a common practice for it to be carried out during festivity and festivals in Tuscany.

Canto alla Paggiola is a classic Tuscan folk song that is sung during the olive harvest. The phrase "Canto alla Paggiola" literally translates to "Song of the Olive Harvest." It is a reflection of the significance of the olive tree in the agricultural tradition of Tuscany.

The Palio Flag-Waving Challenge: During the many festivities that take place around Tuscany, various municipalities host flag-waving competitions. These events are a monument to the historical pageantry that the region has to offer.

Craftsmanship of an Artisanal Nature:

The region known as Tuscany is home to a vast number of artisanal traditions and crafts, with a large number of talented artists working to preserve traditional methods.

Not only do these crafts provide a link to the past, but the works of art that they produce are of the highest possible quality.

Crafting of Leather products in Florence Florence is famous for its leather products, including handcrafted belts, shoes, handbags, and other leather accessories. The Santa Croce neighborhood is famous in especially for its abundance of leather workshops.

Ceramics in Montelupo: The town of Montelupo is well-known for its ceramics, which are characterized by vivid designs and classic motifs. These characteristics give Montelupo pottery their distinctive appearance. Workshops are open for tourists to explore, and they sell one-of-a-kind items.

Marble Sculpture in Carrara Carrara is located in the northern part of Tuscany and is famous for the marble quarries that are located there. White Carrara marble from this area has been mined and worked for ages to produce some of the world's most magnificent sculptures and architectural wonders.

Observances that Have Stood the Test of Time:

The people of Tuscany are fiercely loyal to their traditions, which are deeply ingrained in historical practices and a sense of regional pride. Some of these events have been going on for centuries, yet they are still observed with a lot of zeal today.

This celebration, known as Festa di San Giovanni, is held on June 24 and honors St. John the Baptist, who is considered to be Florence's patron saint. There will be a procession commemorating the past, fireworks, and cultural events.

Festa dell'Uva, also known as the Grape Festival, is an event held in Impruneta, which is located just outside of Florence. Festa dell'Uva commemorates the harvest of grapes and features a procession, wine tastings, and traditional music.

Calendimaggio is a festival that takes place in the springtime in the city of Assisi. This festival is a dynamic and lively celebration that includes a historical pageant, music, and performances from the middle ages.

Religious Practices and Beliefs:

The region of Tuscany has a long history of observance of its religious customs, as seen by the numerous ancient churches and religious festivals that continue to carry significant weight for the populations that live there.

Easter Processions: Easter is commemorated all across Tuscany with processions, religious ceremonies, and pageants that honor the resurrection of Christ. These events take place on Easter Sunday. Several cities in Tuscany, including Florence and Arezzo, are renowned for their ornate festivals.

Pilgrimages: Tuscany is home to a number of different pilgrimage routes, one of which is called the Via Francigena. This route was followed by pilgrims traveling from Canterbury to Rome in the middle ages.

Religious Celebrations The cities, towns, and villages all around Tuscany celebrate their patron saints with annual religious celebrations. Parades, musical performances, and the serving of regional specialties are frequently part of these celebrations.

The traditions and culture of Tuscany are an essential component of what contributes to the region's reputation as being so charming and alluring. The region's gastronomic delicacies, festivals, and folk traditions all showcase the region's profound connection to art, food, and the celebration of life's pleasures. The artisanal craftsmanship of Tuscany is a reflection of the region's devotion to the preservation of traditional methods and the creation of wonderful works of art. In addition, the religious traditions of the region highlight the significance of history and faith in the daily lives of the people who live there. Visitors to Tuscany are immersed in a world where tradition and culture are honored with unyielding passion and a profound sense of pride. This is true whether they are taking a leisurely stroll through the magnificent countryside, relishing the food of Tuscany, or taking part in a vibrant local festival.

Chapter 3

Culinary Delights of Tuscany

Tuscany, which is located in the center of Italy, is renowned not only for the stunning scenery and extensive cultural legacy that it possesses, but also for the excellent culinary traditions that it upholds. The dishes that are created using Tuscan cooking are known for their depth of taste despite their seeming ease of preparation. Tuscan cooking is known for its emphasis on the use of fresh, high-quality ingredients. During this epicurean excursion, we will sample the delectable specialties that Tuscany has to offer, from its well-known cuisine to its magnificent desserts and wines from all over the world.

The Art of Keeping It Simple, That Is What Tuscan Cuisine Is All About

The rustic and agricultural origins of Tuscany are reflected in the food of the region, which is known for its uncomplicated style. The focus is on using fresh ingredients that are acquired from the surrounding area, which lets the food's inherent characteristics come to the fore. Olive oil, bread, wine, as well as a wide variety of vegetables and legumes, are the fundamental components of Tuscan cuisine.

Bread: essential to daily existence

Bread is not considered a side dish in Tuscany; rather, it is an essential component of each and every meal. The traditional bread of Tuscany, known as "pane sciocco," is distinctive due to the absence of salt in its recipe. This custom dates back to the middle ages, when Pisa was the dominant power in the salt trade and levied significant taxes on the commodity. Because of this, the people of Tuscany became accustomed to making do without salt in their bread, and this custom is still followed to this day.

"Ribollita," a hearty vegetable soup, is considered to be one of the most emblematic foods that originates from Tuscany and includes bread. The soup is thickened with the bread that was left over after making it into a supper that is both soothing and delicious.

Pappardelle alla Pomodoro: A Summertime Delight

The delectable soups of Tuscany are an integral part of the region's culinary history; "Pappa al Pomodoro" is an excellent illustration of this. This tomato and bread soup is a classic meal from Tuscany, and it is particularly well-liked during the warm summer months, when tomatoes are at their peak flavor and quality.

It is made with stale bread, tomatoes that have reached their peak ripeness, fresh basil, garlic, and extra-virgin olive oil of the highest quality. The end product is a delicious, hearty soup that is packed to the brim with flavor at every turn of the spoon.

A Refreshing Salad Known as Panzanella

Panzanella is another traditional dish from Tuscany that makes use of stale bread and is a regional favorite. Bread, tomatoes, onions, basil, and cucumbers are all included in this light and refreshing salad, which is then topped with olive oil and vinegar. The meal known as panzanella is extremely popular during the summer months because it features a variety of mouthwatering flavors and textures.

Crostini are the epitome of delicious appetizers

Crostini are thin toasts made from bread pieces, and they are typically used as an appetizer in Tuscany. Because they provide a blank slate on which a variety of toppings can be layered, they are an excellent choice for beginning a meal. Crostini with chicken liver paté (also known as Crostini di Fegatini), tomato and basil (also known as Crostini al Pomodoro), and creamy cheese with truffle (also known as Crostini al Tartufo) are all common toppings for crostini.

The Tuscan antipasto is known as "A Platter of Delights"

The traditional Italian appetizer course, known as antipasto, is interpreted in Tuscany as a varied and scrumptious assortment of regional specialties. It often consists of cured meats like prosciutto and finocchiona (fennel salami), pecorino cheese, vegetables that have been marinated, olives, and crostini, depending on the recipe. This appetizer would go wonderfully with a glass of wine to start.

A Dish That Will Put You at Ease: Pasta and Beans

The dish known as "Pasta e Fagioli" (which literally translates to "pasta and beans") is a traditional dish from Tuscany. Cannellini beans, tubetti pasta, and a delicious broth are the components that go into making this unassuming but satiating dish. This hearty dish is a prime example of the comfort food that can be found in Tuscany.

Traditional Tuscan Meat Dishes, Including Their Famous Steaks

The region of Tuscany is well-known for its traditional meat dishes, one of the most well-known of which is the "Bistecca alla Fiorentina." The classic Florentine steak is a thick T-bone steak that is traditionally prepared using an open flame to cook the meat. Chianina cattle are typically used for this cut of beef. Salt, pepper, and extra-virgin olive oil are the only three ingredients used to season the steak. As a consequence, the surface will be scorched and succulent, while the interior will be rare and soft. It's like something out of a carnivore's wildest dreams.

Another popular meat dish is called "Cinghiale in Umido," which is a stew made of wild boar and cooked over a low heat. A liberal helping of red wine and aromatic herbs contribute to an increase in the depth of flavor and tenderness of the meat.

Tuscan coastal cuisine, with an emphasis on seafood specialties

The coastline of Tuscany is home to a bountiful supply of locally caught seafood, which is honored in a variety of dishes served up all along the shore. A savory seafood stew known as "cacciucco" is prepared by simmering a combination of fish, shellfish, and squid in a broth made from tomatoes along with garlic, chili peppers, and red wine.

Pecorino and Beyond When It Comes to Cheese

The region known as Tuscany is home to a number of distinct cheeses, but "Pecorino" is unquestionably the most revered of all Tuscan cheeses. This cheese made from sheep's milk is available in a variety of flavors, ranging from fresh and mild to aged and pungent. It is a typical component of Tuscan dishes, whether it is grated over pasta, consumed with honey, or included on the traditional cheese platter that is served as part of the antipasto Toscano.

Desserts: The Perfect Ending Touch

Desserts in Tuscany are some of the most delectable in the world, and each one has its own

flavor profile and backstory. "Cantucci" are Tuscan almond biscuits that are typically served with a glass of Vin Santo, which is a sweet dessert wine. They have earned a reputation for having a firm and grainy consistency, making them ideal for dunking in wine.

One such well-liked sweet is the traditional Italian dish known as "Tiramisu," which is composed of alternating layers of ladyfingers dipped in coffee, mascarpone cheese, and cocoa powder. The dessert known as tiramisu is popular all around Italy, but Tuscan restaurants are particularly known for serving it.

Toasting the Region of Tuscany with Wine

Chianti is a type of red wine that is often created from Sangiovese grapes and is considered to be one of the most famous wines produced in

Tuscany. The area known as Chianti Classico, which is situated in Tuscany between the cities of Florence and Siena, is renowned for the quality of its Chianti wines.

Brunello di Montalcino: Brunello di Montalcino is a strong and complex wine recognized for its age potential. This wine is made from Sangiovese grapes alone and contains no other varieties. The village of Montalcino, located in southern Tuscany, is where it originated.

Vino Nobile di Montepulciano is a type of red wine that is mostly produced from Sangiovese grapes. It is named after the town of Montepulciano, which is located in Tuscany. It has a reputation for having a velvety smoothness to its surface.

Super Tuscans are a category of wines that became popular in the 1970s and 1980s. These wines frequently flout the norms of conventional Italian winemaking and are known as "Super Tuscans." It is possible for them to use non-traditional grape varietals and creative maturing processes, which ultimately results in wines that are daring and well acclaimed.

The search for truffles, often known as the culinary treasure hunt

Truffles can be found in copious amounts across Tuscany, particularly the highly sought white truffle. The activity of hunting truffles is a time-honored custom, and the soil in the region's woodlands is well-known for its abundance of truffles. As truffle hunters and their devoted hounds comb the woods in quest of these priceless fungus, truffle hunting is not just a gastronomic adventure but also a cultural experience.

The Farm-to-Table Approach: Supporting Local and Sustainable Agriculture

The "farm-to-table" way of thinking is profoundly embedded in Tuscany's culinary tradition and culture. Ingredients that are seasonal and obtained from the immediate area are prioritized heavily in Tuscan cooking. People are able to purchase fresh, locally farmed vegetables, meat, and dairy goods at farm markets, also known as "mercato contadino," which create a direct link between local producers and consumers.

A great number of Tuscan restaurants adhere to the "farm-to-table" philosophy, which entails the preparation of meals using products obtained from local farms and producers. This dedication to maintaining a sustainable environment and producing high-quality food is one of the defining characteristics of Tuscan cuisine.

Italian culinary customs and celebrations include the following:

The region of Tuscany, along with the rest of Italy, honors a wide range of culinary customs and festivals throughout the course of the year. Locals and tourists alike will get the chance to celebrate the nation's diverse and delicious gastronomic history at these events.

Sagra Festivals Sagra festivals are celebrations of regional cuisine that take place all throughout Italy. You can find Sagras in Tuscany that are centered on particular foods or ingredients, such as truffles, mushrooms, or chestnuts, for example. These festivities provide a wonderful opportunity to sample traditional cuisines of Tuscany and to discover the pleasures of dining with others.

The Palio dei Caci is a cheese-rolling competition that takes place annually in the enchanting town of Volterra, located in Tuscany. As part of the competition to determine who would win the title of champion of the Palio dei Caci, contestants roll enormous wheels of Pecorino cheese down a hill.

This celebration, known as La Sagra del Tordo, is held in Montalcino and honors the local hunting traditions. It features archery competitions, a historical march, and a feast consisting of delicacies made from local game.

The Tuscans commemorate the wild boar, a local delicacy, with a festival called Festa del Cinghiale. The festival is dedicated to delicacies that are created from this game animal. The Festa del Cinghiale is celebrated throughout various villages in Tuscany, and attendees have the opportunity to sample a wide variety of inventive pig dishes.

Participating in Cooking Lessons and Mastering the Art of Tuscan Cuisine

Cooking workshops are a well-liked pastime for tourists who are interested in experiencing Tuscan cuisine in a way that goes beyond the plate. These seminars give participants with hands-on training in the preparation of classic foods from Tuscany. Participants will frequently go to nearby markets to purchase ingredientss, get an understanding of fundamental cooking techniques, and prepare a complete meal from beginning to end. It is an exciting opportunity to take a bit of Tuscany back with you to your own house.

Exploring Tuscany's Viniculture Through Tours and Tastings of Local Wines

Wine lovers from all over the world travel to Tuscany because of the region's stellar reputation as a wine producing area. Visitors can explore the region's vineyards and cellars as well as learn about the process of making wine through participating in wine tastings and tours. These tours provide participants with a deeper appreciation of the region's vinicultural heritage by allowing them to do things like sip Chianti amidst the rolling hills of Tuscany and explore the cellars of Montalcino.

The Tuscan Way of Life: Eating Together and Passing the Bread

In Tuscany, eating is more than just a means of subsistence; rather, it is a revered way of life. Meals are meant to be enjoyed at a leisurely pace, with friends and family gathering together to share anecdotes, laughing, and the great food and wine that is being served.

Gold in its liquid form: Tuscan Olive Oil

In addition to its wine and art, Tuscany is renowned for the quality of its olive oil. The region's fertile ground is ideal for farming olive trees, and the olive oil that is produced as a result of these trees is highly regarded for its superior quality. Olive oil of the extra-virgin variety, also known simply as extra-virgin olive oil, is the major fat used in Tuscan cooking. It gives the food a more complex flavor. Olive oil is considered "liquid gold," and visitors can gain some insight into its creation by partaking in olive oil tastings and tours of olive oil mills.

Tuscany's Gastronomic Traditions and Their International Representation:

The cuisine that originated in Tuscany has made its way around the world, where it has been a source of inspiration for cooks in other countries as well as food connoisseurs. The cuisine, ingredients, and methods of preparation from Tuscany have all made their way into the mainstream of global cuisine, and restaurants serving Tuscan cuisine can be found in cities all over the world.

The Future of Tuscan Cuisine: Combining New Techniques with Age-Old Recipes

Even though it is strongly ingrained in history, Tuscan cuisine continues to change and adapt along with the times. Innovative meals that pay homage to Tuscany's rich gastronomic history are being created by contemporary chefs in the region by combining traditional dishes, ingredients, and preparation methods with current techniques and perspectives.

The farm-to-table mentality practiced in Tuscany is more than just a passing fad; rather, it represents an ongoing commitment to quality and ecological responsibility. The region lays a significant focus on using ingredients that are organic and produced locally, and a large number of the farms and restaurants in the area adhere to environmentally friendly practices.

Tuscany's gastronomic delights and traditions continue to be an integral component of the region's overall cultural character, despite the fact that the region continues to draw tourists and food connoisseurs from across the world.

The culinary delights of Tuscany are a reflection of the region's long and illustrious history, its foundations in agriculture, and its fervent commitment to upholding both quality and tradition. Tuscan food is a celebration of the tastes and ingredients that distinguish this wonderful country, from hearty soups and rustic meat meals to superb wines and delectable sweets. The cuisine of Tuscany includes both savory and rustic dishes.

Tuscan food is preserved not just as a gastronomic experience but also as a cultural and environmental commitment thanks to the farm-to-table concept, the appreciation of local ingredients, and the emphasis on sustainability.

Visitors to Tuscany are welcomed into a world where food is not only nourishment but a celebration of life, community, and the rich tradition of this gorgeous region. Whether they are enjoying a Florentine steak, indulging in a glass of Chianti, or learning the art of Tuscan cooking, visitors to Tuscany are welcomed into a world where food is more than just nourishment.

3.1 Tuscan Cuisine: Simple, Fresh, and Flavorful

The rich agricultural heritage and culinary traditions of Tuscany are reflected in the region's well-known cuisine, which is known for its uncomplicated style and its emphasis on using only fresh, high-quality ingredients. Tuscan cuisine has its origins in the rich areas of central Italy, and it is distinguished by its earthy allure, powerful tastes, and profound respect for the fruits and vegetables of the local seasons. Because of its emphasis on uncomplicated preparation and use of fresh ingredients, Tuscan cuisine has become a favorite among gourmands all over the world. In this investigation, we delve into the heart of Tuscan cuisine, its most famous dishes, and the guiding principles that give the region its own distinct identity in the culinary world.

The Practice of Keeping Things Simple:

The concept of keeping things as simple as possible is fundamental to Tuscan cooking. It is common practice in Tuscan cuisine to construct dishes with a limited number of components, so maximizing the exposure of the unadulterated flavors of the fresh products used. The complexity of the cooking procedures or the intricacy of the garnishes are not as important as the freshness and flavor of the ingredients. This method exemplifies the region's devotion to respecting the natural essence of each component, which results in the creation of dishes that are both reassuring and exquisite despite their apparent lack of complexity.

Ingredients that are Suitable for the Current Season:

The utilization of local, fresh, seasonal produce grown on the fertile lands of Tuscany is honored and celebrated in the cuisine of that region. The agricultural rhythms of the seasons are reflected in the meals of Tuscany, which rely on the wealth of the land for everything from their flavorful tomatoes and fragrant basil to their powerful olive oil and hearty legumes. Not only does the emphasis on locally obtained ingredients improve the flavor of the dishes, but it also encourages a more sustainable and environmentally conscientious approach to the preparation of food.

Bread and Olive Oil: Reasons to Celebrate

Bread and olive oil are essential elements of Tuscan cuisine, both of which have a long and storied history in the region's culinary tradition. The production of the traditional Tuscan bread known as "pane sciocco" is unique in that it does not include the use of salt. This makes it possible for the bread to complement and absorb the flavors of other ingredients in dishes such as the timeless ribollita soup and the invigorating panzanella salad.

Olive oil, sometimes known as "liquid gold," is an indispensable component in Tuscan cuisine. It imparts a robust, fruity flavor to a wide variety of foods, ranging from salads to stews, and is a common term for olive oil.

Typical Flavors Found in Rural Areas:

The flavors of sun-ripened vegetables, aromatic herbs, and meats produced locally are infused into dishes in Tuscan cuisine, which is a magnificent reflection of the region's countryside and its culinary traditions. The rustic traditions of Tuscan farming villages are honored via the preparation of substantial soups and stews, such as pappa al pomodoro and hearty bean stews. These dishes demonstrate the region's profound connection to the land and the harvests that occur throughout the year.

Iconic Dishes Typical of Tuscany:

The ease of preparation and the depth of flavor in Tuscan cuisine are both exemplified by a number of the region's most famous dishes. "Ribollita," a hearty vegetable soup that is supplemented with bread, beans, and seasonal vegetables, shows the custom of making a substantial and delicious supper out of scraps of food that have been left over from other preparations. This hearty tomato and bread soup, known as "Pappa al Pomodoro," highlights the vivid flavors of sun-ripened tomatoes and the aromatic basil, resulting in a dish that is both cozy and reflects the essence of Tuscan cooking.

The utilization of stale bread to produce a dish that is both enjoyable and appropriate for the summertime is exemplified by "Tuscan Panzanella," a refreshing bread salad that is bursting with the flavors of fresh tomatoes, cucumbers, onions, and basil. The "Bistecca alla Fiorentina," a traditional Florentine steak, exemplifies the region's fondness for high-quality meats and straightforward seasoning, which allows the meat's inherent flavors to take the spotlight.

Festivities and Traditions Relating to Food:

The cultural customs and joyful occasions that are celebrated in Tuscany are inextricably entwined with the cuisine of the region. Local food festivals, also known as "Sagras," highlight the different flavors of Tuscan cuisine. These festivals provide a platform for local producers and chefs to share their culinary creations with the community as well as with tourists that are in the area. These events put the spotlight on the region's seasonal vegetables, artisanal cheeses, and world-famous wines, and they provide a complex tapestry of flavors and experiences for people who are passionate about food.

The Classicism of Wines from Tuscany:

The aromas of Tuscan cuisine are excellently complemented by the world-famous wines produced in Tuscany, such as Chianti, Brunello di Montalcino, and Vino Nobile di Montepulciano, among others. These refined wines, which are produced from Sangiovese grapes and aged to perfection, are the perfect complement to the robust tastes of Tuscan cuisine. The result is a delicious harmony of flavor and texture that captures the spirit of the region's rich culinary tradition.

The Tuscan Table: A Feast in Honor of Life and Community in Tuscany:

The act of dining in Tuscany is more than just a gastronomic adventure; rather, it is a festivity that honors life and the community. Meals are revered occasions where loved ones join together to delight in the sumptuous flavors of Tuscan food, trade anecdotes, and make recollections that will last a lifetime. The warmth and hospitality that are characteristic of the Tuscan way of life may be seen reflected in the sociable atmosphere, as well as in the appreciation for good food and company.

The Contemporary Analytical Perspective:

Traditional Tuscan recipes and preparation methods are being rethought by chefs and foodies in order to come up with exciting new meals. This is happening despite the fact that Tuscan cuisine is known for having a gastronomically significant history. A vibrant and interesting culinary landscape that pays homage to the cultural heritage of the region is offered by contemporary Tuscan cuisine, which blends tradition with modernity and offers a fusion of the two.

Cooking Classes and Experiences That Bring the Farm to the Table:

Cooking courses and farm-to-table experiences provide travelers an authentic and hands-on opportunity to master the art of Tuscan cooking. These types of experiences are ideal for tourists who are interested in being fully immersed in the world of Tuscan food. Participants typically begin their exploration of Tuscan cuisine by going to the area's local markets, where they choose their own fresh products and then collaborate with seasoned chefs to produce classic Tuscan dishes. These classes not only provide a more in-depth grasp of the Tuscan cooking techniques, but they also offer a genuine flavor of the culinary traditions that are associated with the region.

Olive oil from Tuscany is known as the "liquid gold" of the region

Olive oil from Tuscany, which is known for its outstanding quality, is an essential component of Tuscan cuisine. It gives each dish a flavor profile that is unmistakably Tuscan. Visitors are able to learn about the creation of this golden elixir by participating in olive oil tastings and touring olive oil mills. This includes learning about the cultivation of olive trees as well as the extraction and bottling processes.

This first-hand experience sheds light on the significance of olive oil in Tuscan cuisine as well as the effort that is put out to ensure that it continues to be of the highest possible quality.

The Legacy of Tuscan Cuisine Beyond All Frontiers:

Tuscan cuisine has made an unmistakable impact on the gastronomic world, serving as an inspiration to cooks and people who are passionate about food all around the world. The meals of Tuscany have been recognized as having crossed cultural barriers due to their ease of preparation, emphasis on using fresh ingredients, and rich flavor profiles. As a result, Italian food has become increasingly popular in countries all over the world. Tuscan restaurants may be found in places all over the world, providing foodies from all walks of life with a taste of the gastronomic legacy of the region.

The cuisine of Tuscany is a celebration of the region's rich agricultural past and culinary traditions. It is distinguished by its uncomplicated style, its use of fresh ingredients, and its intense flavor profiles. Dishes are created that are both soothing and exquisite in their simplicity as a result of the commitment to using food of the highest quality and seasonality, as well as the emphasis on the natural essence of each individual item. The cuisine of Tuscany is more than just a celebration of food; it is also a celebration of life, community, and the abundant gastronomic history of this captivating region. Visitors to Tuscany are welcomed into a world where food is a testament to the flavors, traditions, and the deep connection to the land that characterize the Tuscan culinary identity. Whether savoring a rustic Tuscan soup, indulging in a glass of Chianti, or engaging in a hands-on cooking lesson, visitors are welcomed into a world where food is a testament to the tastes, traditions, and the deep connection to the land that define the Tuscan culinary identity.

3.2 Tasting the Chianti Wines

Chianti is a well-known wine region that can be found in the middle of Tuscany, Italy. It is famed for the great wines it produces as well as the stunning surroundings that surround it. Chianti provides wine lovers with a one-of-a-kind opportunity to embark on a sensory trip through the extensive viticultural heritage of Tuscany thanks to the region's undulating hills, scenery that is covered in vineyards, and old wineries. A tasting in Chianti reveals the region's various terrain, winemaking processes, and the complex flavors that have made Chianti wines a treasure among oenophiles all around the world, from the world-famous Chianti Classico to the eclectic Super Tuscans.

Learning More About the Chianti Region:

The discovery of Chianti's magnificent vineyards, where the Sangiovese grape has the preeminent position, is the perfect way to start a trip around the region. The Sangiovese grape, which is renowned for its vivacious acidity, robust flavors, and exquisite tannins, is the foundation of Chianti wines, helping to define both their one-of-a-kind personality and flavor profile.

Each vineyard and winery in the Chianti region is a treasure trove of sensory sensations thanks to the territory's different microclimates, altitudes, and soil compositions. This contributes to the complexity and diversity of the wines produced in the region.

The Classico Varietal of Chianti:

Chianti Classico is revered for its extensive history, remarkable quality, and distinctive black rooster seal. It is considered to be the heart and soul of the Chianti region. The presence of the black rooster on the label of a bottle of wine denotes that it satisfies the high quality criteria set forth by the Consorzio Chianti Classico. This ensures that the wine inside the bottle is authentically representative of the Chianti Classico region. Chianti Classico wines frequently exhibit hints of rich cherry, plum, and earthy undertones, resulting in a beautiful balance of fruit and acidity that is reflective of the region's terroir as well as the winemaking traditions that have been practiced there.

Introducing: the Super Tuscans

The Chianti region is famous not only for its classic Chianti wines but also for the pioneering Super Tuscans that are produced there. These forward-thinking wines, which are frequently produced through the use of non-traditional grape varietals and procedures for blending, have reinvented Tuscan viticulture and pushed the conventional bounds of winemaking. Wine fans like Super Tuscans because of their robust flavors, complex profiles, and international renown. These characteristics give Super Tuscans the ability to offer a look into the innovative spirit and commitment to perfection that characterizes the region.

Visits to Vineyards and Tastings of Their Wines:

A trip through the illustrious vineyards and wineries of Chianti is an essential component of any excursion that centers on the tasting of wine. Visitors are able to become completely immersed in the process of winemaking thanks to the fact that many of the local wineries give guided tours of their facilities, which range from the vineyards to the cellars. The complexities of the Chianti wines can be better understood via the use of guided tastings, which also offer a sensory adventure that delves into the complex flavors, aromas, and textures that distinguish each vintage. It is common practice for seasoned sommeliers and winemakers to impart some of their knowledge to others, thereby facilitating a more in-depth comprehension of the processes involved in creating wine as well as the distinctive qualities of the wines that are produced in the area.

Food Complements and Other Gastronomic Delights:

The tasting of Chianti wines is typically accompanied by an exquisite selection of delicacies from Tuscan cuisine. The powerful red wines of Chianti are an excellent complement to the region's traditional cuisine, such as the succulent Florentine steak known as bistecca alla Fiorentina or the hearty pasta dish known as pappardelle al cinghiale, which is served with a sauce made from wild pig. The interaction of tastes between the wines and the local cuisine underlines the region's devotion to the art of food and wine pairing, displaying the adaptability of Chianti wines and their capacity to improve the dining experience. In addition, the interplay of flavors highlights the region's commitment to the art of food and wine pairing.

The very definition of hospitality in Tuscany:

Visitors to the region are greeted with the famous warmth and kindness of the Tuscan people,

which is an added bonus to the sensual delights of sampling Chianti wines. The rich cultural past and familial traditions that have created Chianti's viticultural landscape are often revealed through the stories that local winemakers and vineyard owners narrate about the wines they produce and the vineyards on which they grow them. After the last drop of wine has been swallowed, the sociable environment, when combined with the spectacular beauty of the Tuscan countryside, makes for an experience that is unforgettable and that completely immerses oneself in the setting.

Viticulture that is Friendly to the Environment in Chianti:

The adoption of sustainable and organic viticulture techniques by a significant number of Chianti wineries is indicative of their dedication to the responsible management of the region's natural resources and the protection of the environment. These wineries give sustainability a high priority, putting an emphasis on organic agricultural practices as well as renewable energy efforts. This helps to ensure the long-term health and vitality of the ecosystem that the vineyards are a part of. The region's determination to preserve its cultural and environmental heritage for future generations is reflected in its emphasis on sustainable viticulture, which not only contributes to an improvement in the overall quality of the wines but also demonstrates this dedication.

The Chianti Brand Around the World:

Wine aficionados and connoisseurs from all over the world are captivated by Chianti wines because of the indelible impression they have made on the global wine business. Because of the region's dedication to quality, history, and innovation, Chianti wines can be found on the shelves of wine shops and restaurants all over the world. This has helped the region solidify its place as a significant participant in the international wine industry. Chianti wines have a place in the hearts and palates of wine enthusiasts all over the world that is richly merited because to their singular personality and the tremendous workmanship that goes into producing them.

The tasting of Chianti wines is more than simply an experience for the senses; it is also a voyage through the illustrious history of viticulture in Tuscany, as well as its cultural traditions and stunning surroundings. Every bottle of Chianti wine, from the time-honored Chianti Classico to the forward-thinking Super Tuscans, encapsulates the region's commitment to quality, craftsmanship, and a profound connection to the land. This is true whether the wine is a Chianti Classico or a Super Tuscan. A tasting experience in Chianti offers a look into the essence of Tuscan viticulture and the ageless fascination of this enthralling wine area. Whether exploring the vineyards, relishing the local culinary delicacies, or simply basking in the warmth of Tuscan hospitality, a tasting experience in Chianti has something for everyone.

3.3 Olive Oil and Truffle Delights

Not only does Tuscany have a reputation for producing world-class wines, but also for producing great olive oil and truffles because to the fertile land and Mediterranean climate of the region. Tuscany has gained a reputation as a veritable paradise for foodies thanks to the singular way in which its terroir and heritage have been preserved throughout the area. During this mouthwatering excursion, we will investigate the exquisite world of Tuscan olive oil and truffles. We will learn about the processes of olive oil production, the techniques of truffle hunting, and the mouthwatering meals that best highlight these highly coveted components.

Olive Oil, the Tuscan Region's "Liquid Gold"

Olive oil from Tuscany is known as "liquid gold" for a good reason, and this nickname has stuck. The countryside of this area is dotted with seemingly never-ending rows of olive trees, each of which yields a fragrant, opulent, and delicious oil that serves as the foundation for Tuscan cuisine. The finest grade olive oil is extra-virgin olive oil, which is produced from the initial pressing of the olives. Tuscan cuisine makes extensive use of this type of olive oil.

Olive oil production has been a centuries-old tradition in Tuscany, and the methods for cultivating, harvesting, and pressing olives have been handed down from one generation to the next. The end result is a product of superior quality that improves the flavor of dishes both straightforward and complex in their preparation. Olive oil from Tuscany may be used in a broad variety of recipes, ranging from drizzling it over a toasted bruschetta to serving as the foundation for a number of different types of pasta sauces and salad dressings.

Visitors visiting Tuscany have the opportunity to participate in tours of olive gardens and mills, during which they may observe the entire production process, beginning with the gathering of olives and ending with the pressing of oil. These trips provide the opportunity to sample freshly pressed olive oil, an experience that is frequently referred to as the one that is the most genuine and flavorful.

Treasures buried deep underground: truffles

Another delicacy that is strongly ingrained in Tuscan tradition is the use of truffles, which are secretive fungus that have a pungent aroma. The settings that are ideal for growing truffles may be found throughout Tuscany's woodlands, notably in the wooded regions that surround the Apennines. The pursuit of truffles, which is an ancient custom that has been passed down through the years, is an art form in and of itself.

Truffle hunters, also known as "trifolai," travel into the woods accompanied by their particularly trained truffle-hunting dogs, which are often Lagotto Romagnolo or mixed breeds with an acute sense of smell. The dogs are able to pick up on the aroma of truffles that are hidden deep within the forest floor. When it comes to finding these elusive treasures, truffle hunters and their canines have a wonderful working relationship that helps them locate the fungi.

Truffle varieties found in Tuscany include:

The Italian region of Tuscany is home to a number of unique truffle types, each of which has a flavor and scent signature all its own. The "white truffle" (Tuber magnatum), commonly referred to as "Tartufo Bianco," is the type of truffle that fetches the highest price in this part of the world. These truffles have a flavor that is characterized as earthy, garlicky, and complex, and they have a strong scent to go along with it. They are a rare and coveted delicacy. In order to take advantage of the full flavor and scent of white truffles, they are typically shaved or grated over dishes right before they are served.

The black truffle, also known as "Tartufo Nero," is a type of the Tuber melanosporum fungus that can be found in Tuscany. Even though their flavor is more subdued than that of white truffles, black truffles are nonetheless held in extremely high regard in the culinary world. They are commonly used in risottos, pasta recipes, and meat preparations, where they lend a robust and earthy aroma to the meal.

Delights in Truffles Found in Tuscan Cooking:

Truffles are a highly prized component of the food that is prepared in the Tuscan region. They may be used to improve the flavor of a variety of different recipes. In many Tuscan kitchens, truffle-flavored olive oil, truffle paste, and truffle butter are pantry staples. These ingredients allow cooks to impart a hint of earthy truffle flavor into the dishes they prepare.

One of the most well-known foods to feature truffles in Tuscany is called "Tagliatelle al Tartufo." This dish is comprised of fresh tagliatelle pasta, truffle shavings, and olive oil that has been infused with truffle flavoring, and it is served as a pasta dish. This meal perfectly exemplifies Tuscan cuisine, in which the earthy tastes of the truffle are given the prominence they deserve.

Another traditional dish that features truffles is called "Carne al Tartufo," and it is a type of meat dish that is typically created with tender beef or veal and served with a sauce that is based on truffles. This meal does a wonderful job of highlighting the ways in which truffles supplement and amplify the tastes of the meat.

Truffle Festivals: A Gastronomic Occasion to Celebrate

Throughout the course of the year, the region of Tuscany plays host to a number of truffle festivals known as "Sagras." The culture of the region's truffles is being honored and celebrated through these events, which also serve as a venue for truffle aficionados to sample this exceptional delicacy in a variety of prepared foods.

The "Mostra Mercato Nazionale del Tartufo Bianco" in San Miniato is widely regarded as being among the most prestigious truffle festivals in all of Tuscany. This event is a celebration of the white truffle. This event provides attendees with the option to purchase fresh truffles as well as a variety of truffle-themed foods and items, as well as demonstrations on how to find and harvest truffles.

Truffle and Olive Oil Tasting Tours in Tuscany:

In the Italian region of Tuscany, visitors may participate in immersive tours of olive oil and truffle production, which provide an in-depth view into the creation of these gastronomic gems. The culinary component of truffle tours often consists of truffle hunting expeditions accompanied by trained dogs, followed by cooking workshops in which participants learn to prepare dishes that incorporate truffles.

Visitors on olive oil tours are taken to olive orchards and mills, where they are provided with insights into the production process of olive oil. Participants will have the opportunity to sample olive oil that has recently been pressed, as well as learn about the various olive kinds and production methods that go into producing high-quality oil.

Harvesting of Truffles in a Sustainable Manner:

In order to safeguard and maintain truffle populations, Tuscany is placing an increased emphasis on truffle harvesting methods that are environmentally responsible. Hunters of truffles are currently being encouraged to observe truffle seasons, adhere to hunting regulations, and utilize methods that are environmentally benign. These efforts are being made to conserve the natural ecosystem and assure the continued viability of truffle production in the long term.

The Influence of Tuscan Olive Oil and Truffles on the Global Market:

The high quality of olive oil and truffles produced in Tuscany has brought international fame and admiration to the region. Olive oil from Tuscany is highly regarded in culinary circles all over the world because of the fruitiness and complexity of its flavor. Similarly, truffles from Tuscany are a prized delicacy that commands a high price due to their scarcity and opulence. You can find them on the menus of upscale restaurants all over the world, and they captivate the taste buds of gourmands everywhere.

Olive oil and truffles are not only culinary marvels, but also an essential component of the cultural and gastronomic identity of the region of Tuscany known as Tuscany. Tuscany has become a gastronome's dream thanks to the region's commitment to tradition, its mastery of the art of truffle hunting, and its production of olive oil of the highest quality. A culinary trip through Tuscany's olive groves and truffle-laden forests is a sensory study of this exceptional region's gastronomical delights. Whether you are relishing truffle-infused pasta or experiencing the aroma of fresh truffles in the woods, a culinary journey through Tuscany's olive groves and truffle-laden forests is an unforgettable experience.

3.4 Dining in Charming Tuscan Trattorias

In addition to its illustrious past, breathtaking vistas, and top-tier wine production, the region of Tuscany is lauded for the quaint trattorias that can be found across the region. These restaurants institutions that epitomize Italian culture take diners on a gastronomic adventure through Italy's rich culinary history and traditions, where the true spirit of Tuscan cuisine is artfully maintained. Dining in Tuscany is a memorable experience that can be had in a variety of settings, ranging from homey trattorias run by families and tucked away in picturesque villages to lively restaurants in the middle of Florence. In this investigation, we dig into the world of Tuscan trattorias, uncovering the traditions, the food, and the warm hospitality that characterize these enchanting enterprises.

A Trattoria Must Have These Core Components:

A restaurant with its origins in the Italian culinary heritage, a trattoria is a cozy and laid-back establishment that places a premium on authenticity, straightforward preparation, and a strong relationship with the neighborhood it serves. These quaint eateries are well-known for their laid-back attitude, which frequently includes checkered tablecloths, rustic décor, and a pleasant milieu that emanates warmth and comfort for its patrons.

The origin of the word "trattoria" may be traced back to the Italian verb "trattare," which can be translated as "to treat" or "to handle." It reflects the sense of being treated like family, which is appropriate given the setting of the meal. Trattorias are gathering spots for friends and family, where they enjoy delicious cuisine together while making cherished memories.

The Authentic Taste of a Tuscan Trattoria:

In Tuscany, going out to eat at a trattoria is about more than just getting food; it's a beloved way of life. These charming restaurants provide a calm and unhurried atmosphere in which guests may take their time eating their meals, savoring the tastes and practicing the fine art of conviviality.

When you walk into a trattoria in Tuscany, you'll frequently be greeted as if you were a long-lost friend. The crew is noted for their friendliness and genuine hospitality, and they are ready to make your dining experience one that you will remember for a long time. It is not unheard of for the owner or chef of the establishment to come to your table and make recommendations about their favorite dishes or the regional delicacies.

Menus from a Tuscan Trattoria:

The culinary customs of a region are generally reflected in the straightforward nature of the fare served in trattorias. These menus highlight the abundance of fresh, seasonal products that are typically sourced from farms and marketplaces in the surrounding area. The dishes are made with care and accuracy, which enables the inherent flavors of the ingredients to come through in a more pronounced manner.

Pappa al Pomodoro is a Tuscan bread and tomato soup that is commonly served with fresh basil and a drizzle of extra-virgin olive oil. This hearty dish is a joy for those who appreciate the simpler things in life.

A Tuscan specialty, ribollita is a hearty vegetable and bread soup that is traditionally cooked with leftovers, highlighting the thriftiness and resourcefulness that is characteristic of the region.

Tagliatelle al Tartufo is a pasta dish that exemplifies the use of seasonal ingredients and the essence of Tuscan cuisine. It is made with fresh tagliatelle with shavings of black or white truffle.

The hearty Florentine steak known as bistecca alla Fiorentina is traditionally prepared by searing it over an open flame or grilling it, and then simply seasoning it with olive oil, salt, and pepper.

Risotto al Chianti is a traditional Tuscan dish consisting of a silky risotto cooked with Chianti wine, which imparts the dish with the characteristics of the region's most famous wine.

Panzanella is an invigorating bread salad that is traditionally prepared with stale bread, tomatoes, cucumbers, onions, fresh basil, and a light drizzle of olive oil.

Pappardelle al Cinghiale is a meal that features wide strands of pasta topped with a decadent sauce made from wild boar and exemplifies the affection that Tuscans have for game meat.

Crostini are toasted bread pieces that are topped with an assortment of delectable spreads like chicken liver paté or cream that has been infused with truffles.

Tiramisu is a traditional Italian dish that consists of alternating layers of ladyfingers dipped in coffee, mascarpone cheese, and chocolate.

Cantuccini & Vin Santo is a traditional dish from Tuscany that consists of almond biscotti (cantuccini) that have been dipped in Vin Santo, a sweet dessert wine.

The Trattoria Wine List:

The reputation that Tuscany has earned as a wine producing region extends to its trattorias. Here, wine lists typically feature a selection of wines produced in the region, particularly those from the Chianti and Montalcino regions. These wines were selected to pair well with the dishes that are featured on the menu, resulting in an atmosphere that is congruous and pleasurable to dine in. The staff is often informed and happy to offer the ideal wine pairing for your dinner, regardless of whether you prefer a white wine that is crisp and refreshing or a bold red wine.

Trattorias that Are Run By Families:

The preponderance of family-owned and -operated businesses among Tuscan trattorias is one of the most charming elements of these institutions. These trattorias are frequently handed down from one generation to the next, along with the recipes and culinary customs that are treasured and maintained by the family.

It may feel as though you are dining in someone's house when you go to a trattoria that is run by a family, but you will also have the advantage of a trained chef preparing your food. You can taste the passion and pride that these families have invested in their businesses in each and every dish that they serve.

Undiscovered Jewels & Trattorias Slightly Off the Beaten Path:

Some of the most memorable trattorias are frequently located off the main path in less populous towns and villages. This is true even if larger cities such as Florence and Siena provide a wide variety of restaurants to choose from. These hidden treasures may not be featured in guidebooks, but they provide a genuine and personal experience where you can immerse yourself in the culture of the area while savoring food prepared with ingredients gathered from neighboring farms and markets. In addition, they are excellent places to eat.

Festivals held in trattorias:

The region of Tuscany is home to a plethora of festivals that celebrate the culinary customs of the region, and trattoria festivals are not an exception. At these events, which are held to commemorate the art of Tuscan cooking, trattorias from various towns and villages set up booths to display the meals that are considered to be their specialties. Guests can sample a variety of flavors, ranging from those that are straightforward and familiar to those that are daring and unique, all while taking in the joyous mood that is present at these meetings.

Trattorias Often Offer Cooking Lessons:

There are a lot of trattorias in Tuscany that provide cooking classes for anyone who want to learn how to cook in the traditional Tuscan style. Participants are given the opportunity to learn how to produce traditional Tuscan foods through these hands-on experiences, such as making their own pasta, preparing delicious sauces, and preparing mouthwatering desserts. You have the option of going to the area's local markets with the chef to select the fresh ingredients for your supper, and then coming back to the trattoria's kitchen to prepare the meal in its entirety.

Trattorias Must Strive for Long-Term Sustainability:

In the most recent few years, Tuscan trattorias have placed a greater emphasis on being environmentally responsible. A good number of these companies have adopted environmentally friendly methods, such as minimizing the amount of food waste they produce, procuring organic and locally grown ingredients, and conserving energy. These efforts demonstrate the trattorias' dedication to protecting the natural riches of the region and providing support to the community members who live there.

Enjoying a lunch at one of Tuscany's quaint trattorias is about more than simply satiating your appetite; it's about embracing a way of life. These restaurants provide patrons with a taste of the tradition, culture, and hospitality of Tuscany, all while cooking cuisine that celebrate the region's seasonal produce and ingredients. The essence of Tuscan cuisine can be found at trattorias, which range from homey dishes like pappardelle and tiramisu to more refined dishes like bistecca alla Fiorentina. Each encounter is a monument to the rich culinary tradition and the warm embrace of Tuscan hospitality, whether you are dining in a restaurant that is a well-kept secret in a quaint village or savoring classic cuisine in a trattoria that is bustling with activity in the city.

3.5 Preparing Tuscan Dishes: Recipes and Cooking Classes

The cuisine of Tuscany, which is renowned for its uncomplicated nature and concentration on locally sourced, high-quality ingredients, features a delectable assortment of dishes that perfectly embody the spirit of the region's illustrious culinary history. Recipes from the Tuscan region represent the region's strong connection to the land and the seasonal harvests in a variety of forms, ranging from robust soups and savory pasta meals to luscious meats and delectable sweets. Participants are given the opportunity to master the art of producing traditional Tuscan meals from seasoned chefs in a comfortable and friendly setting while taking part in cooking workshops in Tuscany, which offer both an immersive and hands-on experience.

One of the most well-known dishes to come out of Tuscany is called "Ribollita," and it is a hearty soup made with bread and vegetables that typifies the region's economical yet tasty approach to cooking. Another dish that is considered to be a classic is called "Pappa al Pomodoro," and it is a tomato and bread soup that is both straightforward and soothing. It is flavored with the lively flavors of sun-ripened tomatoes and the aromatic basil. "Pappardelle al Cinghiale," a rich and luscious wild boar pasta, delivers a savory taste of Tuscan tradition to those who are fans of pasta.

Participants in cooking classes in Tuscany gain a full understanding of the methods and ingredients that are crucial to Tuscan cooking during their time in the region. Participants will frequently begin by going to the local markets to select fresh produce, meats, and cheeses. By doing so, they will gain an understanding of the significance of using seasonal ingredients in Tuscan cooking. Once participants have returned to the kitchen, experienced chefs will walk them through each stage of the cooking process, providing pointers and advice on how to create realistic flavors and textures. Participants in a cooking class join together to make and enjoy the fruits of their labor, so building memories that will last a lifetime and gaining a better appreciation for the culinary traditions of Tuscany. Cooking classes foster a sense of camaraderie and community.

Chapter 4

The Language of Love in Tuscany

Not only is Tuscany famed for its breathtaking scenery, historic cities, and rich cultural legacy, but it is also renowned for the language of love that seems to pervade every corner of the region. Tuscany is an amazing region located in the center of Italy. In this investigation of 3,000 words, we are going to look into the profound link that exists between Tuscany and the idea of love, and we are going to deconstruct the singular aspects that add to the region's appeal as a romantic destination. We will explore the many facets of the landscape of love in Tuscany, from the lilting tones of the Tuscan dialect to the enticing aromas of the region's cuisine and the fervent artwork that has evolved from the region's cities.

The Melody of Love Is Spoken in the Tuscan Dialect

Language is widely regarded as the most significant manifestation of a culture's underlying values, and for the people of Tuscany, language itself is an incarnation of love. The Tuscan language, also referred to as "Toscano," is renowned for having lyrical and poetic elements, which make it an effective vehicle for conveying a variety of feelings, especially those associated with love. The melodic intonations, gentle consonants, and flowing vowels of the Tuscan dialect create an environment of romance and passion that is unequaled.

Poets of distinction, such as Dante Alighieri, Petrarch, and Boccaccio, wrote some of their most famous works in the enticing Tuscan language. This is where the poetic history of the Tuscan dialect may be found. Their poetry, letters, and stories all ooze a profound sense of love and yearning, which helped pave the way for the region's image as a romantic destination. When listening to or speaking this entrancing accent, which appears virtually tailor-made for the declaration of love, one cannot help but feel the stirring of the heart.

The Beauty and Charm of Italy's Tuscan Countryside

The stunning scenery of Tuscany acts as a canvas on which nature paints its own version of a declaration of love. The lovely landscape, which includes rolling hills, vineyards, and quaint villages, seems to have been designed specifically with romance in mind. The natural splendor of the area is best exemplified by the well-known Val d'Orcia, which is included as a UNESCO World Heritage site. Feelings of affection and tranquility are evoked by the landscape's softly rolling hills, which are dotted with cypress trees and interspersed with fields of sunflowers. Numerous artists, poets, and lovers have been moved to create by the breathtaking beauty of these places, and those individuals' hearts have been won over as a result.

The architecture of Tuscany, with its old villages and rustic stone farmhouses, contributes significantly to the region's already alluring allure as a romantic destination. Under the warm Tuscan sun, small, quiet alleyways, secret courtyards, and charming piazzas provide the ideal setting for couples to stroll hand in hand or share a passionate kiss as they bask in the warmth of the region.

The Romance of Food in Tuscany's Traditional Cooking

The ease, sincerity, and depth of flavor that are hallmarks of Tuscan cooking have earned it acclaim all over the world. In Tuscany, the act of sharing a meal is more than just a gastronomic pleasure; rather, it is a public confession of love and a celebration of being together. The openness, sincerity, and ardor with which people in Tuscany approach their romantic relationships are reflected in the manner in which they cook and share their cuisine.

Not only are dishes such as ribollita, pappa al pomodoro, and pici pasta with wild boar sauce excellent, but they are also a monument to the love that Tuscans have for their region and the traditions that they have passed down to them. These recipes have been handed down from generation to generation, and their preparation is a labor of love that frequently requires the participation of the entire family. An event that is both intensely emotional and uniting is when people share a meal by breaking bread together and taking their time enjoying each bite.

The region of Tuscany is also renowned for producing wines of international renown, such as Chianti, Brunello di Montalcino, and Vernaccia di San Gimignano, amongst others. These wines from Tuscany are illustrative of the idea that over the course of time, both love and wine can develop and become more profound. The undulating vineyards that blanket the region are not only a source of livelihood, but also a metaphor of the fertile ground from which love, like the best grapes, can bloom. Not only do the vineyards provide a source of income, but they also symbolize the fertile ground.

The Creativity of Tuscany and the Art of Love

Some of the most renowned artists in the history of the world have made their homes in Tuscany; the works of these artists have long been associated with feelings of love and longing. It was in Florence, Italy, that the cultural movement known as the Renaissance got its start, and it was during this time that creative masterminds such as Leonardo da Vinci, Michelangelo, and Botticelli emerged. These artists created masterpieces that continue to inspire and stir powerful emotions, most commonly those revolving around love and the appreciation of beauty.

Both "The Birth of Venus" and "Primavera" by Botticelli show idealized concepts of love and beauty, with the feminine form serving as the focal point of each of the paintings' respective compositions. These paintings have come to be regarded as iconic symbols of the celebration of love and desire that occurred during the Renaissance.

Dante Alighieri's "Divine Comedy" is a piece of literature that narrates the story of his search for his beloved Beatrice as he travels through Hell, Purgatory, and Heaven in an effort to find her. The narrative is an enduring investigation of love, devotion, and the nature of the human experience since it is interwoven with the tremendous love he had for her throughout its entirety.

The Cinematic Romance of Tuscany

The seductive appeal of Tuscany has not only been immortalized in works of art and literature, but it has also established itself as a mainstay in the world of film. Numerous movies that center on the topic of love have used the region's stunning landscapes, historic towns, and romantic atmosphere as the setting for their stories.

Under the Tuscan Sun, which was released in 2003 and was based on the book of Frances Mayes, is considered to be one of the most iconic movies that takes place in Tuscany. The protagonist of this tale is a recently divorced American lady who, on a whim, decides to purchase a villa in Tuscany, setting her on a path toward both personal growth and romantic fulfillment. The film does an excellent job of showcasing the region's natural beauty as well as the curative power of love.

Another well-known film is "A Room with a View" (1985), which was adapted from a novel written by E.M. Forster. It chronicles the narrative of a young Englishwoman's journey of self-discovery and love while she is traveling throughout Italy, with a significant portion of the film taking place in the lovely town of Florence. The movie takes place in Italy. The film takes place in the beautiful environment of Tuscany, and its themes revolve around love, culture, and social standing.

The existence of the film industry in Tuscany is not restricted to projects in Hollywood. Italian filmmakers, like their American counterparts, have praised the location for its enchanting atmosphere. One movie that fits this description is called "Il Postino" (1994), and it follows the story of a postman who meets and falls in love with a local woman while he is delivering letters to the great poet Pablo Neruda. The film portrays the essence of love, poetry, and the Italian way of life through its setting on the island of Procida, which is located not too far from Tuscany.

Festivals in Tuscany: A Celebration of Love

The allure of Tuscany is heightened by the fact that the region plays host to a plethora of festivals and events that center on love and passion. One of these events is the Feast of St. Valentine, which is held in Terni, which is a town in the southern part of Umbria and is located not too far from the border with Tuscany. Terni, which is thought to be the birthplace of Saint Valentine, the patron saint of love and lovers, is a particularly romantic location on the 14th of February due to the fact that he is associated with the city.

Festa della Rificolona, which takes place once a year in Florence, is an enchanted festival that

honors the city's long-standing traditions as well as its relationship to love. The custom of commemorating the birth of the Virgin Mary is what drew inspiration for the festival known as "rificolone," which included the lighting of lanterns. The streets of Florence are filled with the entrancing glow of these lanterns, which creates an atmosphere that is both romantic and celebratory.

The famous Palio di Siena horse race, which takes place twice yearly in Siena, is another event that symbolizes the love and passion of Tuscany. This race takes place twice yearly in Siena. The Palio is a vivid show of the love and allegiance that Sienese people have for their neighborhoods, and it is also a true reflection of the violent rivalries and passions that exist amongst the city's several contrade, often known as districts.

Tuscany's Many Romantic Love Tales

Throughout the course of history, Tuscany has served as the setting for a countless number of real-life love stories, each of which has its own special allure and mystery. These love stories have been imprinted on the past and the culture of the area, and they have become a component of the region's romantic legacy.

The romance between Dante Alighieri and Beatrice Portinari is one of the most well-known and well-known love stories associated with Tuscany. The unrequited love that Dante had for Beatrice, a woman whom he had just a few brief encounters with, is at the center of the poet's greatest work, the "Divine Comedy." Their history has come to represent the concept of love that is beyond comprehension and beyond one's grasp, a topic that continues to enthrall romantics all over the world.

Francesco and Bianca, both of whom were members of the influential Medici family in Florence, are the subjects of another well-known love story from Tuscany. Bianca Cappello, a Venetian beauty, captivated the heart of Francesco, also known as Francesco de' Medici, who fell hopelessly in love with her. Because Francesco was already married to his first wife, their passionate love affair was considered scandalous during that time period.

In the end, they tied the knot, and theirs is a love story that is also entwined with political drama and heartbreak. Their turbulent relationship continues to pique the interest of historians as well as fans of romantic comedies.

A Destination for Couples Seeking Romance, Tuscany

For many years, couples looking for a romantic trip have chosen Tuscany as their destination of choice. It is the ideal place for couples to make their own unique and unforgettable memories thanks to the region's historic cities, opulent countryside homes, and world-class restaurants.

People frequently refer to Florence as the "heart" of Tuscany because of the city's rich artistic and cultural traditions as well as its charming atmosphere. Couples may experience the city's rich history and cultural past by visiting the Uffizi Gallery, walking down the Arno River, and sharing a gelato in the shade of the Ponte Vecchio. All of these activities can be done while in Florence.

Agriturismi, which literally translates to "farmhouse accommodations," are scattered across the Tuscan countryside and provide visitors a taste of rural life as well as a tranquil respite from the rush and bustle of everyday activities. Intimate moments may be had in abundance in Tuscany, whether they be spent sipping wine in a vineyard, taking a relaxed bike ride through the rolling hills, or simply appreciating the peace and quiet of the countryside.

The coastal regions of Tuscany, such as the Argentario Peninsula and the Tuscan Archipelago, both offer beachside getaways that are ideal for romantic getaways. These areas are perfect for married couples who share a passion for the water and want to experience the region's rich cultural heritage at the same time.

Love Lessons Learned in the Tuscan Countryside

The region of Tuscany may teach visitors important lessons about love that go beyond the romantic. A deeper understanding of love, relationships, and perhaps life itself can be gained from the region's cultural and historical features.

Both the cuisine and the style of life in Tuscany place a strong emphasis on being unpretentious and true to oneself. This might be interpreted as a metaphor for love, which suggests that it ought to be forthright, honest, and genuine to who it is. Love, much like a dish from Tuscany that has been expertly made, does not require a lot of embellishment in order to be satisfying and nourishing.

Connection to the Land The people of Tuscany have a great connection to their land, and this connection serves as a reminder of how important it is to maintain a sense of one's own roots and to remain linked to the earth. It is necessary to remember where you came from and to keep a connection to your own identity even if you are sharing your life with another person. This is especially important in romantic relationships.

Passion and Expression Both the melodic aspects of the Tuscan dialect and the artistic legacy of the region underscore the significance of passion and expression in romantic relationships. It is not enough to merely have the emotion of love; this feeling should also be shared and honored. Love ought to be a creative force in our lives, just like Botticelli's paintings and Dante's writings were creative forces in their own eras.

Time and Patience: Just as Tuscan wines get better with age, we are reminded that love, too, can develop and become more profound with time and patience. In a culture that values quick gratification, Tuscany serves as a reminder that there are certain things that are worth patiently waiting for and cultivating over time.

Community and Tradition: The celebrations of love, such as the Palio di Siena and the Feast of St. Valentine, highlight the importance of community and tradition in romantic relationships. Love is not merely a personal experience; rather, it permeates all aspects of culture, society, and history. The relationships that hold two people together can be strengthened via shared experiences of joy and affection.

The deep connection that Tuscany has always had with the concept of love can be seen not only in the region's picturesque landscapes, mouthwatering cuisine, and rich creative past, but also in the region's very culture and sense of self. Love, in all of its guises, is said to flourish in this part of the world because of the people who live there, their history, and the customs that have been passed down for generations.

Tuscany captures the essence of love in a variety of ways: the poetic quality of the Tuscan dialect; the breathtaking landscapes; the delectable cuisine; the passionate art; the real-life love stories that have unfolded here; and so on. It is a place that never fails to invigorate us and serve as a constant reminder of the splendor and power of love in all of its myriad guises.

Travelers and lovers will continue to be lured to Tuscany, where they will find not only a site of beguiling beauty but also a profound connection to the language of love. Tuscany is known for its wine, which has a long history of being associated with romantic love. The enduring charm of Tuscany serves as a reminder that love, much like a well-aged wine, only improves with the passage of time, and that in the end, what really matters is not the destination but the journey.

Tuscany will always be there, whispering the sweet language of love to those who seek it, whether you are strolling hand in hand through the streets of Florence, eating a romantic lunch in a Tuscan trattoria, or gazing out over the rolling hills at sunset. So, whether you are doing any of these things, Tuscany will always be there.

4.1 The Musicality of the Italian Language

It is not for nothing that Italian is frequently referred to as "the language of music" due to the extraordinary musicality of the language. This Romance language is praised for having a rhythmic cadence, melodic intonation, and rich phonetics, all of which combine to make it a pleasure to both listen to and speak. During this investigation into the melodic beauty of the Italian language, we will delve into the fundamental aspects that contribute to its cultural relevance as well as its influence on the fields of art and music.

The Sounds of Italian, an Exercise in Phonetic Elegance

The melody of the Italian language is inextricably linked to the phonetics of the language. The language of Italian is distinguished by the way its vowels and consonants combine in such a way as to provide a balance between soft and sharp sounds. This harmony is achieved through a delicate balance, similar to that of a musical composition in which a variety of instruments contribute to the overall harmony.

The musical aspects of the Italian language are enhanced by the fact that its pronunciation system is straightforward and consistent. The pronunciation of each letter is the same across the language, which makes it user-friendly and straightforward for people who are not native speakers. This method of accurate pronunciation is absolutely necessary in order to keep the musical flow of the language intact.

The Rhythmic Heartbeat of Italian Music Is Called Melodic Intonation

The melodic intonation of the Italian language is one of the aspects that sets it apart from other languages. It is well known that people who speak Italian have the capacity to transmit feeling as well as meaning through the rise and fall of their intonation. This melodic nature infuses regular discussions with a one-of-a-kind musicality, transforming even the most mundane
 exchanges into seeming like poetry dialogues.

The Italian language makes use of a method known as stress accent, in which particular syllables within a word are emphasized by employing a change in pitch or volume in the speaker's voice. The language takes on a more melodic quality as a result of this accentuation, which also makes it easier to convey nuances of feeling, emphasis, and intent. It's almost as if each sentence had its own musical score, complete with crescendos, decrescendos, and other dynamics that communicate emotion.

A Vocal Symphony Featuring the Melodic and Harmonious Sounds of Vowels

Vowels play an important part in the Italian language and contribute to the lyrical sound of the language. The vowel sounds in Italian are articulated with a high level of clarity and precision, despite the fact that there are just a few of them. Because each vowel sound can be articulated independently, it is possible to create euphonic pairings and diphthongs in this language. The musicality of the language is heightened by the importance placed on the quality and purity of the vowels.

Vowel sounds of the Italian language are widely regarded as among the most beautiful in the entire world. The openness and purity of vowels like as "a," "e," and "o" makes it possible to create a rhythm that is continuous and flows smoothly. Due to the fact that many people find this quality endearing in the Italian language, it is frequently used as a language of choice for lyrical expressions, poetry, and music.

The Rhythmic Pulse Comprised of Consonant Harmony

Consonants in Italian also contribute to the language's musicality, in addition to the vowels' mellifluous qualities. Consonants are pronounced with precision and clarity, and the rhythmic pulse of the language is created by the consonants' and vowels' harmonious interplay with one another. Consonants are employed in order to highlight particular syllables and improve the cadence of the sentence as a whole.

The use of consonants in the Italian language is well-balanced, avoiding an overabundance of harshness or abruptness. Because of this equilibrium, the transition from one sound to the next in the language is seamless, giving the impression that one is listening to a river of speech. The absence of the heavy glottal stops found in certain other languages when articulating consonants is one factor that contributes to the musicality of the language as a whole.

Poetry with Rhythm: The Italian Language in Literature

The literary world has been profoundly influenced by the melodious quality of the Italian language. Because of the rhythmic and melodic aspects of the language, Italian literature, and particularly poetry, has been lauded for a very long time for its capacity to express profound feelings and vivid imagery. This is particularly true of Italian poetry. Through the poetry that they wrote, Italian poets such as Dante Alighieri, Petrarch, and Giovanni Boccaccio displayed the language's capacity to evoke feelings of both passion and beauty.

The "Divine Comedy," which was composed by Dante some time in the 14th century, is still considered to be one of the most famous works of Italian literature. Not only is the poem revered for the profound religious subjects it explores, but also for the poetic and musical qualities it possesses.

Dante is known for his use of the poetry style known as terza rima, which comprises a series of rhymes that weave in and out of each other to create a musical flow throughout the poem. The rhythmic structure of terza rima, when combined with the melodic Italian language, results in "The Divine Comedy" being an outstanding example of literary music.

Petrarch, who is most known for his sonnets and canzoni, wrote works that addressed concepts related to love and beauty. The musicality of Petrarch's poetry, which includes rhyme schemes and meter that have been meticulously designed, accentuates the feelings that he is trying to portray. Because of the musicality of the Italian language, his poetry have been recognized all over the world as emblematic expressions of love and yearning.

Expressions of Opera: Italian in Musical Operatic

Opera is sung in Italian, and the musical features of the Italian language have had a significant impact on the development of classical music throughout the world. Operas, such as those written by composers such as Verdi, Puccini, and Rossini, are renowned for the emotive Italian lyrics and powerful music that they combine in their works. The combination of the Italian language and classical music results in an experience that is mesmerizing and profoundly moving for all parties involved, including the musicians and the listeners.

In order to perfect their Italian pronunciation and vocal delivery, opera singers frequently undergo extensive training. Singers are able to convey a wide range of emotions with their voices thanks to the melodic intonation of the language and the rich vowel sounds it contains. Language is a crucial part of the operatic experience because it enables actors to convey the intensity, drama, and complexity of their characters. Italian is an essential language.

For instance, "La Traviata," which was composed by Verdi, is a well-known opera that exemplifies the interaction between the Italian language and music. The poetic beauty of the language in which the soaring arias and passionate duets are performed lends an additional layer of depth to the emotional impact of the music. The Italian libretto provides an additional layer of emotional depth to the music, which together create an experience that is really immersive.

Italian Identity through the Lens of Language as a Cultural Identifier

The cultural identity of Italy is imbued with a profound sense of harmony, which is reflected in the melody of the Italian language. People from many different parts of the world and walks of life are brought together via a shared understanding of the language. It is a wellspring of national pride and contributes to the cultivation of a sense of shared heritage and identity among Italians.

The musical elements of Italy's language have had a significant impact on the country's long and illustrious history of music and art. The Italian language continues to play an essential role in the operatic heritage despite the fact that Italian opera in particular has left an unmistakable impact on the rest of the world. The continued popularity of Italian opera, with performances being held in famous locations all over the world, is evidence of the nation's deep commitment to its language.

The Appeal of Italian Around the World: Italian, the Language of Passion

The melodic quality of the Italian language contributes to its widespread popularity. It is frequently understood to be a language of ardor, romance, and beauty, which strikes a chord with individuals hailing from a variety of cultural origins. This appeal is not limited to music and literature but extends to ordinary communication, where the language's melodic properties may make even banal talks appear beautiful. This appeal is not limited to music and literature but extends to everyday speech.

The melodic appeal of Italian is what draws many people to study and speak the language, since it is widely regarded as one of the most attractive languages to both listen to and speak. People frequently discover that the musicality of the Italian language enthralls them, regardless of whether they are studying the language for the sake of travel, business, or personal enrichment.

A symphony of sound and expression, the Italian language is distinguished by its phonetic refinement, melodic intonation, and rhythmic poetry. Because of its poetic aspect, it has become an effective tool for communicating feelings, relating stories, and producing works of art. The musicality of the Italian language is demonstrated by works of Italian literature and opera, and the cultural value of the language goes well beyond the borders of Italy.

The power of language is demonstrated by the capacity of Italian to infuse both feeling and beauty into even the most mundane of communications. It serves as a useful reminder that language is not only a medium for the transmission of information; rather, it is a channel via which individuals can establish more profound and significant bonds with one another. The Italian language serves as a useful reminder that how we talk can be just as important as the words that we choose, and that language, in its most developed form, has the potential to be a wellspring of creative ideas and an outlet for artistic expression.

4.2 Love and Romance in Italian Culture

Love and passion are inextricably intertwined with the Italian way of life. Love is at the center of Italian culture, as seen by the passionate embraces of lovers that can be seen in the charming streets of Rome as well as the lyrical displays of affection that can be found in Italian art and music. In the course of this investigation, we will delve into the profound link that exists between love and the culture of Italy, and we will unearth the various ways in which love is honored, expressed, and adored all over the nation.

The sweet life of romance is known as "la dolce vita"

It is well known that Italians have a lust for life and an appreciation for the finer things in life; love is no exception to this rule. The idea of "la dolce vita," also known as "the sweet life," is profoundly embedded in Italian culture. It refers to many areas of life, including love and romance, and it embraces the entire country. The Italian culture places a strong emphasis on living in the present and appreciating the value of meaningful relationships with others.

Relationships of a romantic nature are considered to be an essential component of "la dolce vita." Italians are well aware of the significance of cultivating love and romance in their lives, and they do it in a variety of ways, including doing evening "passeggiatas" (strolls) down streets with cobblestones and gathering together for meals in quaint trattorias. The Italian way of loving urges couples to appreciate every time together and to find happiness in the uncomplicated joys of being in each other's company.

Amore — Love as a Common Linguistic Denominator

The term "amore" comes from the Italian language and means "love." It is understood all around the world as a global statement of affection. The concept of love is accorded a significant amount of importance in Italian society, and this applies not just to romantic partnerships but also to the ties that bind families and friends together. Many people believe that love is one of the most profound and meaningful experiences one may have in their lifetime.

Passion is a trait that is commonly associated with Italians, and this passion can be seen in the manner in which they express their love for one another. Since the time of Dante Alighieri and Petrarch, the art of writing love letters and romantic poetry has been a treasured heritage in Italy. The lyrical character of the Italian language makes it particularly well-suited for portraying the breadth of human experience and the ferocity of love.

The Craft of Enticement: Italian Romance as Depicted in Film and Literature

The Italian culture has been responsible for the creation of some of the most famous love stories in the history of literature and film. There are many stories about love and romance in Italian culture.

Some of the most famous examples include "Romeo and Juliet" by William Shakespeare, which takes place in Verona, and "The Leopard" by Giuseppe Tomasi di Lampedusa, which is about a passionate love affair.

The subject of love has been portrayed in a meaningful way on the big screen in a number of films, including those produced in Italy. Films such as "La Dolce Vita," "Cinema Paradiso," and "The Bicycle Thief" are able to depict the complexity and beauty of human relationships, which contributes to the worldwide obsession with Italian romance. The fascination of many of these cinematic love stories is heightened by the fact that they are set in Italy, specifically in the country's entrancing towns and landscapes.

Love as Depicted in Italian Art, the Romance of Art

The celebration of love and romance is a central theme throughout the history of Italian art. Art has been used for a very long time as a means for expressing and immortalizing love in its many forms. Some of the first examples of this can be seen in Botticelli's "The Birth of Venus" and Caravaggio's "Amor Vincit Omnia" (Love Conquers All).

In particular, the art of the Italian Renaissance investigated concepts such as love, beauty, and the connection between people. Figures that were commonly entwined in passionate embraces were depicted in works of art such as paintings and sculptures. Love, whether it be divine or worldly, was an important topic that was explored in the works of painters such as Raphael, Titian, and Leonardo da Vinci.

One of the most well-known love stories in Italian art is that of Paolo and Francesca, which Dante Alighieri described in his work "Divine Comedy." Numerous artists, most notably Dante Gabriel Rossetti and Jean-Auguste-Dominique Ingres, were inspired by their tragic love affair to create paintings that capture the moment. As a result of these artistic interpretations, the story of Paolo and Francesca has become a symbol of love that is both forbidden and passionate.

The Romantic Tongue: Italian (also known as the Language of Love)

The very nature of the Italian language is such that it lends itself to professions of love and passion because of its inherent romanticism. Because of its lyrical features, melodic intonation, and euphonic vowel sounds, it is considered to be one of the most romantic languages in the entire world. The lyrical and expressive manner in which Italians communicate is another factor that contributes to the overall allure of the culture.

The expressions of love and adoration used in Italian are both beautiful and passionate. Expressions of affection and real feeling, such as "Ti amo" (I love you) and "Amore mio" (my love), are common in Italian conversation. The act of expressing one's love for someone in Italian is an expression that is both personal and cultural at the same time.

Weddings are a traditional way of celebrating love in Italian culture.

Weddings in Italy are lavish affairs that celebrate the bride and groom's love for one another and their families. The participation of a person's ancestors and close relatives in the wedding service is a clear indication of the significance of the family unit in Italian culture. The value of love and commitment is symbolized by a number of traditions and customs that are observed during weddings, which are typically elaborate and expensive affairs.

The custom of showering visitors with "confetti," also known as sugared almonds, is one example of such a tradition. These almonds serve as a metaphor of the sweet life that the newlyweds will enjoy together. The importance of food and love in the lives of Italians is demonstrated by the lavish wedding feast, which is filled with mouthwatering dishes prepared in the Italian tradition. The addition of music and dancing at Italian weddings contributes to the joyous and enchanting mood of the celebration.

Local Love Across All of Italy in a Romantic Novel

The numerous regions that make up Italy each have their own distinct ways of expressing love and devotion. Gondola rides and masquerade balls are just two examples of the romantic activities that have helped turn Venice into a mecca for couples from all over the world. Couples who are looking for a romantic getaway will find the undulating hills, vineyards, and quaint villages of Tuscany to be an appealing backdrop for their trip.

The city of Naples, with its lively street life and people who are passionate about what they do, emits a sense of affection and coziness. Both in literature and in real life, many different love stories have been inspired by Sicily's rich history as well as its spectacular landscapes.

The expression of Love as a Form of Art

Love and passion are not merely components of Italian culture; rather, they constitute an art form that is performed and celebrated on a daily basis. The Italians have a well-developed awareness that love is not merely a feeling but also a way of life. It is the secret to living "la dolce vita" and savoring every moment, whether it be a shared meal, a sweet hug, or a passionate expression of adoration. It is the key to experiencing "la dolce vita."

The strong connection that Italian culture has always had to love and romance serves as a good reminder that these emotions are universal and do not recognize national boundaries. Love is a potent and transformational force, and Italian culture encourages us to appreciate and express it with the same fervor and ardor that have characterized the nation over the course of its history.

4.3 Romantic Phrases and Expressions

The capacity of language to convey feelings of love, passion, and affection makes it a potent tool. Romantic words and expressions provide us the opportunity to communicate our most profound sentiments and feelings to the people we hold most dear. These words have the power to rekindle the flames of love and deepen the links between couples, regardless of whether they are spoken gently at an intimate moment or written down in a letter that is written from the heart. In the course of this investigation, we will delve into the entrancing world of romantic phrases and expressions, demonstrating how they can evoke feelings of love and affection for one another.

1. "I Love You"

    The power contained in the three simple words, "I love you," cannot be overstated. They are able to communicate feelings that are at once the most profound and the most universal, transcending both language borders and cultural divides. It doesn't matter what language you speak—"Ti amo" in Italian, "Je t'aime" in French, or "Te amo" in Spanish—they all mean the same thing. These words are a proclamation of love and the basis upon which all manifestations of romantic love are constructed.

2. "You Complete Me"

    This iconic line from the film "Jerry Maguire," which was delivered by Tom Cruise, encapsulates
    the concept that love may bring about a sense of completion and fullness in one's life. When you tell someone, "You complete me," you are acknowledging that they are the person who fills in the gaps in your life and provides you with a sense of wholeness and satisfaction.

3. "My Heart Belongs to You"

    This expression is a beautiful way of expressing the profound affection and dedication you feel for a particular person. It gives the impression that your entire heart, which is where your feelings and affection are stored, is devoted to the person you love the most. A sincere expression of your emotional connection is to say something along the lines of "My heart belongs to you."

4. **"You Are the Love of My Life"**
   When you say to someone, "You are the love of my life," you are acknowledging that you have a special and irreplaceable space in your heart for that person. It is an indication of a love that is profound and everlasting, one that is unaffected by the passage of time or the conditions of life.

5. **"You Make My Heart Skip a Beat"**
   This statement perfectly depicts the exhilaration and heart palpitations that can be brought on by love. It gives the impression that being close to someone you care about may be an exciting and exhilarating experience, as if the mere presence of that person causes your heartbeat to speed up.

6. **"You Are My Sunshine"**
   This heartfelt expression is a dedication to the person in your life who brightens it up and makes it seem more welcoming. Your significant other brings more light into your life than the sun does during the day. A heartfelt and endearing declaration of love and gratitude, "You are my sunshine" is often heard.

7. **"You're the One I Dream About"**
   Dreams frequently contain revelations of our most private aspirations and yearnings. When you tell someone, "You're the one I dream about," you're letting them know that they hold a significant position not only in your conscious but also in your heart and thoughts. Even your subconscious may be thinking about them.

8. **"Forever and Always"**
   A vow of undying love and devotion is conveyed by the use of the phrase "forever and always" in a pledge. It is a sign that your love is steadfast and unwavering, and that it will be able to weather the passage of time.

9. **"You're the Most Beautiful Person I've Ever Met"**
   This expression goes beyond merely referring to a person's outward look to communicate the idea that the person's inner beauty and personality are what make them the most alluring to you. It's the kind of flattery that warms your own being.

10. **"In Your Arms, I Find Home"**
    When you feel at home, you are feeling secure, at ease, and completely like yourself. This idiom conveys the sentiment that being encircled by the arms of one's significant other evokes feelings of acceptance and safety.

11. "Every Moment with You Is a Treasure"
    The value of time spent with a loved one cannot be overstated. This proverb emphasizes the importance of appreciating and making the most of every minute spent together. It is an indication of the caliber of the time that was spent together.
12. "You Are the Music of My Heart"
    This figurative expression likens the person you love to music, which is something that has the capacity to arouse strong sensations and emotions. It gives the impression that being in their presence is like listening to a lovely song that plays in your heart.
13. "I Totally Adore You"
    The emotional confession of intense love and affection that "I adore you" carries with it. It goes beyond the basic expression of "I love you" and conveys a profound regard and fondness for the person to whom it is addressed.
14. "You're the Spark in My Life"
    The statement "your beloved is the spark that ignites the flames of love and passion" compares the person you love to a spark. It gives the impression that they infuse your life with a sense of vitality and excitement.
15. "You Are My Soulmate"

The concept of having a "soulmate" refers to having a profound and meaningful connection with another person. Declaring that another person is your "soulmate" means that you believe they are your "perfect match," that you intend to spend the rest of your life with them, and that your souls are in tune with each other.

Words have the capacity to captivate, connect, and deepen the link between two people. This power is especially potent in the arena of love. Romantic words and expressions enable us to explain the beauty and depth of our sentiments, so generating an environment of love and affection that stays in the hearts of people who hear them. Romantic phrases and expressions can be found in literature, music, and film. These words are a monument to the enduring strength of love and the many ways that it may be conveyed. Whether whispered in a private moment or shared with the world, these words are a testament to the power of love.

4.4 Love Stories and Legends from Tuscany

Since ancient times, the charming area of Tuscany in central Italy, which is recognized for its picture-perfect landscapes, medieval cities, and rich cultural history, has served as the setting for ageless love stories and legends. These tales of romance, passion, and unrequited love have worked their way into the very fabric of Tuscan society, giving depth and fascination to this enthralling region in the process. During this excursion, we will delve into some of the most compelling love stories and legends from Tuscany. Each of these tales is a testament to the eternal power of love, and they will serve as our point of departure.

1. Pasticceria Paolo e Francesca
   One of the most well-known love stories to come out of Tuscany is the sad story of Paolo and Francesca, which Dante Alighieri memorialized in his work "Divine Comedy." During the 13th century, Paolo and Francesca were residents of the city of Pisa. They belonged to the Malaspina family and lived there. The fact that Francesca was married to Paolo's brother Gianciotto made it difficult for them to be open about their love affair. The plot takes a dark and sad turn when Gianciotto finds out that they are in love with one another and, overcome with wrath, decides to kill them both. Dante comes face to face with the doomed lovers in the second circle of Hell. Here, they are doomed to spend eternity being buffeted by the winds, which symbolizes the turmoil caused by their unrequited love.
2. The Illusion of Francesco de' Medici and Bianca Cappello
   During the 16th century, Bianca Cappello, a noblewoman from Venice, and Francesco de' Medici, the Grand Duke of Tuscany, were involved in a passionate and tumultuous love affair. Due to the fact that Francesco was already married to his first wife, Joanna of Austria, their union was fraught with political drama and rumors of scandal. After she passed away, he wed Bianca, which caused a commotion within the Medici family as well as in other circles. The unsolved circumstances surrounding Bianca's passing, in addition to Francesco's unexpected dying, lent an air of mystique to their narrative and gave rise to rumors of poisoning and a possible plot. The passionate affair that took place between Bianca and Francesco has never ceased to captivate both historians and romantics.
3. The Folklore of the Old Bridge of Florence
   The historic Ponte Vecchio Bridge in Florence is supposed to have been the setting for a passionate love story. Benvenuto Cellini, a young goldsmith, was said to have been hopelessly in love with a stunning Florentine woman, according to the legend. To gain her favor, he designed a golden padlock for the bridge that served as a representation of his love for her. The padlock was placed on the railing of the bridge, and as a symbol of their devotion to one another, couples began connecting their own padlocks to the railing. Today, as a continuation of this age-old custom, lovers from all

over the world fasten padlocks to the railings of the Ponte Vecchio as a declaration of their undying devotion to one another and as a symbol of Florence's ongoing appeal as a romantic destination.

4. **The Romantic Complicated Tale of Dante and Beatrice**
   Beatrice Portinari was a woman who Dante Alighieri saw only infrequently during his lifetime, although the famous poet and author of "The Divine Comedy" was profoundly in love with her. During his lifetime, he only saw her a few times. The remembrance of Beatrice served as the inspiration for some of Dante's most exquisite lyrics, and she became the muse for Dante's poetry. Their love, which was never returned in life, was immortalized in Dante's works, where he presents Beatrice as a symbol of holy love that can never be attained. Despite the fact that their love was never returned in life, it was. This strong bond between Dante and Beatrice has become both a symbol of sublime and eternal love and one of the most acclaimed love stories in all of Italian literature.
5. **The Tale of the Island of Elba and Its Legend**

Isola d'Elba is an island located off the coast of Tuscany, and it is the setting for an enthralling legend about love and yearning. According to the legend, a young fisherman by the name of Agostino fell in love with the stunning nymph Elba, who resided in the seas around the island. Elba's feelings for Agostino were so strong that she underwent the transformation into a mermaid so that she could be with him. It was believed that their love was so strong that even after they had passed away, they continued to protect and watch over the island, making sure that it thrived and thrived well into the future.

The myths and legends of love that come from Tuscany are a testimony to the eternal power of love and its capacity to enthrall the human heart. These stories, which may be distinguished by tragedy, intrigue, or lifelong passion, have become an essential component of Tuscan culture. They lend depth and richness to the romantic attraction of the country. Tuscany, with its breathtaking landscapes and historic cities, continues to inspire and fascinate lovers, writers, and dreamers, which helps to ensure that the tradition of love in this amazing region will continue for generations to come.

Chapter 5

Tuscan Villas and Retreats

Tuscany is a region in central Italy that is renowned for its mouthwatering cuisine, visually stunning scenery, and culturally significant history. It is also the location of some of the most seductive and enticing villas and retreats that can be found anywhere in the world. These accommodations, which are scattered among undulating hills, attractive vineyards, and ancient towns, provide guests with a one-of-a-kind and all-encompassing experience that combines the friendliness of Italian hospitality with the peace and quiet of the Tuscan countryside. In this exhaustive guide, we will delve into the attractiveness of Tuscan villas and retreats, covering their history, architecture, amenities, and local experiences, as well as their vital contribution to the cultural fabric of the region.

1. The Inheritance of Tuscan Villas: An Overview of Their Historical Development
   The history of the Tuscan villas extends back centuries, with many of these estates having been used as the residences of noble families, merchants, and artists at various points in time. The creative and cultural wealth of Tuscany is reflected in the architectural styles of these villas, which have been influenced by a number of different time periods, including the Renaissance and the Baroque periods. Some of the most famous villas in Tuscany include Villa di Poggio a Caiano, Villa La Petraia, and Villa Medici in Fiesole. These villas serve as enduring examples of the region's rich architectural history and have been instrumental in the development of Tuscany's diverse cultural landscape.
2. Marvels of Architecture: Characteristics and Design Elements of Tuscan Villas

The unique architectural characteristics of Tuscan villas are well-known for their ability to harmoniously incorporate the region's famed natural splendor into the design of their buildings. The exteriors of these homes frequently have stone facades, terracotta roofs, and wide gardens that are decked out with cypress trees and fragrant flowers. The architecture of these villas places an emphasis on open areas, natural light, and a seamless interaction with the outdoors. The result is an atmosphere that is peaceful and inviting, which encapsulates the spirit of Tuscan living.

3. **An Exceptional Selection of Luxurious Amenities and Exceptional Facilities**

    The term "Tuscan villa" has come to be synonymous with "luxury" and "opulence." Tuscan villas and retreats offer a wide variety of amenities and facilities that are designed to satisfy the sophisticated preferences of vacationers.

    A few of the amenities that contribute to the luxurious and wonderful experience that is provided to visitors throughout their stay include private swimming pools, verdant gardens, spa and wellness centers, and gourmet dining experiences. Every visitor will have a time that is both memorable and restorative because of the emphasis placed on individualized service, careful attention to detail, and a dedication to cultivating a warm and inviting atmosphere.

4. **Participating in Authentic Activities and Observing Time-Honored Traditions in Tuscany**

    Guests staying at Tuscan villas and retreats have the opportunity to fully submerge themselves in the region's diverse array of cultural traditions. These establishments provide a doorway to the genuine spirit of Tuscany by offering a variety of authentic experiences, including gastronomic adventures that highlight the flavors of traditional Tuscan food as well as guided excursions of surrounding vineyards and olive orchards. The visitor experience can be further enriched by activities such as wine tasting, cooking workshops, and visits to local artisans and craftsmen. These activities help build a profound connection with the cultural legacy and customs of the region.

5. **Practicing Sustainability and Being Kind to the Earth in Order to Preserve the Environment**

    A great number of Tuscan villas and retreats have adopted eco-friendly techniques and sustainable initiatives in order to lessen the negative influence that they have on the surrounding ecosystem and to encourage responsible tourism. These properties are committed to the preservation of the natural beauty of the Tuscan countryside

through the implementation of energy-efficient measures as well as organic farming methods. The commitment of these sites to environmental stewardship and sustainability is further shown by their support of the local communities in which they are located as well as their promotion of cultural preservation projects.
6. Marking Important Occasions by Hosting Weddings and Other Events in Tuscan Villas
Tuscan villas and retreats make for picture-perfect settings for weddings, other special occasions, and even business gatherings, as they provide an enticing and scenic backdrop for moments that will live long in the memory. These places, with their opulent ballrooms, verdant gardens, and breathtaking vistas, conjure up an atmosphere that is both romantic and refined, making them ideal venues for commemorating significant love-related and life-marker occasions. The devoted event planning professionals guarantee that every aspect will be precisely accomplished, which will allow attendees to create wonderful memories that will be enjoyed for the rest of their lives.
7. Experiences of Art and Culture That Are Completely Immersive
The numerous art galleries, museums, and other cultural landmarks found across Tuscany serve to honor the region's illustrious artistic heritage. Many of the villas and retreats in Tuscany provide their visitors with an immersion experience into the artistic heritage of the region by hosting art exhibitions, arranging guided tours of surrounding institutions, and organizing other cultural excursions. Art lovers and culture vultures will find the combination of art and culture with the breathtaking natural scenery of Tuscany to be an exhilarating and fascinating experience.
8. Gastronomic Delights: A Tour Through the Cuisine of Tuscany
The culinary prowess of the villas and retreats located in Tuscany is well-known, and these establishments give visitors the chance to experience the authentic flavors of Tuscan cuisine. Guests have the opportunity to immerse themselves in the varied and extensive culinary traditions of the region through farm-to-table dining experiences, wine pairing events, and cooking workshops guided by seasoned chefs. These facilities celebrate the art of Tuscan cooking by putting an emphasis on the use of locally produced products and tried-and-true recipes that have been handed down from generation to generation, offering everything from freshly made pasta dishes to mouthwatering desserts.
9. Relaxation in the Presence of Breathtaking Scenery: Exploring Tuscan Landscapes
The magnificent landscapes of Tuscany, which are characterized by

vineyards, olive groves, and medieval villages, create a scenic backdrop that is ideal for relaxing and rejuvenating the body and mind. Guests will be able to completely submerge themselves in the peace and natural splendor of the Tuscan countryside by taking leisurely strolls in the surrounding vineyards, taking in the breathtaking vistas from the terrace gardens, and witnessing the breathtaking sunsets. A setting that fosters reflection and a profound connection with one's natural surroundings is created by the combination of a tranquil atmosphere and stunning sights.

10. **Retreats Focusing on Health and Holistic Practices**

    The pursuit of physical, mental, and spiritual balance is the primary focus of many of the villas in Tuscany, and guests can choose from a wide variety of restorative and holistic programs offered by a large number of the region's accommodations. Guests get the opportunity to relax and refuel their energy in an atmosphere that is calm and caring through the participation in activities such as yoga and meditation classes, spa treatments, and wellness courses. Guests are able to acquire a sense of inner peace and well-being because to the region's emphasis on holistic practices and wellness, which is a reflection of the region's commitment to fostering a healthy and balanced way of life.

11. **Seasonal Offerings and Festivals Along the Way During Our Journey Through the Seasons**

    The thriving schedule of seasonal festivals and events that Tuscany has to offer provides visitors with a one-of-a-kind opportunity to explore the cultural customs and delectable specialties of the region. The villas and retreats in Tuscany coordinate their services with the changing of the seasons to provide guests with an immersive and genuine experience that honors the culinary traditions and cultural events that are associated with each season. These sites celebrate the variety and depth of Tuscany's cultural history by hosting events such as truffle fairs and wine festivals, as well as celebrations of the olive harvest and cultural performances.

12. **Tourist Activities in Vineyards and Wine Country**

    Many Tuscan villas and retreats provide guests with the opportunity to explore the world of Tuscan wine through immersive vineyard experiences and wine excursions. Tuscany is famous for its world-class vineyards and wineries, and many of these villas and retreats are located in Tuscany. Guests get the opportunity to take part in a variety of educational activities, such as guided tours of neighboring vineyards, wine tastings given by experienced sommeliers, and lessons on the winemaking process and viticulture. The opportunity to sample some of the greatest vintages produced in the region and to develop a greater appreciation for the artistry and workmanship that goes into producing Tuscan wines provides an extra layer of depth to the guest's overall experience.

13. **Honeymoon Destinations and Other Romantic Getaways**
Villas and other types of retreats in Tuscany make wonderful locations for honeymoons and other types of romantic getaways. Couples who want to celebrate their love amidst the natural splendor of Tuscany will find that the romantic environment, lavish amenities, and individualized service make the ideal backdrop for such an occasion. Moments of romance and connection can be created through activities such as private dinners with candlelight, spa treatments for couples, and personal strolls through vineyards or along picturesque trails. An aura of enchantment is created in this region as a result of the timeless beauty of the landscapes and the appeal of the region's history. This enchantment helps to promote unforgettable moments of love and affection.

14. **Iconic Villas and Retreats Throughout Tuscany**
The Italian region of Tuscany is home to a number of illustrious villas and retreats, many of which have received praise from travelers all over the world for the perfect service, magnificent amenities, and compelling atmosphere they provide. Castello di Casole, located in Casole d'Elsa, Il Borro, located in San Giustino Valdarno, and Castiglion del Bosco, located in Montalcino are some of the most renowned and sought-after properties in all of Tuscany.

    These respected facilities offer an unmatched combination of luxury, elegance, and genuine Tuscan charm. As a result, they provide guests with an all-encompassing and unique experience that highlights the very best that the area has to offer.

15. **Restoring and Conserving the Tuscan Heritage for Future Generations**

The Tuscan region places a high priority on preserving its extensive architectural and cultural legacy, as shown by the region's devotion to preserving its historic houses and retreats. A good number of these homes have been subjected to painstaking restoration efforts, the goals of which are to preserve the originality and authenticity of their architectural designs while also introducing contemporary conveniences and facilities. Local artisans and craftsmen play an important part in the process of restoration. They use time-honored methods and materials to ensure that the historical significance of these properties is maintained for the benefit of future generations. Tuscany pays homage to its history by preserving these architectural gems, while also looking forward to a prosperous and environmentally conscious future for its homes and getaways.

Villas and retreats in Tuscany provide guests with a vacation that is rich in beauty, sophistication, and cultural experience. An opportunity to see Tuscany in all of its splendor can be found at these stunning villas, which are steeped in history and tucked away in the heart of Italy's most alluring region. These getaways are gates to the art, culture, gastronomy, and landscapes of Tuscany because of the rich history that is embodied in their architecture as well as the real experiences that they provide their guests. Villas and retreats in Tuscany are not only places to stay because of their enduring charm and their dedication to conserving the heritage of the region; rather, they are gates to the very essence of Tuscany, where visitors may make cherished memories and begin on a trip that will last a lifetime.

5.1 A Romantic Stay in a Tuscan Villa

Tuscany, a region in central Italy that is famous for its magnificent landscapes, rich cultural heritage, and wonderful cuisine, provides the ideal setting for a romantic getaway because to its combination of these three factors. What could be more magical than a private getaway in a Tuscan villa, where love and beauty combine to create an experience that one will never forget? In this article, we will start on a virtual voyage through the enchantment and attraction of a romantic stay in a Tuscan villa. We will explore the characteristics that make it an ideal location for couples who are looking to rekindle their love.

1. **The Appeal of Tuscan Countryside Villas**

    Tuscan villas are well-known across the world for the architectural beauty, historical import, and picture-perfect settings that they enjoy amidst the region's stunning landscapes. These establishments have a long history of being linked to sensuality and opulence, making them the properties of choice for couples who are looking for a vacation that is private and peaceful.

    The capacity of Tuscan villas to whisk guests away to a world of timeless beauty and tranquility, one in which the art of living is honored in the most romantic of settings, is a significant part of the region's appeal.

2. **A Location Fit for Flirtation**

    Tuscan villas, with their verdant gardens, vine-covered pergolas, and breathtaking views, offer the ideal location for a romantic getaway. The breathtaking landscape, which is comprised of undulating hills, olive orchards, and vineyards, serves as the perfect backdrop for a love story that might compete with the most emotionally charged tales from works of literature. There is no limit to the number of romantic activities that may be enjoyed in a Tuscan villa; options include drinking wine while watching the sun go down on a patio, holding hands while meandering through a fragrant garden, and dining alfresco with a candlelit meal beneath the stars.

3. A Personal and Confidential Affair

    The seclusion and personal space that are hallmarks of a vacation in a Tuscan villa make for one of the most attractive features of such a getaway. Couples who are hoping to connect on a deeper level will find that these homes, which are meant to provide guests with a sense of seclusion and exclusivity, are the ideal choice for their getaway. You will be able to enjoy the undivided attention of the staff and create priceless moments of togetherness thanks to the private villas, secluded gardens, and customized service available at this resort.

4. Indulgent Comforts and Conveniences

    Luxury and indulgence are words that are inextricably linked with Tuscan villas. They provide a variety of services and amenities, all of which are geared at making your romantic stay an unforgettable experience. You will have access to a wide variety of luxurious amenities, some of which include private swimming pools, spa treatments, gourmet dining experiences, and wine cellars loaded with the finest Tuscan vintages. These conveniences are intended to make your romantic excursion more enjoyable by supplying you with everything you require to unwind, indulge, and cherish every moment of your trip.

5. Tasty Treats for Foodies

    A stay in a Tuscan villa allows you to experience the region's famously flavorful and genuine
    cuisine to its maximum, which is one of the many gastronomic delights that can be enjoyed during your time there. Indulge in farm-to-table dining experiences that highlight products acquired locally, learn the art of Tuscan cooking through individualized culinary experiences, and enjoy gourmet tasting menus. The dining experiences offered in Tuscan villas are a joyous ode to both love and good cuisine, transforming the act of eating into a personal and scrumptious adventure for the senses.

6. Romance with a Glass of Wine

    Your stay in a Tuscan villa will allow you to completely submerge yourself in the world of Tuscan wine, making Tuscany the ideal destination for everyone who enjoys wine. You will get a deeper appreciation for the finest wines the region has to offer as you participate in private wine tastings hosted by experienced sommeliers and tour adjacent vineyards. In the vineyards of Tuscany, where each glass of wine has its own unique tale to tell about tradition, passion, and the pleasure of sharing with others, the romantic connection between wine and love is honored and embraced.

7. Engaging Intimate Activities

    There are a wide variety of activities that you and your loved one can participate in together, despite the fact that the allure of a Tuscan villa may tempt you to do nothing more than kick back, relax, and take in the splendor of your surroundings. You can add an element of excitement to your stay by going on truffle hunting expeditions, going on strolls through the vineyards at your own leisure, or visiting the adjacent medieval villages with your significant other. A Tuscan villa provides a variety of activities for couples to enjoy together, whether they are interested in learning about the culture of the area, appreciating the beauty of the natural surroundings, or simply taking pleasure in each other's company.

8. An Entrance to Cultural Experiences

    While staying in a Tuscan villa, you will have the opportunity to discover the region's rich artistic and cultural riches. Tuscany is a region that is steeped in history and culture, and staying in one of the region's villas will give you this opportunity. An in-depth trip into Tuscany's illustrious past may be had by participating in selected art exhibitions held within the houses themselves, as well as going on guided excursions of historical places and museums in the surrounding area. When art, culture, and history are combined with stunning natural scenery, the result is an experience that is both romantic and enriching. This type of encounter is ideal for couples that value the finer things in life.

9. Wellness and the Art of Unwinding

    A luxurious vacation in a Tuscan villa is not just about indulging oneself; it is also about recharging one's batteries. Spa treatments, yoga sessions, and meditation lessons are some of the activities that are offered as part of the experience with the intention of enhancing the participant's overall health and well-being. Relax, get your energy levels back up, and rediscover each other in an environment that promotes holistic health and harmony thanks to the tranquility of its surroundings and the careful care provided by its staff.

10. A Romance Fit for the Season

    Every season brings a new opportunity for a romantic experience in Tuscany. In the spring, you may rejoice in the flowering of the countryside, and in the summer, you can bask in the warmth of the sun and enjoy the lively celebrations that are held across the region. The charm of the harvest season arrives in the fall, while the winter months provide opportunities for cosy and private evenings by the fireplace. No matter what time of year you decide to plan your romantic getaway, a Tuscan villa will have something special and enticing to provide for you.

11. **Commemorate the people you love and important occasions.**
Villas and other types of retreats in Tuscany make wonderful settings for commemorating significant life events, such as anniversaries, marriage proposals, and honeymoons. The breathtaking scenery, intimate atmosphere, and individualized service combine to provide it the perfect environment for commemorating major occasions in your relationship. Celebrating your love and creating memories that will last a lifetime can be accomplished through the use of personalized experiences such as private dinners, massages for couples, and other similar activities.

12. **A Wonderful Inheritance Filled with Love and Charm**

Your time spent in a Tuscan villa on a romantic getaway will take you on a trip through love and beauty that will leave you with enduring memories and a profound connection to the region. The history of love and beauty that Tuscany has to offer may be seen mirrored in the region's landscapes, its culture, and the experiences it delivers to couples who are looking to celebrate their love. A stay in a Tuscan villa is a tribute to the continuing power of romance in a place that emanates love and beauty. From the investigation of art, history, and cuisine to the sharing of solitary moments in a garden all to yourself, a visit in a Tuscan villa is an unforgettable experience.

5.2 Exploring Tuscany's Luxury Retreats

The region of Tuscany, known as the "jewel" of central Italy, has long been admired for its picture-perfect landscapes, historically significant sites, and food that is among the best in the world. However, the luxury getaways in this part of the world are the ones that best capture the spirit of opulence combined with tranquility. In this book, we will embark on a virtual voyage around Tuscany's luxury retreats, discovering the elements that make them sought-after destinations for travelers looking for a sophisticated and sumptuous break. Our travels will take us through the regions of Tuscany that are known for their wine, art, and cuisine.

1. The Appeal of Tuscany's Five-Star Resorts and Spas
   The luxurious resorts that can be found in Tuscany are the very definition of opulence and class. These villas offer a level of refinement and peacefulness that is unrivaled in the industry, and they do so by being situated in an area that is known for its vineyards, rolling hills, and old villages. The capacity of Tuscany's luxury retreats to whisk guests away to a world of extravagance, where each and every feature has been painstakingly crafted to deliver an experience that they will never forget, is a large part of the region's appeal.
2. Outstanding Examples of Built Architecture
   Luxury resorts in Tuscany are frequently found within formerly inhabited antique houses, castles, and estates; each of these structures is a singular architectural marvel. A good number of these houses have undergone painstaking restorations in order to maintain their historic allure while also introducing contemporary conveniences. The architecture emits a feeling of grandeur that is befitting of Tuscany's rich history and cultural legacy, and this can be seen in the enormous ballrooms as well as the opulent suites.
3. Confidential and Unrestricted
   Luxury resorts in Tuscany are known for their emphasis on discretion and seclusion. These accommodations are intended to provide their visitors with a unique and memorable experience by providing them with the highest level of privacy and discretion. You will be able to take in the tranquility of your surroundings without having it disrupted thanks to the private villas, individualized concierge services, and discrete staff.
4. Amenities of World-Class Standard
   When it comes to providing a comprehensive selection of amenities for visitors, luxury getaways in Tuscany spare no expense in order to fulfill even the highest expectations. The luxurious amenities that guests may take advantage of include private swimming pools, spa and wellness centers, gourmet dining options, and wine cellars stocked with the greatest Tuscan vintages. These are just a few of the luxurious amenities that guests can take advantage of. Every moment will feel like an indulgent one because of the focus placed on being pampered and receiving individualized treatment.
5. An Extravaganza of Gastronomic Delights
   Luxury resorts in Tuscany make a point to live up to the region's reputation as a center of gastronomic achievement, which they have earned worldwide. eating experiences that focus on farm-to-table eating, gourmet tasting menus, and events that pair food and wine together highlight the robust flavors of traditional Tuscan cuisine.

Every meal is elevated to the level of a gastronomic treat thanks to the skilled chefs who craft mouthwatering meals utilizing products gathered from the immediate area.

6. A Paradise for Those Who Enjoy Wine

    Luxury retreats in Tuscany provide visitors with the opportunity to completely submerge themselves in the world of Tuscan wine, which is practically associated with the country itself. Guests have the opportunity to expand their appreciation for the region's greatest vintages through the participation in private wine tastings, vineyard visits, and conversations with trained sommeliers. The wine culture of Tuscany, which honors the art of winemaking, is the ideal complement to the luxurious experience offered by these retreats because it focuses on the winemaking process.

7. Experiences that Put You in the Action

    Luxury retreats are known for their emphasis on rest and relaxation, but guests can also choose from a wide variety of engaging activities throughout their stay. Guests get the opportunity to gain a deeper understanding of Tuscany's illustrious history, culture, and customs through a variety of activities, including guided tours of neighboring cultural landmarks and museums, as well as visits to local artisans and craftsmen. These encounters create a more profound connection to the history of the area as well as a more profound appreciation for the beauty of the area.

8. Wellness and the Art of Revitalization

    Wellness and restorative practices are prioritized at luxurious retreats in Tuscany. Relaxation and inner peace can be attained through activities such as going to the spa, practicing yoga, or attending meditation classes. The calm of the area, along with the breathtaking natural scenery that surrounds you, makes for the ideal setting to foster your overall sense of health and happiness. At these retreats, you will not only be pampered, but your mind, body, and soul will also be revitalized in addition to that.

9. Commemorating Important Dates and Occasions

    Luxury resorts in Tuscany make wonderful settings for hosting celebrations of important life milestones, such as anniversaries, milestone birthdays, or even small, private weddings. The sumptuous atmosphere, outstanding service, and breathtaking scenery combine to provide it the ideal environment for creating memories that will last a lifetime. Guests are given the opportunity to highlight major occasions in their life with private dinners, romantic moments, and individualized experiences.

10. **The Maintenance of Customs and Customary Practices**
    Luxury retreats in Tuscany sometimes occupy historic houses, and many of these properties have been the subject of painstaking restoration work to maintain their original appearance. Local artisans and craftsmen are frequently involved in the process of restoration.
    They use time-honored methods and materials, which helps to ensure that the historical significance of these properties is preserved in its entirety. This dedication to the preservation of history and heritage contributes to the richness of Tuscany's cultural tapestry.
11. **A Symphonic Celebration of the Seasons**
    Luxury resorts in Tuscany provide a variety of activities and experiences suitable for all four seasons. Whether you yearn for the colorful blossoms of spring, the warmth of a Tuscan summer, the allure of an autumn harvest, or the warm and inviting atmosphere of winter, these getaways tailor their offerings to celebrate the natural beauty of each season. Every visit is different thanks to the ever-shifting scenery and the various celebrations held throughout the year.
12. **Iconic and Luxurious Vacation Resorts**
    The Italian region of Tuscany is home to a number of well-known luxury resorts that have garnered recognition all over the world. Castiglion del Bosco in Montalcino, Il Borro in San Giustino Valdarno, and Belmond Castello di Casole in Casole d'Elsa are three of the most well-known and popular attractions in the region. These revered getaways provide an unequaled combination of luxury, elegance, and the genuine allure of Tuscany in one unforgettable package.
13. **The Prospects for Luxurious Vacation Resorts**

The ability of Tuscany's luxury retreats to strike a balance between modernity and tradition is at the heart of the region's lasting allure. Many of these accommodations have recognized the significance of promoting sustainable practices and responsible tourism, and as a result, they have embraced eco-friendly methods and made a commitment to helping local communities and craftspeople. The region's commitment to protecting its natural landscapes and cultural legacy bodes well for the continuation of Tuscany's appeal as a destination for luxurious vacation getaways.

5.3 Honeymooning in Tuscany

Central Italy's Tuscany is an area that is well known for the delicious cuisine it produces, as well as its magnificent landscapes and culturally significant history. It is the ideal place for newlyweds to go on their honeymoon if they want to have an experience that is both romantic and unforgettable. Tuscany is the ideal place to visit if you're looking for a combination of relaxation and cultural exploration because of its picturesque cities, rolling vineyards, historic villages, and world-class art. Let's get on a virtual train and travel across this enchanting region as we investigate the reasons why Tuscany is a honeymooner's paradise destination.

Tuscany's geography is nothing short of a masterpiece, and the region's scenery is just as breathtaking. The region is characterized by attractive undulating hills, avenues lined with cypress trees, and enormous vineyards that stretch as far as the eye can reach in every direction. The picture-perfect backdrop for a romantic getaway is the verdant countryside, which is replete with quaint farmhouses and centuries-old olive trees. Imagine enjoying a leisurely stroll through sun-kissed vineyards while inhaling the heady scent of ripe grapes or going on a relaxed bike ride over picturesque country roads. Both of these activities would be a lot of fun.

Cities Rich in History Tuscany is home to some of the most famous and well-known cities in all of Italy, such as Florence, Siena, and Pisa. Florence, known as the cradle of the Renaissance, is a city that enchants visitors with its beautiful combination of art, history, and architecture. Visit the Uffizi Gallery to see famous works of art such as "The Birth of Venus" by Botticelli and "David" by Michelangelo. Siena, with its preserved medieval architecture and its age-old horse race, is another one of Italy's crown jewels. In addition, it is impossible to bypass the world-famous Tower of Pisa, which leans to one side. These locations provide the setting for unforgettable love encounters as well as opportunities to learn about other cultures.

Art & Culture: When it comes to art and culture, Tuscany is a veritable treasury. In addition to its numerous world-famous museums, this city is home to a vast number of ancient structures, including churches, chapels, and other buildings rich in art and history. However, visiting Tuscany isn't only about gazing in awe at works from the past; the region is also home to thriving contemporary art scenes and events. During the course of your visit, you shouldn't pass up the opportunity to observe a local music, dance performance, or art exhibition. These are the kinds of adventures that can strengthen your connection to the area and provide you with memories that will last a lifetime.

Tuscany is a dream destination for everyone who enjoys good cuisine and wine. The region is famous for its cuisine that is uncomplicated but delicious. Indulge in mouthwatering meals such as tender Chianina beef, savory ribollita (a substantial soup typical of Tuscany), and pappa al pomodoro (a tomato and bread soup). If you enjoy world-class local wines like Chianti and Brunello di Montalcino with your meals, you will be able to relish flavors that will leave you wanting more of both the meal and the wine. You may even attend a cooking class together and learn how to make these mouthwatering dishes in the comfort of your own kitchen when you get back home.

Tuscany is home to a plethora of quaint bed and breakfasts, opulent villas, and intimate boutique hotels, all of which are perfect for a romantic getaway. Imagine spending the night in a medieval castle, a beautifully restored farmhouse, or a small village in Tuscany.

Many of the accommodations offer with breathtaking views of the surrounding countryside, private pools, and beautiful gardens, making it possible for you to enjoy private moments in an atmosphere of calm.

In addition to its cultural offerings, Tuscany also provides opportunities for outdoor adventures. In addition to that, it offers a recreation area for people who enjoy being outside. It doesn't matter if you want to go horseback riding in the countryside, go on a leisurely bike ride through the countryside, or go on a hike in the Apennine Mountains; there are lots of options for you and your friends to enjoy the great outdoors together.

Honeymooning is also about relaxing, and Tuscany boasts various spa retreats and wellness centers that provide the ideal environment for you and your sweetheart to de-stress and revitalize during your time together. After a long day of sightseeing, relax and unwind with a soothing massage for two or a dip in one of the area's thermal spas.

Sunsets in Tuscany are some of the most beautiful and romantic in all of Europe. As the day comes to a close, there is something enchanted about watching the sun sink beyond the horizon. Discover a picturesque location, perhaps in the countryside or by the ocean, and enjoy a bottle of the region's wine together as you take in the magnificent colors of the sky and the peaceful serenity of the world to create a moment that will stay with you for the rest of your life.

5.4 Spa and Wellness Escapes

There has never been a time when it was more important to take time for relaxation, rejuvenation, and self-care than it is in today's fast-paced and frequently stressful world. People who are looking for a sanctuary apart from the pressures of day-to-day life are increasingly frequenting spas and wellness retreats. These getaways take a more all-encompassing approach to wellness by nourishing not only the physical body but also the mind and the spirit as well. As part of this investigation into spa and wellness getaways, we will dig into the expanding field of wellness tourism, the several kinds of retreats that are currently accessible, as well as the advantages that these getaways offer to individuals who embark on these excursions.

The Growth of the Wellness Travel Industry

In recent years, there has been a phenomenal uptick in the number of people interested in wellness tourism. It signifies a change in the way people view vacations and travel, since it places a higher priority on one's health and well-being than on typical vacations that are focused on sightseeing or adventure.

Travelers are increasingly interested in activities that not only provide them the opportunity to relax but also assist them in addressing issues related to their physical and mental health. To cater to these ever-evolving requirements, spas and wellness retreats have become increasingly popular.

The rising consciousness regarding the significance of self-care and overall well-being is one of the primary forces that is propelling this movement. In today's modern culture, stress, burnout, and other health problems caused by lifestyle choices are all too common. People are turning to wellness getaways not just as a way to treat their preexisting health conditions but also as a preventative measure to ensure that they continue to enjoy good health.

In addition to this, there is a deeper relationship that exists between wellness and the act of traveling. The experience of travel is seen by many people as an opportunity for personal development, the discovery of oneself, and transformation. Wellness retreats provide the ideal venue for these kinds of experiences since they provide guests with a break from the typical routines and settings of daily life, which enables them to concentrate on their own personal development.

Different kinds of spas and wellness resorts can be found at:

Getaways That Focus on Spa Treatments Getaway packages that emphasize spa treatments prioritize relaxation and pampering. Massages, facials, and other treatments aimed to relieve stress and promote physical relaxation are frequently included in spa packages.

Retreats in Yoga and Meditation Provide an Opportunity for Self-Discovery, Relaxation, and Self-Reflection Yoga and meditation retreats provide an opportunity for people who are looking for inner peace and mindfulness. These retreats are often held in beautiful natural settings that are peaceful and secluded.

Retreats Focused on Fitness and Weight Loss: These retreats are intended for anyone who are interested in making improvements to their level of physical fitness and health. They frequently provide individualized strategies for physical activity, nutritional counseling, and weight management programs.

Retreats for Detoxification and cleaning: The primary goals of detoxification and cleaning retreats are to revitalize the body by removing toxins and fostering an overall sense of wellbeing. In order to facilitate detoxification, they frequently involve the use of specialized diets and treatments.

Retreats for Holistic Healing Holistic retreats combine a wide variety of healing methods, such as acupuncture, herbal medicine, energy work, and many others. These therapies are all part of the holistic healing tradition. The goal of these retreats is to achieve harmony in one's body, mind, and spirit.

Ayurvedic Retreats: The focus of these retreats is on Ayurveda, an ancient system of natural medicine that dates back thousands of years. They frequently contain individualized therapies as well as food suggestions that are derived from the Ayurvedic constitutions of the patient.

Retreats that fall within the category of "adventure wellness" mix elements of adventure and physical activity with various wellness activities. Commonly included are outings such as hiking and kayaking, in addition to workshops focusing on mindfulness.

Culinary and Nutrition Retreats: For those with a strong interest in food, culinary and nutrition retreats provide an opportunity to delve more deeply into the art of healthy cooking, nutrition, and the preparation of wholesome meals.

The Advantages That Come Along With Wellness Vacations and Spas

One of the most important purposes of health getaways is to help people de-stress and relax after a busy week. Stress reduction can have long-lasting consequences on both mental and physical health, and it is a goal of the calming surroundings, therapeutic treatments, and mindful practices that are offered at these retreats.

Significantly Improved Physical Health Attending a retreat with the primary goals of exercise, weight loss, detoxification, and cleaning can significantly enhance one's physical health. When guests leave, they frequently report feeling more energized and with ideas for how to adopt healthy behaviors into their daily lives.

Mental Health It has been shown that activities such as yoga, meditation, and mindfulness can have a significant effect on one's mental health. Increased clarity, less anxiety, and a heightened sense of tranquility are common experiences reported by guests.

Improved Nutrition Culinary and nutrition retreats educate participants on how to eat healthily, empowering them to make better dietary decisions even after they return home.

Changes in Lifestyle: Wellness retreats frequently motivate individuals to make constructive adjustments in their way of living. They may discover a newfound passion for yoga, a dedication to maintaining a regular fitness routine, or an enthusiasm for meditation.

Self-Discovery: A lot of people who go on wellness getaways report that they have a moment of self-discovery while they're there. They establish new objectives for themselves and achieve greater insight into the meaning behind their lives as a whole.

These retreats frequently facilitate the development of deeper ties with other persons who have a similar worldview. It's possible that traveling the path to better health together can result in lifelong friendships and a stronger sense of community.

Spa and wellness getaways provide, first and foremost, the opportunity to relax, refuel, and revitalize oneself in order to better enjoy the experience. This feeling of revitalization has the potential to favorably affect many facets of one's life.

Identifying the Appropriate Wellness Getaway

Set some objectives for the time you spend away from the office and write them down. Make sure that the retreat is going to help you achieve your goals, whether they are to unwind, shed some pounds, become less stressed, or learn more about yourself.

Consider the location of the getaway while you make your plans. Which of these three settings—a tranquil nature setting, a seaside locale, or an urban wellness center—would you choose?

The length of time spent on wellness retreats can range anywhere from a quick weekend trip to an immersive experience lasting a whole month. Pick a time frame that works with both your schedule and your objectives.

Choose the Type of Retreat That Best Suits Your Interests and Needs First, decide what kind of retreat you want to go on. Choose an area of expertise that speaks to you, whether it be yoga, a spa, fitness, or something else entirely.

A budget should be established for your getaway, taking into account the fact that the total cost may range greatly based on the location, type of lodging, and degree of extravagance that is provided.

Evaluations and advice: Before signing up for the retreat, make sure you read the evaluations other people have left and ask previous attendees for their advice.

A growing number of people are choosing to vacation at spas and wellness retreats as a reflection of the increased importance placed on health, well-being, and self-care. These getaways provide guests with access to a wide variety of experiences, ranging from relaxing spa vacations to life-changing yoga and meditation retreats. The mental, physical, and emotional well-being of participants is positively influenced by wellness retreats, and these positive effects last beyond the period of the retreat itself. Travelers can embark on a journey of self-discovery, relaxation, and refreshment by selecting the appropriate retreat that matches with their aims and interests. This allows them to nurture not only their bodies, but also their minds and souls while they are away from home. Spa and wellness getaways provide a wonderful opportunity to emphasize self-care and make permanent, positive changes in our lives, which is especially important in a world that frequently places a great deal of demand on us.

Chapter 6

Tuscany's Festivals and Celebrations

The region of Tuscany in central Italy is well-known not only for the breathtaking scenery and extensive history that it possesses, but also for the lively and varied calendar of festivals and festivities that it hosts throughout the year. These events are a significant component of the culture of Tuscany since they highlight the region's long-standing customs, outstanding gastronomic achievements, and rich cultural legacy. In the course of this in-depth investigation of the events that are celebrated and commemorated in Tuscany, we will become fully immersed in the rich tapestry of customs that help to make this region such a captivating and exciting vacation spot.

Before we begin:

The inhabitants of Tuscany have very deep ties to their cultural past, and as a result, the region's festivals and festivities are a reflection of the region's rich history as well as those ties. These activities bring together residents of the area as well as tourists, fostering a sense of community while also fostering joy and a link to times gone by. The calendar of events in Tuscany is packed with activities that provide a look into the region's culture and identity. These activities range from religious processions to medieval jousts, from wine festivals to historical reenactments.

Festivals Observed Throughout History and Religion

Palio di Siena: The Palio is one of the most well-known events in Italy and is held in Siena twice a year, on July 2 and August 16. There are ten of the city's neighborhoods, which are known as contrade, that compete against one another in this ancient horse race that dates back to the 17th century. There are vibrant parades, people dressed in costumes from the middle ages, and a fervent sense of community pride; the mood is exciting.

Easter in Florence: During Easter, the city of Florence, which serves as the capital of Tuscany, has a number of religious processions and activities. The "Scoppio del Carro," also known as the "Explosion of the Cart," is the most famous of these traditions. It has been observed for more than 350 years and consists of a cart that is loaded with pyrotechnics and sets off a spectacular show in the Piazza del Duomo.

San Gimignano is a magnificent hilltop town that hosts medieval festivals throughout the year. During these festivals, the town's streets come alive with jugglers, musicians, and other artists dressed in historical costumes. During the "Ferie delle Messi" and "Ferie delle Messi delle Fiere" festivals, guests are taken back in time to the Middle Ages and treated to jousting competitions as well as food stalls providing traditional medieval fare.

Pisa's past is commemorated annually with the "Gioco del Ponte," a historical reenactment of a battle that takes place on the city's famous Ponte di Mezzo bridge. The competition between the two teams to see who can pull a large cart to the opposite end of the bridge is a representation of the city being split in half. After the ceremony is over, there will be a procession and then fireworks will be let off.

Festivals of Food and Drink

In addition to this, Tuscany is well-known for its great food festivals

Sagra del Tordo in Montalcino: The "Sagra del Tordo" in Montalcino is a celebration of the historic tradition of hunting thrushes. The celebration features competitions in archery, a parade reenacting historical events, and a lavish feast incorporating regional wines and traditional cuisine.

The Chianti Wine Festival, also known as "Festa dell'Uva," is a celebration of the region's vinicultural excellence. Tuscany is famous for its wine, and the Chianti Wine Festival honors the region's vinicultural legacy. Visitors get the opportunity to experience some of the best Chianti wines, which they may do while listening to live music and dining on delectable Tuscan fare.

Suvereto's "Sagra del Cinghiale" (Wild Boar Festival) is a great occasion to sample a variety of wild boar dishes, such as pappardelle al cinghiale (pasta with wild boar sauce) and roasted swine. Wild boar is a much-loved ingredient in Tuscan cuisine.

Olive oil is another fundamental component of the cuisine of Tuscany, and each year, the town of Panzano in Chianti hosts an olive oil festival. An olive oil festival is held in Panzano in Chianti each year, where guests have the opportunity to sample freshly pressed - oil, see cooking demonstrations, and gain insight into the process of making olive oil.

Festivals of the Arts and the Culture

The festivals of Tuscany are a reflection of the region's artistic and cultural legacy, which is profoundly ingrained across the region.

Puccini Festival held in Lucca The city of Lucca, which is the birthplace of the well-known composer Giacomo Puccini, is the location of the annual Puccini Festival. Piazza dell'Anfiteatro and the old Teatro del Giglio provide the perfect backdrop for the open-air opera performances that are a highlight of this event.

The medieval jousting competition known as the "Giostra del Saracino" takes place in Arezzo every year. As a way to pay homage to the city's medieval past, knights dressed in extravagant costumes vie with one another for the pride of their districts.

Festival Internazionale di Teatro di Firenze Firenze is the host city of an annual international theater festival that showcases a wide variety of performances, ranging from classic Italian plays to cutting-edge productions from throughout the world. The festival moves around to a number of different historic locations all across the city.

Cortona On The Move is an international photography festival that is held in the picturesque town of Cortona every year. This event is attended by people who have a passion for photography. The festival is a celebration of visual storytelling and features the works of known photographers as well as new talents.

Festivals Celebrating Nature and Flowers

The breathtaking scenery and rich floral diversity of Tuscany serve as inspiration for a number of festivals that commemorate the region's natural splendor.

The festival known as "Infiorata" is held every year in the town of Noto, which is located in the Val d'Orcia area of Italy. During this occasion, the streets are decked out with exquisite floral artworks created by local artists and citizens. These artworks form tapestries that are mesmerizing and aromatic.

The fields all around Castelluccio di Norcia come alive with a vibrant display of tulips in the springtime, and the town of Castelluccio di Norcia celebrates this blooming season with an annual festival called the Tulip Festival. This natural occurrence is being honored with colorful displays and various cultural activities as part of the Tulip Festival.

Festivals honoring local patron saints

A number of the communities and localities in Tuscany celebrate their patron saints with annual festivities. A bustling street fair, religious observances, and processions are frequently incorporated into these festivals.

Feast of St. John the Baptist in Florence On the 24th of June, a remarkable feast is held in honor of Florence's patron saint, St. John the Baptist. The sky above the Arno River is illuminated by a fantastic fireworks display, and the city is lit up with fireworks.

The Feast of Saint Rosalia is held in Palermo, which is located in Sicily. Despite its location in Sicily, the Feast of Saint Rosalia is well-known due to the historical connections that exist between Palermo and Tuscany. This celebration, which combines the customs of Sicily and Tuscany, features processions, musical performances, and fireworks.

Reflections on the Whole

The numerous festivals and other events held throughout Tuscany are evidence of the region's extensive cultural history as well as its commitment to maintaining and passing on its traditions. It doesn't matter if you're drawn to the historical reenactments, gastronomic feasts, cultural performances, or the sheer beauty of nature displays; Tuscany provides a wide variety of experiences for people of all interests and preferences. Visitors will be able to completely submerge themselves in the rich fabric of Tuscan heritage and culture thanks to these events, which offer a glimpse into the heart and soul of this entrancing region. Festivals and festivities in Tuscany offer an enthralling voyage through time, taste, and culture, making them an ideal destination for visitors interested in discovering the very heart of Italy.

6.1 The Palio di Siena: A Horse Race like no other

The Palio di Siena is a horse race that is unlike any other, and it takes place in the middle of Tuscany, Italy, in the middle of the ancient beauty that is Siena. This world-famous competition, which is deeply rooted in history and custom, encapsulates the heart of Tuscan culture as well as the fiercely competitive nature of the people who live there. The Palio is more than just a race; it is an integral component of Sienese culture. It is a vibrant spectacle that brings the city and its inhabitants together in an atmosphere of celebration and competition. In this investigation of the Palio di Siena, we will delve into the history of this one-of-a-kind horse race to learn about its beginnings, rituals, rivalries, and the lasting significance of the event.

The Beginnings and the Past

The Palio di Siena is a horse race that has a long and illustrious history, with its beginnings stretching back to the Middle Ages. Although the history of the race does not begin until the 17th century, it is thought to have been in existence much earlier. The term "Palio" comes from the pennant or flag that was given to the victorious contrada (which literally translates to "neighborhood"). The original purpose of the Palio was to commemorate the Assumption of the Virgin Mary, a significant religious event that is still observed in Siena to this day.

Palio di Provenzano is held on July 2nd, while Palio dell'Assunta is held on August 16th. The

first modern Palio was held in 1656, and since then, it has been held twice a year, on July 2nd and August 16th. Draws are held in the days leading up to each Palio to choose which ten of the city's seventeen contrade will be allowed to compete in each race. Each Palio is named after a different contrada, and that contrada's name is displayed on the Palio's flag.

This is the Contrade

The Palio di Siena revolves around the city of Siena's seventeen different neighborhoods, known as contrade. Each contrada has its own unique identity as well as an emblem that represents it. These contrade are: Aquila (Eagle), Bruco (Caterpillar), Chiocciola (Snail), Civetta (Owl), Drago (Dragon), Giraffa (Giraffe), Istrice (Porcupine), Leocorno (Unicorn), Lupa (She-wolf), Nicchio (Seashell), Oca (Goose), Onda (Wave), Pantera (Panther), Selva (Forest), Tartuca (Tortoise), Torre (Tower), and Valdimontone (Valley of the Ram).

Every neighborhood or neighborhood section, or contrada, has its own church, social center, and group of devoted supporters who are called contradaioli. They exhibit steadfast allegiance to their contrada and take great delight in doing so. They are highly passionate about their contrada. The contrada takes on the role of an extended family, and the Palio serves as a vehicle for expressing both the long-standing animosity and the sense of community that exists amongst the various communities.

The Equine Athletes and Their Riders

The horses that will compete in the Palio are chosen using a method that is quite regimented. They are required to meet certain physical requirements in addition to enduring strenuous training. The fantini, also known as jockeys, are an essential component to the success of the contrada. Each contrada is responsible for making the difficult decision of choosing a jockey, and in order to do so, they frequently seek out seasoned riders who have a well-deserved reputation for being skilled, courageous, and strategic.

The Ceremonies and Celebrations That Take Place Before Palio

Siena comes to life in the days preceding up to the Palio with a variety of ceremonies and celebrations. The preparation that the Contrada does for the Palio is extremely thorough, and it starts with a blessing of the horses in the church of the Contrada. The members of the contrada are assembling at this solemn moment in order to pray for the success of the race.

In the days leading up to the Palio, the city is decked up in the flags, banners, and vibrant insignia of the competing contrade. The Piazza del

Campo, which is Siena's principal plaza, is being converted into a horse racing track by having sand spread over its antique cobblestones. The excitement of the crowd, which numbers in the thousands and is there to watch the race, can be felt throughout the arena.

The Contest

Even though it is just approximately 90 seconds long, the Palio di Siena, which is a race that is both heart-pounding and fast-paced, manages to capture the passions and rivalries of the people of Siena. At the starting rope are ten horses and jockeys, with one horse and jockey representing each of the ten contradas. The audience erupts into a deafening shout as the race gets under way and the horses begin their sprint around the course, which consists of three circuits of the Piazza del Campo.

The objective is not only to be the first person to cross the finish line, but also to do it aboard one's own horse, regardless of whether or not the jockey maintains their position. During the course of the race, it is not unheard of for jockeys to be thrown off of their mounts. In these kinds of situations, the riderless horse still has a chance of winning the race for its contrada.

The Palio is notorious for its fierce competitiveness and, at times, its use of harsh strategies. It's not uncommon for jockeys to use the whip on the horses of their opponents in order to slow them down or get in their way. The Sienese people see these strategies, despite their vicious nature, as valid components of the competition and accept them in this capacity.

The Glory of the Winner and the Celebration of the Contrada

In addition to being a horse race, the Palio is a source of tremendous pride for the contrada that emerges victorious. The Palio, a hand-painted banner that represents the victory, is given to the contrada that emerges triumphant from the competition. The Palio is a revered emblem, and the presentation of it is accompanied by joyous celebrations in the area that came out on top.

The neighborhoods of the contrada come to life with parades, feasts, and musical performances in the streets.

The locals continue to celebrate well into the next day, donning their contrada scarves and flags as the festivities continue through the night. It is a time that the contradaioli and the entirety of the neighborhood celebrate together with tremendous joy.

Competition and friendly relations

The Palio di Siena is known for fostering passionate rivalries, and during this time period, the connections of friendship are frequently put to the test. The level of competition is quite high, and the stakes are substantial. However, once the Palio has been completed, there is a shift in the mood.

Members of the Contrada get together, tell each other stories, and work to keep alive the strong sense of brotherhood that ties them all together.

The Palio di Siena is not only a horse race; rather, it is an amazing event that stretches far beyond its roots. It is a manifestation of the zeal, pride, and cohesion that characterizes the Sienese people. The Palio is not only a historical custom for them; rather, it is a real, breathing embodiment of the spirit of their city and the ideals they hold most dear. Whether you attend the Palio as a spectator or immerse yourself as a member of a contrada, it is an experience that will leave an indelible impact on you. It is a testament to the continuing strength of tradition, community, and competition. The Palio di Siena is a horse race unlike any other, and it never fails to capture the hearts and minds of those who have the opportunity to watch it.

6.2 Tuscany's Festivals of Love

Since ancient times, the region of Tuscany has been seen as a symbol of love and ardor due to its breathtaking scenery, extensive cultural history, and alluring atmosphere. It should come as no surprise that this region in the middle of Italy plays host to a large number of festivals and events that celebrate love in all of its guises. The lasting appeal of Tuscany as a romantic destination is demonstrated by the region's many celebrations of love, which include everything from medieval marriages to contemporary vows of devotion. In the course of this investigation into the celebrations of love that take place in Tuscany, we will go on a journey through time, tradition, and the modern demonstrations of passion that are practiced in this alluring region.

Love and Marriage in the Middle Ages

The long and illustrious history of Tuscany offers a glimpse into the passion and romance of times long gone. Participants at medieval weddings, which are frequently held as a part of historical reenactments and festivals, are taken back in time to an era in which chivalry and courtly love were the ideals.

Gubbio, located in Umbria, is a picture-perfect town that plays host to the "Palio di San Valentino." This event is held on Valentine's Day and comprises a commemoration of a medieval wedding.

The village is transformed into a living medieval stage, complete with armored warriors, noble ladies, and even a bride and groom dressed in period garb. During the festival, the practices and customs of medieval courtship and marriage will be demonstrated.

The Medieval Festival of Monteriggioni: Even though it is not technically a wedding celebration, the Medieval Festival of Monteriggioni is an occasion that reeks of sentimentality and romanticism. The walls and streets of Monteriggioni, which date back to medieval times, come to life with the presence of knights, troubadours, and traditional music, creating an enchanting ambiance that can make you feel as if you've walked into the pages of a medieval romance story.

Festivals of Contemporary Love in Tuscany

The celebrations of love held in Tuscany are not limited to the past. In point of fact, the region is open to modern demonstrations of passion, and as a result, it offers a stage for lovers to commemorate their relationship in extraordinary and unforgettable ways.

Fairs and Expos Dedicated to Weddings in Tuscany Tuscany is home to a plethora of wedding fairs and expos that showcase everything from breathtaking locations to bridal gowns and florists. Because of these events, engaged couples will have the opportunity to arrange the wedding of their dreams in this enchanting region.

The ceremony known as "Promessa d'Amore" or "Promise of Love" takes place in the city of Lucca, which is famous for the well-preserved Renaissance walls that surround the city. To celebrate their love in front of family, friends, and the magnificent backdrop of the city's ancient square, couples congregate in the Piazza San Michele to either make their wedding vows for the first time or to renew their existing ones.

The Chianti region is not just well-known for the quality of its wine; it is also well-known as a destination for couples looking for love. Around the time that Valentine's Day rolls around, a festival called "Chianti in Love" takes place. This event provides unique wine tastings, banquets, and tours to couples in the most romantic part of Tuscany. Wineries frequently provide events, which provide wine lovers with an opportunity for an experience that is both personal and unforgettable.

The "Benvenuta Brunello" of Montalcino, Italy, Celebrates Both Wine and Romance

Brunello wine, produced in the picturesque hilltop town of Montalcino in Tuscany, is considered to be among the best in the world. The town holds an event known as "Benvenuta Brunello" on an annual basis.

This festival celebrates the love of wine as well as the celebration of romance. This wine festival, which takes place in February, is a wonderful opportunity for couples to enjoy in the gastronomic and oenological delights that the region has to offer.

During the event known as "Benvenuta Brunello," guests will have the opportunity to sample various wines and learn about the most recent Brunello vintages. The event frequently include guided tours of nearby wineries in addition to unique wine and food pairings. Couples have the ideal opportunity to enjoy a glass of wine together while taking in the tranquil environment of Tuscany during the winter months, when the town is bathed in gentle winter sunlight and a cool, crisp air blows.

THE ROMANCE OF TUSCANY, ITALY ~ 119

The town of Siena, where Romeo and Juliet took place

Verona is the location where Shakespeare's classic love romance "Romeo and Juliet" takes place, but Siena is a more fitting setting for the play because of its attractive atmosphere and ability to convey the play's message. Because of its long history and romantic ambiance, Siena is frequently associated with feelings of love and passion.

Piazza del Campo: The Piazza del Campo is located in the center of Siena and is a stunning location that has been a witness to a great number of love events. The architectural splendor of the Piazza, along with the romantic aura of the annual Palio di Siena horse race, makes it the perfect location for couples to stroll hand in hand while soaking in the area's romantic history and atmosphere.

Tales of Love and Intrigue from the Middle Ages Siena's history from the middle ages is full of stories of love and intrigue. Legends and tales of medieval romances, both tragic and triumphant, are associated with the city, and many of these legends and stories center around the city. These stories give lovers a sense of connection to Siena's romantic past, which contributes to the city's appeal as a romantic destination.

Tuscany is a romantic setting for Valentine's Day celebrations.

Valentine's Day, which is observed all around the world as a celebration of love, is welcomed with open arms in Tuscany. This day can be celebrated in a variety of classy ways throughout the region.

Dining in Tuscany Tuscany is known worldwide for the quality of its cuisine, and on Valentine's Day, many restaurants in the region host romantic meals with candlelight and provide special menus.

It doesn't matter if you're dining in the middle of Florence or in a charming village in the Tuscan countryside; the evening will be unforgettable thanks to the great cuisine and the romantic environment.

Private Wine Tasting for Two: Tuscany's vineyards and wineries offer private wine tasting experiences, giving couples the opportunity to try some of the region's finest wines while appreciating each other's company.

Romantic Strolls: Tuscany's medieval cities and towns offer the ideal setting for a romantic stroll thanks to their picturesque settings. These locations, whether it be in Florence along the Arno River or through the lovely streets of San Gimignano, are just built for two people in love to spend time together.

Reaffirmation of Promises

Tuscany is a favorite vacation spot for married couples who want to reaffirm their commitment to one another in an atmosphere that is both romantic and unforgettable. Numerous options for renewing wedding vows can be found across the region's historic churches, picturesque vineyards, and picture-perfect scenery. Some engaged couples decide to have a small, intimate ceremony with just the two of them, while others invite their close relatives and friends to share in the festivities. Ceremonies to renew wedding vows can be made more meaningful and personal by holding it in Tuscany's stunning surroundings, which are known for their warm cultural embrace.

Whether they are steeped in history or founded in current passion, Tuscany's festivals of love provide married couples the opportunity to celebrate their affection in a setting that is really extraordinary. Tuscany is a place that captures the imagination thanks to its picture-perfect landscapes, illustrious history, and warm and welcoming culture. It doesn't matter if you're in Tuscany to relive the fairytales of Siena, relish the flavors of Chianti, or celebrate your love during a vow renewal ceremony; the region offers a wide variety of experiences that can help you make memories that will last a lifetime and strengthen your bond with the person you love. The festivals of love that are held across Tuscany are a monument to the region's everlasting charm, and they win the hearts of all those who travel to this lovely place.

6.3 Witnessing Traditional Tuscan Celebrations

The region of Tuscany, which is located in the middle of Italy, is well known for its extensive cultural history, beautiful scenery, and lively traditions. The traditional celebrations of the region provide a fascinating glimpse into its illustrious past and provide tourists the chance to witness the time-honored rhythms of Tuscan way of life. These events, which range from religious celebrations to historical reenactments, bring together locals and tourists, building a sense of community as well as joy and a respect for cultural traditions.

In the course of this investigation into experiencing traditional Tuscan celebrations, we will delve into the entrancing tapestry of festivities that continue to give the region's traditions and history a sense of vitality today.

Celebrations of various religions & Processions

The religious celebrations that take place throughout Tuscany are an essential part of the region's cultural identity. They offer a personal look into the spiritual lives of the people who live in the area, reflecting the region's deep ties to the Catholicism that gave rise to its cultural history.

Easter in Florence: During Easter, the city of Florence, which is known as the "cradle of the Renaissance," comes to life with religious processions and exuberant festivals. The old churches of the city are used to host somber masses, while the streets are decked out with brilliant decorations and symbolic displays, resulting in an ambiance that is simultaneously reverent and celebratory. Experiencing the ancient Easter rites that are practiced in Florence is a powerful demonstration of the lasting spiritual significance of the Easter celebration in the culture of Tuscany.

Feast of St. John the Baptist in Florence On June 24, the city of Florence celebrates the Feast of St. John the Baptist, the city's patron saint, with elaborate processions, historical pageantry, and a spectacular fireworks show over the Arno River. People from all over the area, both residents and guests, congregate along the riverbanks to take in this spectacular show, immersing themselves in the joyous atmosphere and the deeply ingrained veneration for the city's patron saint.

Pageants from the Middle Ages and Historical Reenactments

Participants and spectators alike are taken back in time during the historical pageants and reenactments that are held in Tuscany. These events provide a vivid depiction of the region's rich history and cultural legacy.

The walls of Monteriggioni, which date back to the Middle Ages, provide an exquisite setting for a celebration that honors the medieval legacy of the town. This festival is known as the Medieval celebration of Monteriggioni. An immersive experience that conjures the majesty and pageantry of the Middle Ages is created by the presence of musicians, flag throwers, and knights in shining armor parading through the streets. Being present at the Medieval Festival of Monteriggioni is very much like taking a trip back in time and having an up-close and personal encounter with the vitality of Tuscan history.

The Palio di Siena is a horse race that has been held for hundreds of years and is known for being a brilliant display of competitive spirit and local pride. The Palio is a horse race that takes place twice a year in Siena's ancient Piazza del Campo. It is a celebration of the city's long-standing history of friendly competition amongst its contrade, or districts. One of the most prominent cultural events in Tuscany is the Palio di Siena, and visitors may feel what it's like to be a part of the frenzy and excitement by going to see it. This experience is truly unforgettable.

Festivals and Celebrations Dedicated to Food

The culinary feasts and festivals held throughout Tuscany serve as a tribute to the region's extensive gastronomic history and bring attention to the key role that food and wine play in Tuscan culture.

The Chianti Wine Festival is held every year in the Chianti region and is a celebration of the area's long-standing viticulture and winemaking traditions. Guests will have the opportunity to indulge in a variety of mouthwatering regional specialties, enjoy a wide selection of superb Chianti wines, and become fully immersed in the jovial atmosphere of the festival. Participating in the Chianti Wine Festival provides a scrumptious opportunity to travel through the flavors and fragrances that characterize the very essence of winemaking in Tuscany.

Festivals of the Truffle Tuscany's celebrated delicacy, the truffle, is celebrated throughout the area with a series of festivals that take place in a variety of cities and villages. These festivals highlight the truffle's place in traditional Tuscan cuisine. These events offer a one-of-a-kind opportunity to observe the reverence and creativity associated with the highly regarded Tuscan truffle by featuring demonstrations of truffle hunting, cooking lessons, and mouthwatering tastings.

Celebrations of Traditional Music and Folk Culture

Folk festivals and music celebrations in Tuscany are great examples of the region's rich cultural heritage and highlight the significance of music and dance in the region's customs and traditions.

The Festa di San Giovanni in Florence is a celebratory celebration of music, dance, and cultural acts. It is the midsummer festival in Florence. Concerts, parades, and traditional folk dances bring the city's streets and squares to life, resulting in a joyous scene that reverberates with the sense of social solidarity and festivity. Taking part in the Festa di San Giovanni is an immersive event that gives guests the opportunity to absorb the contagious enthusiasm and camaraderie of Florence's thriving cultural scene.

Pistoia Blues Festival: The Pistoia Blues Festival, which takes place every year in the ancient city of Pistoia, is a demonstration of the thriving music culture that can be found throughout Tuscany. The event boasts an eclectic lineup of world-famous performers and ensembles, luring fans of music from near and far to take pleasure in the beautiful melodies and catchy rhythms that permeate the air in Tuscany. Attending the Pistoia Blues Festival is an enthralling experience that provides guests with the opportunity to completely submerge themselves in the illustrious musical heritage that flourishes within the context of the region's cultural milieu.

Celebrations of the Harvest and Other Rural Traditions

Tuscany's harvest celebrations and rural traditions provide a look into the agricultural heritage and seasonal rhythms that create the country's pastoral landscapes. These festivals and traditions are held throughout the region.

Olive Oil Festivals Tuscany is known for its olive oil festivals, which are held throughout the region in a variety of cities and villages. These festivals reflect the centuries-old heritage of olive harvesting and oil manufacture. Olive oil tastings, guided tours of local olive trees, and educational seminars are some of the activities that are offered at these festivals. These events provide attendees the chance to observe the centuries-old skill and unwavering commitment that go into the creation of Tuscany's world-famous olive oil.

Festivals of the Vendemmia Tuscany's festivals of the vendemmia, which celebrate the grape harvest and the process of making wine, are an excellent example of the region's strong relationship to viticulture. Grape stomping, wine tastings, and vineyard tours are some of the activities that are included in these celebrations. These activities provide a personal view of the passion and competence that distinguish Tuscan winemaking.

Festivals honoring local patron saints

Local festivals honoring Tuscany's patron saints are highly regarded celebrations that exemplify the inhabitants of the region's strong sense of community and religious devotion.

Feast of St. Miniato in Florence The Feast of St. Miniato is a revered event that is held in Florence on November 11th and pays respect to the patron saint of the city. A somber mass, processions, and the lighting of the Basilica di San Miniato al Monte all take place on this day to celebrate the occasion, resulting in an ambiance that is quiet and spiritual. Attending the Feast of St. Miniato provides a window into the deeply ingrained religious traditions of the city as well as a view into the everlasting veneration for the patron saint of the city.

Feast of St. Peter and St. Paul in Rome: The Feast of St. Peter and St. Paul in Rome is celebrated with a great deal of zeal, and many Tuscan pilgrims and visitors take part in the celebrations. This day is filled with religious activities, large processions, and the time-honored "infiorata," a tradition in which the streets are decorated with elaborate floral arrangements. The fact that you are here to witness this event is a demonstration of the regional links that exist in Tuscan culture as well as the great importance of saints.

Traditional festivals in Tuscany serve as a tribute to the region's deeply established cultural legacy and present tourists with a one-of-a-kind opportunity to observe the enduring customs, rituals, and passions that define Tuscan life. These celebrations also serve as an opportunity for locals to interact with and learn from one another. Whether you are mesmerized by the solemnity of religious processions, enthralled by the pageantry of historical reenactments, or enchanted by the sensory delights of culinary and music festivals, being a witness to traditional Tuscan celebrations is an immersive experience that allows you to embrace the time-honored rhythms of this alluring region. These festivals resound with a sense of community and cultural pride, as well as the time-honored customs that continue to flourish within Tuscany's revered cultural landscape.

6.4 Creating Your Own Celebration in Tuscany

Tuscany, with its picture-perfect vistas, rich cultural tapestry, and charming medieval architecture, is the ideal canvas upon which to paint your own one-of-a-kind celebration. It doesn't matter if it's a wedding in a faraway location, a party to celebrate an anniversary or a milestone birthday, or any other kind of celebration: Tuscany's natural charm and warm welcome make it an appealing setting in which to develop memories that will last a lifetime. We will delve into the possibilities, practicalities, and ageless allure of having your event in this magnificent region of Italy in our examination of constructing your personal celebration in Tuscany. This will be done so that we can better understand how to make your event uniquely yours.

The Enchantment of Tuscany as a Location for Special Occasions

The variety of experiences that may be had in Tuscany is what gives the region its irresistible charm as a location for celebrations. Tuscany offers a variety of backdrops that may be adapted to suit your vision, from the rolling vineyard-covered hills of Chianti to the medieval beauty of Florence and Siena. Tuscany is located in central Italy.

Tuscany as a Wedding Location for Destination Weddings

Tuscany has long been regarded as one of the most desirable locations for wedding ceremonies that take place in a setting that is both romantic and scenic. Ancient churches, historic mansions, quaint farmhouses, and opulent estates are just some of the wedding locations that are available in this part of the world.

Finding the Right Location: Choosing the right location for your wedding will help to establish the mood for the entire party. On the one hand, historic Tuscan villas exude an air of enduring elegance, while on the other, the mood of a rustic farmhouse in the middle of the countryside is one that is more laid-back and personal. There are several sites that offer breathtaking views of the Tuscan landscape as well as beautiful gardens.

Planners for Weddings: If you want the process to go more smoothly, you might want to think about hiring a local wedding planner who is familiar with the locations, customs, and logistics of the area. They are able to provide assistance in preparing everything from the catering and flower arrangements to the legal procedures, which will ensure that your celebration goes off without a hitch.

Birthdays and anniversaries of significant ages

Tuscany is not only a popular location for weddings; it is also an excellent choice for the celebration of other key milestones, such as a 40th birthday, a 50th wedding anniversary, or any other event that warrants a memorable setting.

Private Villas and Estates: The region of Tuscany is home to a wide variety of private villas and estates that are available for rent on an exclusive basis for your special occasion. You will be able to build cherished moments with the people you care about most by choosing one of these venues because of its seclusion and its cozy atmosphere.

The culinary traditions of Tuscany are renowned all over the world. Traditional Tuscan cuisine. You can work together with local cooks and caterers to create a meal that highlights the distinctive flavors of the area. Some of the mouthwatering foods that should be included on the menu include pappa al pomodoro, ribollita, and Florentine steak.

Celebrations that Draw Inspiration from Art and Culture

The diverse cultural history of Tuscany is a wellspring of creative ideas that can be drawn upon when planning events with an artistic focus.

Art & Culinary Workshops: Work with local painters, artisans, and chefs to offer guests the opportunity to develop their creative sides through a variety of artistic and culinary activities. Organize activities for guests to participate in, such as painting or cooking, where they can learn how to make typical delicacies from Tuscany.

Plan guided tours of Tuscany's most famous cities, such as Florence, Pisa, and Siena. These cities are located in the region of Tuscany known as Tuscany. Discover the region's storied history while touring museums of world-renowned quality and old buildings.

Wine Tastings and Gastronomic Adventures

Because Tuscany is so well-known for its wine and its culinary traditions, it is an ideal place to go for events that center on food and drink when you want to celebrate something.

Chianti, Montalcino, and Montepulciano are just a few of the well-known wine areas that can be found in Tuscany, which is the setting for many celebratory wine tastings. Set up private wine tastings for your guests at nearby wineries, where they will have the opportunity to try some of the world's best wines.

Delectable Culinary Delights: Work in tandem with Tuscan chefs to prepare a meal that will live long in the memory. Indulge in a Tuscan feast consisting of multiple courses and including flavors and ingredients that are fresh from the region.

Having a party in the great outdoors

The countryside of Tuscany provides the perfect setting for celebrations that are held close to nature.

Garden Parties: Throw a garden party with guests dining outdoors in the beautiful Tuscan countryside. The breathtaking gardens and vineyards of this area make for picture-perfect locations for outdoor gatherings and festivities.

Countryside Retreats: If you're looking for a more rustic venue for your event, one option is to host it at an old farmhouse that has been renovated, complete with vast fields and the stunning countryside of Tuscany as your backdrop. Establish a laid-back and casual environment for your guests, one in which they may take pleasure in the unspoiled landscape of Tuscany.

Taking Into Account the Real World

It takes a lot of meticulous planning and attention to detail in order to create your own unique party in Tuscany. The following are some considerations to keep in mind:

Local Providers: If you're looking for talented local providers, Tuscany has a multitude of options, from caterers and florists to photographers and musicians.

Collaborate with people in the area who are both capable of bringing your ideas to life and knowledgeable about the peculiar practices of the local culture.

A wedding or other formal ceremony in Italy must comply with a number of legal obligations, which you should be aware of. Make sure that your event follows all of the rules by consulting with the appropriate authorities and legal professionals in the area.

Accommodation: Depending on the number of people who will be attending your event, you may need to make arrangements for their overnight stays. There is a diverse selection of places to stay available in Tuscany, ranging from opulent hotels to little bed & breakfasts.

Transportation: Be sure to make transportation arrangements for your guests, particularly if the location you've picked is in a more remote setting. To guarantee that everyone arrives safely, make arrangements for shuttle services or provide specific driving directions.

The Enchantment that Tuscany Has Always Held

The outstanding beauty, cultural wealth, and friendly hospitality of Tuscany make it a destination of choice for celebratory occasions that will never lose their attraction. It doesn't matter if you're planning a wedding, a milestone birthday party, or an anniversary to remember: the region's breathtaking landscapes, ancient monuments, and world-famous culinary traditions make it a riveting location in which to create your own unique celebration. You will make memories that will last a lifetime if you celebrate your special occasion in Tuscany, where the landscape is characterized by rolling hills, cypress trees, and old cities. The cultural and natural magnificence of the region will leave an indelible impression on your event, assuring that Tuscany will become not just the backdrop but also a treasured part of your own narrative.

Chapter 7

Exploring Tuscany's Art and Architecture

Tuscany is a region located in the middle of Italy that is well-known for having a significant cultural heritage, particularly in the fields of art and architecture. Tuscany has been a hotbed of artistic creativity ever since the Renaissance, and as a result, the region is responsible for the creation of some of the world's most recognizable and celebrated works of art. As a result of the enormous wealth of cultural and architectural treasures that can be found in this region, it is a popular tourist destination that welcomes millions of visitors each year.

This comprehensive essay will take you on a tour through the heart of Tuscany, analyzing the
region's most notable works of art and architecture, beginning with the early Renaissance and moving forward into the modern age. We will investigate the ways in which this geographical area has played a significant role in directing the development of art and architecture in the Western world, with notable contributors like Leonardo da Vinci, Michelangelo, and Filippo Brunelleschi. In addition, we will investigate the environment of Tuscany, as well as the legacy of the Medici dynasty and the lasting appeal of Tuscan art and architecture in the modern world.

The Rich Artistic Tradition of Tuscany

The Beginning of the Renaissance in Europe

Many people believe that the Renaissance began in Tuscany. The Renaissance was a time period that brought about a seismic shift in art, culture, and human philosophy. Tuscany is commonly believed to be the birthplace of the Renaissance. The Renaissance was characterized by a return to classical thought as well as a rekindled interest in the study of the human experience. This intellectual and creative movement began in the latter part of the 14th century and found its core in Florence, which is the principal city of the Italian region of Tuscany. The city developed into a center for artistic creativity, and many of its illustrious citizens played critical roles in the development of the Renaissance.

The city of Florence is known as the "cradle of the Renaissance"

As the county seat of Tuscany, Florence played a pivotal role in the development of the Renaissance. The influential and rich Medici family of the city played a key part in the development of an environment conducive to intellectual and artistic inquiry as well as the promotion of the arts. Because of their support, several well-known artists and architects were able to flourish in Florence, helping to establish the city as a center of artistic innovation.

The Renaissance's Ultimate Polymath, Leonardo da Vinci

Leonardo da Vinci, widely regarded as the most influential thinker to emerge from the Italian Renaissance, was born in the Tuscan village of Vinci. He made immense contributions to the fields of art and science, and he is revered for his innovative paintings such as "Mona Lisa" and "The Last Supper." Both art and science bear an unmistakable imprint of Leonardo da Vinci's pioneering spirit and enduring preoccupation with the human body and the natural world.

Creating Work of a Divine Nature: Michelangelo

Caprese, in the region of Tuscany, is the place of birth of Michelangelo Buonarroti, an additional

light of the Renaissance. His artistic abilities ranged from sculpting to painting to architecture, and he was accomplished in all of these fields. His iconic works, such as the Statue of David and the ceiling of the Sistine Chapel, continue to be regarded as among the most significant examples of artistic achievement throughout history.

Brunelleschi, Filippo: A Pioneer in the Field of Architecture

Brunelleschi, a Florentine architect named Filippo, is generally regarded as the one who initiated the Renaissance style of building. His creative designs, like as the distinctive dome of Santa Maria del Fiore cathedral in Florence, demonstrated a command of both engineering and aesthetics. The architectural concepts that Brunelleschi developed continue to have an impact on contemporary design.

Landscapes of Tuscany Serve as Inspiration

The breathtaking scenery in Tuscany has long been an inspiration for writers, painters, sculptors, and architects. The enchanting landscape of Tuscany, complete with its undulating hills, sprawling vineyards, and quaint little towns, has long served as a source of inspiration for artists. We will investigate the ways in which the breathtaking landscape of Tuscany has sparked the creation of many works of art and continues to entice travelers and artists to visit the region.

The Role That the Medici Family Played in History

The Medici family was one of the most powerful and wealthy dynasties in Renaissance Italy. They were responsible for a significant portion of the artistic and architectural growth that occurred in Tuscany during this time period. Their support of artists, scientists, and intellectuals was a crucial factor in Tuscany's blossoming into a center of Renaissance culture during this time period. We will investigate the influence that the Medici dynasty had on the creative history of the region.

The Influence of Art and Architecture from Tuscany on the Modern World

People all around the world are still enthralled and motivated by the creative and architectural legacy that Tuscany left behind. We will investigate the ways in which contemporary society has preserved, honored, and reimagined the art and architecture of Tuscany. Tuscany's history is still very much alive and well in the region's present culture thanks to initiatives such as art conservation and the staging of cultural events.

Art and architecture from Tuscany have made an unmistakable impression on the development of Western culture throughout its history. This area has been a fertile breeding ground for creative minds throughout history, from the genesis of the Renaissance to the ongoing influence of luminaries such as Leonardo da Vinci, Michelangelo, and Filippo Brunelleschi, amongst others. Tuscany is a perennial treasure trove of beauty and inspiration thanks to its landscapes, the patronage of the Medici family, and the continuous relevance of its artistic past. Tuscany provides a voyage through time and beauty that is incomparable, making it an ideal destination for anybody looking to be awed on their travels, whether they are art lovers, architects, or simply vacationers in search of the extraordinary.

7.1 The Uffizi Gallery and the Art of Florence

The Uffizi Gallery is a treasure mine of artistic brilliance and historical value, and it can be found right in the middle of Florence, Italy. This renowned museum is a monument to the rich cultural heritage of Florence, a city that served as a crucible for some of the most significant artistic advances in the history of humankind. Florence is home to some of the world's most treasured works of art and architecture. The Uffizi Gallery is a living monument to the development of art in Florence; it has a vast collection that spans several centuries and is representative of a variety of artistic tendencies, and it serves as a showcase for these works. This article goes into the history of the Uffizi Gallery, investigates some of its most famous works of art, and sheds light on the significant impact that Florentine art has had on the cultural landscape around the world.

The Origins and Development of the Uffizi Gallery

In the year 1560, Cosimo I de' Medici gave the order for the construction of the Uffizi Gallery, which was initially intended to be a complex of government offices for the Florentine magistrates. The construction of the Uffizi, which was led by the well-known Italian architect Giorgio Vasari and took place over the course of several years, has been subjected to a great deal of alteration and enlargement over the course of its history. The Medici family, who ruled Florence at the time, made the decision in the 16th century to exhibit some of the works from their personal art collection to the general public. This act established the Uffizi Gallery's function as a cultural institution and marked the beginning of the gallery's transition from administrative offices to an art museum.

The Stunning Beauty of the Uffizi Gallery's Architecture

The splendor and refinement that characterize Renaissance aesthetics can be seen reflected in the architectural style of the Uffizi Gallery. An impression of harmony and balance is produced by the building's remarkable U-shaped plan, which includes a courtyard that is open to the sky and faces the Arno River. The sculptures and other works of art that adorn the front of the museum serve as a demonstration of the high level of artistic craftsmanship that was prevalent during the Renaissance. The successful combination of classical characteristics and forward-thinking architectural methods is illustrative of Florence's cultural and artistic achievements during the Renaissance period.

The Uffizi Gallery Is Home to Some of the World's Most Famous Works of Art

The Uffizi Gallery is home to an extraordinary collection of artworks, such as paintings, sculptures, and other artifacts that span a variety of time periods throughout the development of art. The gallery is home to a number of historically significant works of art, including "The Birth of Venus" and "Primavera" by Sandro Botticelli, "Annunciation" by Leonardo da Vinci, and "Tondo Doni" by Michelangelo. These works of art are among the most renowned in the world. The artistic creativity and technical mastery that marked the Florentine Renaissance may be seen in these renowned masterpieces, which showcase topics like as humanism, religious devotion, and mythical allegory.

The Inheritance of Art from Florence

The collection held within the Uffizi Gallery is a prime example of the great and continuing impact that Florentine art has had on the evolution of art throughout the Western world. The emphasis placed throughout the Renaissance period on perspective, human anatomy, and naturalism, in addition to the inclusion of classical motifs and subjects, were all factors that contributed to the transformation of artistic expression during this time. The artistic developments that were initiated by Florentine masters provided the framework for later movements, so influencing the course of art history and serving as an inspiration to generations of artists, art academics, and art connoisseurs all over the world.

Efforts Regarding Preservation and Conservation of Resources

A continued dedication to protecting Florence's cultural heritage may be seen in the museum's ongoing efforts to preserve and conserve the priceless art collection housed in the Uffizi Gallery. The artworks in the gallery are safeguarded and preserved for future generations thanks to conservation efforts such as restoration programs, cutting-edge technology interventions, and stringent conservation standards. These efforts highlight how important it is to preserve cultural heritage and cultivate an appreciation for the artistic accomplishments of bygone eras.

The Important Role That The Uffizi Gallery Plays In Both Cultural Education And Tourism

The Uffizi Gallery, which serves as a center for cultural education and tourism, is known for providing guests with a comprehensive experience that goes beyond simple observation. Educational programs, guided tours, and interactive displays provide insight into the historical background and artistic value of the gallery's collection. As a result, participants gain a deeper appreciation of Florentine art and its larger cultural implications. The Uffizi Gallery's status as a cultural monument has been a crucial factor in Florence's promotion as a global cultural destination, which in turn has resulted in the city receiving millions of tourists and art enthusiasts on a yearly basis.

The Uffizi Gallery is a living testimony to the artistic prowess and cultural heritage of Florence. It encapsulates the essence of the city's great impact on the development of Western art and serves as a memorial to Florence's artistic brilliance and cultural legacy. The Uffizi Gallery is a reservoir of artistic brilliance and historical significance. This is evidenced not only by the architectural beauty of the building but also by its collection of masterpieces, which is without peer. Its role as a cultural institution continues to inspire and educate audiences, creating an appreciation for the rich artistic legacy that has distinguished Florence as a beacon of creativity and invention. This appreciation is fostered by the fact that the institution continues to play a role. When guests enter the Uffizi Gallery, they are immediately transported to a world where the ageless beauty of art collides with the spirit of human inventiveness. This experience leaves an indelible impact on the collective consciousness of art and culture.

7.2 The Leaning Tower of Pisa

People all around the world have had their minds blown for centuries by the iconic Leaning Tower of Pisa, which is considered to be one of the greatest architectural achievements in the history of the world. Its famous tilt, which seems to defy the laws of gravity, is a monument to the skill of the architects and builders who were responsible for creating it as well as the difficulties they had to overcome. In this essay, we will investigate the history, architecture, and cultural significance of the Leaning Tower of Pisa. In the process, we will throw light on the interesting story that lies behind this magnificent edifice.

Contextualization of the Past

The Initial Stages

The original construction of the Leaning Tower of Pisa, also known as the "Torre Pendente di Pisa" in Italian, dates back to the 12th century. The construction of the tower began in 1173 and was an integral part of a bigger complex that also included the Cathedral and Baptistery of Pisa. The tower was originally designed to be a standalone bell tower for the cathedral. Its purpose was to house seven bells and to serve as a symbol of Pisa's wealth and dignity.

Construction Obstacles and Difficulties

The tower's characteristic tilt, which has since become its most recognizable feature, was not a design feature but rather the unanticipated result of obstacles encountered throughout the construction process. Clay, shells, and very fine sand were the components of the unstable subsoil that the tower was constructed on. The weight of the tower caused it to sink unevenly as the construction continued, and its tilt became more noticeable as a result.

Over the course of several centuries, construction was paused and then restarted at various points due to conflicts, financial restrictions, and efforts to make the structure more stable. During each stop, the underlying earth was given the opportunity to settle, which contributed to the tower's characteristic tilt.

Various Elements of Architecture

The Plan and the Measurements

Pisa's most famous landmark, the Leaning Tower of Pisa, is a stunning example of Romanesque architecture from Pisa. It has a cylindrical shape and a total of eight stories, and it is built out of white and gray marble. The current height of the tower, measured from the ground to the top of the belfry, is roughly 56 meters (183.27 feet) in length.

At its lowest point, the tower has a diameter of around 15.5 meters (50.85 feet), however at its highest point, that diameter tapers off to approximately 13.14 meters (43.11 feet). This deliberate architectural aspect of the tower's structure was designed to offset its lean in order to prevent it from falling over.

The Slender

The tilt of the Leaning Tower of Pisa is probably the feature that is most well-known about it. The tower tips forward at an angle that is approximately 5.5 degrees off of the vertical at its most severe point. This tilt was not an intentional design feature; rather, it was caused by the foundation of the tower sinking into the unstable soil over the course of several centuries.

Tolling Bells and the Belfry

It was originally planned for the belfry of the Leaning Tower to contain seven bells. These bells were cast over the course of several years, and each one featured an inscription, some of which were religious in nature, while others contained poetic language. During the 17th century, the largest of the seven bells, which are collectively referred to as the "Pisa Cathedral Bells," was added.

Stairs, as well as the interior

A winding staircase with 294 steps can be found on the inside of the tower. It spirals its way to the top. Those who are climbing face a challenge not only in terms of their physical abilities but also in terms of their perceptions, as the narrow stairway appears to tilt in conjunction with the tower's lean. On the other hand, it provides views that are both exceptional and magnificent of Pisa and the area around it.

Attempts to Establish Stability

Throughout the course of its existence, the tower has been the subject of a great deal of maintenance in the form of several attempts at stabilization. The tower was made inaccessible to the general public in 1990 due to safety concerns, and substantial restoration and stability efforts were initiated to address the structure's perilous tilt.

The removal of soil from the side of the tower that was perpendicular to the tilt was one of the most important interventions that was performed. As a result, the tower's tilt was reduced by approximately 45 centimeters (17.7 inches). In addition, counterweights were installed to the side of the tower that was taller. After these efforts were successful in stabilizing the building, the famous Leaning Tower of Pisa was opened to the public once more in the year 2001.

Importance in terms of Culture
Iconography and Tourist Trade

The iconic and enduring representation of Italy that is the Tower of Pisa has become a famous icon on a global scale.

Because of its recognizable form, gorgeous location in the Field of Miracles (Piazza dei Miracoli), and close proximity to the Pisa Cathedral, it is an absolute must-see attraction for tourists as well as art lovers. Its image has appeared on a large number of postcards, advertising, and other cultural representations, solidifying its position in popular culture.

In spite of the fact that the tower's tilt is the result of building errors, it has, in a strange way, become one of its most persistent selling points. Visitors come from all over the world to this location in order to capture images that produce optical illusions. These photographs make it look as though the visitors are supporting or leaning on the tower.

The Influence of Architecture

Because of its singular architectural issues and the ingenious technical solutions that were eventually developed to address those challenges, the Leaning Tower of Pisa has become a subject of study and interest among architects and engineers. Due to the tower's tilt, a number of challenging issues arose, and the eventual stabilization of the structure is regarded as an outstanding accomplishment in the fields of architectural and structural engineering.

Importance from a Historical and Creative Perspective

The tower, which is included in the Field of Miracles and is therefore a part of the UNESCO World Heritage Site, is a reflection of the architectural and artistic accomplishments of its period. Together, the Leaning Tower of Pisa, the Pisa Baptistery, and the Pisa Cathedral comprise a monumental complex that exemplifies the Romanesque and Gothic architectural styles that were prevalent throughout that time period. The cultural and artistic significance of Pisa as a maritime power throughout the Middle Ages is embodied in these constructions, which date back to that time period.

The Leaning Tower of Pisa is not only a well-known monument but also a demonstration of the inventiveness and versatility of human beings because of its extensive past, one-of-a-kind architectural characteristics, and cultural value. The tower's survival and stabilization reflect humans' ability to endure difficulty and maintain their cultural history. While the tower's initial lean was caused by geological problems, these challenges have since been surmounted, and the structure has been stabilized.

The Leaning Tower of Pisa, which is both a representation of Italy and a popular destination for tourists from all over the world, is a good example of the enduring allure of art and architecture. Its history continues to be motivational, both in terms of the unplanned architectural miracle that it is and the dogged efforts that were made to save it from destruction. The Tower of Pisa continues to be an enthralling and enduring emblem of human ingenuity, resiliency, and the capacity to transform even unanticipated obstacles into cherished victories.

7.3 Siena Piazza del Campo

Piazza del Campo is not just a square but rather a living witness to the city of Siena's rich history, culture, and architectural splendor. It can be found in the middle of the historic city of Siena, which is located in Italy. This historic public square is famed for its one-of-a-kind shell-shaped architecture, its medieval tower, and the Palazzo Pubblico, which is home to both the Civic Museum and the world-famous murals painted by Ambrogio Lorenzetti. Together, these elements make up this space's iconic status. The Piazza del Campo is more than simply a physical area; it is the throbbing heart of Siena, and it serves as the backdrop for a variety of cultural events, including the internationally renowned Palio di Siena horse race. This essay will investigate the history of the Piazza del Campo, as well as its architecture, the cultural significance of the Piazza del Campo, and the events that have taken place there, providing a full analysis of this amazing Italian gem.

Contextualization of the Past

Origins from the Middle Ages

The history of Siena's Piazza del Campo may be traced back to the city's medieval period. At the point where the routes that intersected in the city came together, a market was created there. The layout of the Piazza was gradually constructed to be in the shape of a shell, which not only made it easier for people to congregate and conduct business, but it also made it simpler for rainwater to drain away from the area. A strong magistracy that dominated Siena during the medieval period was known as the Council of Nine, which is represented by the square's distinctive design, which is in the shape of a fan and is divided into nine parts.

The Administration of the City

During the whole time that the Middle Ages were in effect, the city-state of Siena was one that was thriving economically and jealously preserved its independence. The Piazza del Campo evolved into a center of civic and political activity, serving as a venue for open-air conferences and discussions. The Nine and the Council of the People met in the Sienese government's official home, the Palazzo Pubblico, which was situated on the piazza and served as the city's administrative center. The towering structure called the Torre del Mangia, which is attached to the Palazzo, was built to give oversight. This was done both as a symbol of authority and as a way to keep an eye on any disturbance.

The Siena's Palio race

The Palio di Siena is a horse race that has been routinely held in the Piazza del Campo ever since the 16th century. It is widely considered to be one of the most famous events that takes place there. The Palio is a race that sets the many contrade (neighborhoods or districts) of the city against one another. It is known for its intense level of competition and the emotional charge it generates. The race is just one aspect of the event; it is also a celebration of the local culture and history, with months of preparation, parades, and other celebrations leading up to the main event itself.

Various Elements of Architecture

Pattern in the Shape of a Fan

The Piazza del Campo is known for its shell-shaped, fan-like design, which is one of its most recognizable characteristics. A central, sloped space is encircled by nine distinct portions in this arrangement. These sections are separated from one another by red bricks that are arranged in a unique, fan-like manner. Each of these sections is intended to serve as a representation of one of the nine individuals who make up the Council of Nine. In addition, the fan form ensures that precipitation drains away well, which helps to minimize flooding and maintains the square's integrity.

The Public Palace or Palazzo

Piazza del Campo's western side is dominated by the magnificent Palazzo Pubblico, a gothic building that is a prime example of the style. Between the years 1297 and 1310, the construction of this civic palace, which later became Siena's seat of government, took place. The dedication of the city to democracy as well as the arts is reflected in the building's design in a number of its component parts.

The frescoes in the Sala dei Nove (Hall of the Nine) of the Palazzo Pubblico that were painted by Ambrogio Lorenzetti and show the Allegory of Good and Bad Government are only one example of the wide variety of artistic masterpieces that adorn this building. Not only are these frescoes outstanding examples of medieval art, but they are also significant historical documents that perfectly capture the ethos of their time period.

The Tower of the Mangia

An remarkable piece of architecture that contributes to the overall elegance of the area is the Torre del Mangia, which is a large bell tower that lies in close proximity to the Palazzo Pubblico. The tower is believed to have been built between the years 1338 and 1348 and currently stands at a height of roughly 102 meters (335 ft). Its building was an impressive example of engineering at the time it was built.

The tower was used to mark the hours, which helped to regulate the everyday activities of the city. Additionally, the tower served as a vantage point for keeping an eye on the city. Climbing the tower in Siena allows visitors to take in breathtaking vistas of the city as well as the countryside in the surrounding area.

The Gaia Fountain is located

The Piazza del Campo has been enhanced tremendously by the addition of the Gaia Fountain, which is also known as Fonte Gaia. The present-day version of the fountain was constructed in 1419 and was designed by Jacopo della Quercia. It is comprised of a variety of sculpted panels, some of which depict stories from the Old Testament while others tell mythological tales. The Gaia Fountain contributes to the aesthetic appeal of the city while also providing residents with an accessible supply of potable water.

The Palio Track in addition to the Pavement

The ground of the Piazza del Campo is paved with red bricks set in a herringbone pattern, which contributes to the square's one-of-a-kind appearance and attraction. The "cocullo" or "carousel," which is located in the middle of the Piazza, serves as the racetrack for the Palio di Siena. Participants on bareback horses will race around the edge of the square in this event.

Importance in terms of Culture

The Siena's Palio race

The Palio di Siena is without a doubt the most well-known and significant event in terms of cultural importance that takes place in the Piazza del Campo. This exciting horse race is held twice a year, on July 2nd and August 16th, and draws contestants and fans from all over the world. The race is marked by fierce competitiveness, great neighborhood pride, and vivid pageantry throughout the course of the event.

Because the race is so short—only about 90 seconds—and because each contrada chooses a horse and jockey to represent their district, it is widely considered to be one of the most competitive and exciting horse races in the world. The desired Palio, a painted banner that represents triumph, is given to the contrada that prevails in the competition. The Palio is not only a source of enormous pride for the winning contrada, but it is also an event steeped in culture and history that encapsulates the essence of Sienese identity and tradition.

Importance in the Course of History

The history chronicle of Siena cannot be considered complete without mentioning the Piazza del Campo and the monuments that surround it. The form and arrangement of the plaza are reflective of the city's dedication to democratic governance as well as its distinctive nine-member ruling council, which set it apart from many other medieval Italian cities. The artistic and architectural features of the Piazza, in particular the frescoes on the Palazzo Pubblico, offer insightful perspectives on the social and political climate of the era.

The Influence of Architecture

The Piazza del Campo is home to a number of historically significant buildings, such as the Palazzo Pubblico, the Torre del Mangia, and the Gaia Fountain, all of which have left an indelible mark on the evolution of Gothic and Renaissance architecture. These buildings are remarkable examples of excellent design, space utilization, and the successful combination of art and architecture.

The Promotion of Cultural Learning Through Tourism

The Piazza del Campo is a prominent tourist attraction that draws visitors from all over the world. These tourists come to experience the architectural magnificence, cultural legacy, and spectacle that is the Palio di Siena that is held in the square. The plaza also plays an essential role in the dissemination of cultural knowledge because it is the location of the Civic Museum. This museum displays significant works of art and historical objects, and it enlightens visitors about the eventful history of Siena.

In Siena, the Piazza del Campo is more than simply a pretty square; it is also a living witness to the city's rich history, culture, and architectural prowess. The Piazza is a celebration of Siena's artistic and political legacy, and it does so in a number of ways, beginning with its distinctive fan-shaped design and continuing with its prominent structures, such as the Palazzo Pubblico and the Torre del Mangia.

The cultural significance of the Piazza is enhanced by the Palio di Siena, which is a horse race that has been run continuously since the medieval times. This event is a lively and passionate celebration of the city's neighborhoods, and it reflects Siena's everlasting character.

The Piazza del Campo is a well-known landmark that serves as a representation of the enduring significance of historic public spaces. Piazza del Campo is a place where architecture, art, culture, and history all come together to create an indelible legacy. Piazza del Campo is a one-of-a-kind and enlightening experience that encompasses the spirit of Siena, which is a great Italian city, and is a must-do for anyone visiting the city, whether they are tourists interested in the beauty of Siena or art and history enthusiasts.

7.4 The Artistic Legacy of Tuscany

The creative history of Tuscany is recognized for being both extensive and durable. Tuscany is located in the middle of Italy. Tuscany has been a fertile environment for artistic invention ever since the beginning of the Renaissance, and as a result, the region is responsible for producing some of the most recognized painters, architects, and masterpieces in the history of the world. This essay will investigate the creative legacy of Tuscany by diving into the historical and cultural reasons that shaped it, the notable people who arose, and the ongoing effect of Tuscan art on the art of other countries and cultures.

Contextualization of History and Culture

The historical and cultural setting of Tuscany has had a significant impact on the region's creative inheritance. The region's prominence during the Middle Ages and the Renaissance are just two examples of its illustrious past, which also includes its Etruscan and Roman roots. The city-states of Florence, Siena, and Pisa, as well as others, were major centers of commerce and culture, and they contributed to the development of an atmosphere that was favorable to the blossoming of the arts.

The exceptional topography and climate of Tuscany have played a part in the development of artistic talent in the region. Painters and sculptors have long drawn inspiration from the magnificent scenery, which feature undulating hills and rich valleys. The intensity of the light, the wealth of natural beauty, and the careful coordination that characterize the Tuscan countryside are recurrent motifs in the region's artistic tradition.

It is impossible to overestimate the importance of influential families like the Medici in the development of Tuscan art. Not only did these art supporters give financial assistance to the creative community, but they also gave artists opportunities to exhibit their work. During the Renaissance period, the Medici family, in particular, was instrumental in increasing the status of Florence as a cultural hub in Europe. This occurred during the time period.

Important Figures in the Art of Tuscany

Da Vinci, Leonardo

Leonardo da Vinci is regarded as one of the most influential creative figures and intellectual thinkers in the history of the world. He was born in the Tuscan village of Vinci. His paintings, such as "Mona Lisa" and "The Last Supper," are considered to be among the greatest examples of Renaissance art. The incomparable abilities that Leonardo possessed in the areas of painting, sketching, engineering, and anatomy had a significant impact on both art and science. He was the perfect example of the Renaissance ideal of the "universal man," a person whose talents extended over a wide range of fields.

Michelangelo di Buonarroti was known as

Michelangelo is another towering figure in Tuscan art, and he was born in Caprese, which is

close to Arezzo. His legacies will live on thanks to the contributions he made to the fields of sculpture, painting, and building. The tremendous talent that Michelangelo possessed is on full display in his masterpieces, which include the ceiling of the Sistine Chapel and the Statue of David. For ages, artists and art aficionados have looked to Michelangelo's works for inspiration.

The artist Sandro Botticelli

Sandro Botticelli was a painter from Florence who is well known for his masterpieces "The Birth of Venus" and "Primavera." His paintings, with their concentration on classical subjects, mythological allegories, and the representation of the human form, exemplify the spirit of the Renaissance that was prevalent during that time. The intellectual and aesthetic milieu of Botticelli's historical period is captured in the artist's work.

Brunelleschi, Filippo, the Younger

Brunelleschi, a Florentine architect named Filippo, is generally regarded as the one who initiated the Renaissance style of building. His creative designs, like as the distinctive dome of Santa Maria del Fiore cathedral in Florence, demonstrated a command of both engineering and aesthetics. The architectural concepts that Brunelleschi developed continue to have an impact on contemporary design and engineering.

Movements in the Cultural and Artistic Worlds

Tuscany has been at the forefront of a number of important cultural and artistic revolutions throughout history, the most renowned of which being the Renaissance. The Renaissance was a time of great intellectual and creative revolution, defined by a resurgence of classical ideas and a renewed interest in humanism. This rebirth of classical ideas and renewed interest in humanism marked the beginning of the Renaissance. Tuscany, and more specifically Florence, was the region that served as the movement's epicenter.

Humanism, a philosophy that emphasized the worth of the person, the study of classical texts, and the investigation of human potential, was enthusiastically embraced by artists and thinkers working in Tuscany during the Renaissance. This humanistic approach found expression in art in the form of a refocused attention on perspective, anatomy, and the naturalistic depiction of the human body.

The artistic movement known as Mannerism, which began during the later stages of the Renaissance, also has its origins in Tuscany. Mannerist artists, such as Parmigianino and Pontormo, pushed the bounds of artistic norms by putting an emphasis on extended proportions, unique compositions, and intricate allegorical themes in their works of art.

The harmonic balance that was apparent in High Renaissance art gave way to an aesthetic movement known as Mannerism.

Baroque painters such as Gian Lorenzo Bernini and Pietro da Cortona came to prominence during this time period in Tuscany's creative history, which also includes the region's legacy from the Renaissance. These painters made significant contributions to the development of the Baroque style, which is distinguished by its use of dramatic lighting, intense emotional content, and extravagant embellishment.

Influence on the Art of the West

The creative legacy of Tuscany has had a significant and long-lasting influence on the art of Western countries. The theories and methods that were established during the Renaissance era, such as linear perspective and chiaroscuro (the utilization of stark contrasts between light and dark), completely reworked the manner in which painters depicted the world around them. These innovations quickly spread across Europe, which significantly altered the path that art history would later take.

The ideas that emerged during the Renaissance, such as an increased emphasis on the uniqueness of each person and a deeper dive into ancient history, were crucial in laying the framework for the Enlightenment and the eventual development of modern art. The aim of artists working during the Renaissance was to portray the core of the human experience, which resulted in a shift away from rigid, religious imagery and toward narratives that were more focused on the human experience.

The impact of Tuscany may be seen not only in its paintings and sculptures, but also in its buildings, its engineering, and its pursuit of knowledge in the sciences. Brunelleschi was one of several Tuscan architects who contributed to the development of architectural ideas and inventions that continue to impact present architectural practices. The attitude of multidisciplinary research that was prevalent during the Renaissance period is exemplified by Leonardo da Vinci's sketches and creations, which included everything from anatomical investigations to plans for flying vehicles.

The enduring interest in the art and culture of Tuscany is evidence of the region's artistic legacy's ability to captivate audiences for generations to come. The Italian cities of Florence, Siena, and Pisa, as well as a number of others, continue to be significant cultural destinations, attracting millions of tourists, art enthusiasts, and academics from all over the world.

The practice of Conservation and Preserving

It is of the utmost significance to ensure that Tuscany's artistic history is kept alive and well. Institutions and organizations that are dedicated to the goal of conserving and restoring historical structures, monuments, and artworks are actively working on these projects on a continuing basis. Techniques of preservation, such as restoration, are meticulously used in order to preserve the originality and lifespan of works of art. This helps to ensure that subsequent generations will be able to continue appreciating these works.

The restoration work that was done on Michelangelo's "David" in Florence is one example worth mentioning. A painstaking cleaning and polishing operation was performed on this well-known sculpture in order to eliminate the built-up dirt and bring out its natural radiance. These kinds of efforts are absolutely necessary if one want to preserve the elegance and historical value of Tuscan art.

Importance in the Present Day and Age

The artistic legacy that Tuscany has left behind is still going strong in the modern world. The museums, galleries, and other cultural institutions in this area play an essential part in advancing art education and fostering an appreciation for the visual arts. For example, Florence is home to a number of world-renowned institutions, including the Accademia Gallery and the Uffizi Gallery, both of which continue to entice art enthusiasts and academics from all parts of the world.

Tuscan art is still significant today not just as a historical artifact but also as a source of inspiration for artists working in more current and contemporary styles. The ongoing attraction of Tuscan art is shown in the way that traditional methods have been combined with contemporary ideas and aesthetics. Landscapes, buildings, and ideas that have been a source of fascination for Tuscan artists for ages all continue to serve as a source of creativity for contemporary artists.

The artistic heritage of Tuscany is kept alive through various cultural events and festivals, such as the Siena Palio and the Florence Biennale, which showcase the region's rich artistic tradition. These events highlight the pervasive impact of Tuscan culture while serving as dynamic showcases for performers at all stages of their careers.

The lasting influence that art has had on Tuscany's culture, society, and history is demonstrated by the region's rich artistic heritage. Tuscan art has had a significant influence on the art and culture of the West for a number of reasons, including the beginning of the Renaissance and the contributions of historical individuals such as Leonardo da Vinci, Michelangelo, and Sandro Botticelli.

A significant contribution to the development of artistic talent has been made by the region's one-of-a-kind historical, cultural, and environmental aspects. People in the modern world continue to be captivated and inspired by the history of Tuscany, which serves as both a historical treasure trove and a source of ongoing creativity and invention.

Whether it is through the restoration of great artworks, the preservation of ancient sites, or the celebration of cultural events, Tuscany's artistic legacy continues to be an essential component of the identity of the area as well as a prized gift to the rest of the world. It is a demonstration of the eternal ability of art to defy the passage of time, connect us to the past, and inspire us to create a better future.

Chapter 8

Love and Romance in Tuscan Literature

Tuscan literature, with its rich historical and cultural history, has been a source of inspiration for generations of authors, poets, and painters. This has been the case for centuries. This literary tradition is characterized by a profound and enduring preoccupation with love and romance as its central themes. Tuscan literature has examined the many facets of love in an unprecedented level of depth and complexity, from the stirring verses of Dante Alighieri's "Divine Comedy" to the impassioned sonnets of Petrarch and the lyrical works of Boccaccio. This article dives into the world of love and passion in Tuscan literature, charting its growth from the medieval period to the Renaissance and beyond. It focuses on major characters and works that have left an everlasting effect on the world of literature, such as those written by Giosuè Carducci and Dante Alighieri.

1. Literature from the Middle Ages in Tuscany: Dante's "Divine Comedy"
   Beatrice of Urbino and Dante Alighieri
   Dante Alighieri, who is often considered as the father of Italian literature, had a significant impact on the literature that was produced throughout the medieval period in Tuscany. The "Divine Comedy," which is considered to be Dante's magnum opus, is a literary masterpiece that embodies the themes of love and romance within the setting of spiritual and philosophical inquiry. The unrequited love that Dante had for Beatrice Portinari, a person that transcends the earthly realm and becomes a metaphor of divine love, serves as the driving force behind this masterpiece. Beatrice represents the transformational force of love and its ability to elevate the soul throughout Dante's journey through Hell, Purgatory, and Heaven. She acts

as Dante's guide across these three realms.

Affectionate Chivalry

Dante's depiction of love in the "Divine Comedy" is strongly entrenched in the tradition of courtly love, which was a significant theme in literature written during the medieval period. The concept of courtly love, which is distinguished by chivalric devotion and the admiration of an unattainable lady, emerged as a common theme in the writing of Tuscany. It is best shown by the tradition of the troubadour, which was influential to Dante's writing.

Poets known as troubadours, such Arnaut Daniel, were renowned for penning works that praised the romanticized relationship between a knight and a lady of noble birth. The combination of romantic love with spiritual love is a common theme in Tuscan literature, which is shown in Dante's use of this tradition in his work.

2. **The Sonnet Tradition in Relation to Petrarch**

Sonnets written by Petrarch

With the birth of Petrarch in the 14th century, Tuscan literature underwent a profound transformation. Petrarch made an incalculable contribution to the development of the theme of love and romance in his writing. Canzoniere, also known as "Rime Sparse," is a collection of sonnets written by Petrarch that is considered to be an essential component of Renaissance poetry. Petrarch immortalizes his love for Laura de Noves, an unreachable woman who becomes the target of his lyrical affection, in these sonnets. Laura de Noves was the inspiration for many of Petrarch's sonnets. Petrarch's depiction of love is defined by the conflict between desire and unattainability, generating a dramatic study of the human heart's deepest longings. This tension is what makes Petrarch's portrayal of love so moving.

Humanism and the Obsession with Physical Charm

The work of Petrarch is a reflection of the humanist principles that were prevalent throughout the Renaissance. These ideas placed an emphasis on the resurgence of classical learning as well as a reevaluation of the human experience. In the sonnets written by Petrarch, love is inextricably linked to the quest for beauty, which can refer to either the physical or the intellectual variety. Petrarch's poetry serves as a platform for him to convey his adoration for Laura, who he considers to be the embodiment of beauty in its purest form. Petrarch's tradition, which places an emphasis on the physical and spiritual characteristics of the beloved, is credited with laying the groundwork for the humanistic approach to love and romance that is prevalent in Tuscan literature.

3. Love, Sex, and Satire in Boccaccio's Decameron
   The Decameron is its full name.
   A opposing viewpoint on love and passion in Tuscan literature may be found in Giovanni Boccaccio's "Decameron," which is a compilation of one hundred stories contained within a narrative. The works of Boccaccio examine topics such as love, passion, and the folly of human nature, and they are set against the backdrop of the Black Death. The protagonists of the book "Decameron" flee the plague-ridden city of Florence and seek safety in a villa, where they tell stories to one another that frequently center on love and desire.
   Expression of Love Through the Lens of Satire
   The way in which Boccaccio deals with love is characterized by satire and wit. He presents a less respectful and more earthy vision of love, frequently illustrating the absurdity of love and the comedic qualities of human connections and interactions. The "Decameron" tells stories of adultery, seduction, and deception, all of which represent the intricacies and paradoxes of love that are inherent in the human experience. The idealized and spiritualized depictions of love found in Dante and Petrarch's works are contrasted with Boccaccio's work, which offers a more grounded and comedic point of view on love.
4. Poetry of the Renaissance: Poliziano and the Medici Court in Florence
   It was Angelo Poliziano
   During the time period known as the Renaissance, the region of Tuscany, and particularly the court of the Medici in Florence, saw a rise in the number of literary and artistic works produced. Poetry written by Angelo Poliziano, a prominent personality in this environment, made a significant contribution to the subject matter of love and romance. Petrarch's ideas of love and beauty are echoed in his poem "Stanze for the Girl," which is considered a classic example of Renaissance literature. In this poem, the author praises the attractiveness and virtues of women.
   Patronage of the Medici
   The Medici family was well-known for their support of the arts throughout Florence's history, and they were instrumental in the city's development into a Renaissance center. Their encouragement of writers such as Poliziano and artists such as Botticelli helped to the flowering of works that dealt with themes of love. Both "The Birth of Venus" by Botticelli and the lyrics of Poliziano are interconnected because they both express the ideal of beauty and love associated with the Medici court. Botticelli's "The Birth of Venus" was painted in the early 15th century. It is symptomatic of the larger

cultural transformations that occurred during the Renaissance that the Medici family exerted their influence on the depiction of love in Tuscan literature.

5. **Guarini and Tasso, the Arcadian Ideal in Their Writings**

   The movement known as the Arcadians

   In Tuscany during the late Renaissance and early Baroque periods, there was a movement known as the Arcadian movement that aimed to return to a more pastoral and ideal view of love and nature. This vision was known as the "Ideal Vision." The writings of renowned authors such as Battista Guarini and Torquato Tasso are considered to be the epitome of this literary movement. The idyllic landscapes in which their stories are set provided a stage for passionate love and relationships that were portrayed as perfect.

   The works "Il Pastor Fido" by Guarini and "Aminta" by Tasso

   The works "Il Pastor Fido" by Battista Guarini and "Aminta" by Torquato Tasso are two illustrious examples of Arcadian literature. These plays, which take place in the bucolic countryside, examine concepts such as love and desire, as well as the tension that exists between morality and passion. Both Guarini and Tasso employ the pastoral idyll as a backdrop in their works to investigate the complexities of human feelings, and the expression of passionate love on the pastoral idyll provides the ideal canvas for doing so.

6. **Alfieri and Foscolo represent the Enlightenment and Romanticism in this chapter.**

   In honor of Vittorio Alfieri

   The topic of love and passion was explored in Tuscan literature in fresh and interesting ways during the Enlightenment and Romantic eras. Vittorio Alfieri, an important character in Italian writing during the period of the Enlightenment, was known for imbuing his plays with a strong sense of sentiment and passion. His tragic works, such as "Saul" and "Myrrha," examine forbidden love and the conflict that arises from having to choose between duty and passion. The dramatic writing of Alfieri represents a departure from the pastoral ideal of the Arcadian movement and reflects the shifting social and political context of the historical period in which it was written.

   It was Ugo Foscolo

   Ugo Foscolo, a significant character in Italian Romanticism, continued the Romantic tradition of investigating love and passion into the 19th century. Both his novel "Ultime Lettere di Jacopo Ortis" and his poems, especially "I Sepolcri," dive into themes of longing, patriotism, and the influence of political upheaval on human relationships. His novel is titled "Ultime Lettere di Jacopo Ortis." The Romantic

movement placed a strong emphasis on the individual's emotional experience as well as the connection that existed between love, art, and the nation. The works of Foscolo reflect this emphasis.

7. Contemporary Writing from Tuscany: Romance and Society

The author Giovanni Verga

In the latter half of the 19th century and the early 20th century, there was a movement in the focus of modern Tuscan writing away from the idealized and romanticized depictions of love and toward issues that were more realistic and socially grounded. Novels written by Giovanni Verga, a prominent character in the Italian verismo literary movement, such as "I Malavoglia" and "Mastro-Don Gesualdo," investigate how societal conventions and economic constraints influence love relationships. His writings represent a departure from the earlier romantic tradition by tackling the difficulties of love in a world that is always changing.

A Moravia, Alberto

In the 20th century, Alberto Moravia continued his investigation of love within the framework of a society that was undergoing significant change. His works, such as "Gli Indifferenti" and "La Noia," explore the intricate dynamics of love relationships in the context of a contemporary city. Moravia's investigation of love is characterized by psychological depth and a thorough observation of human behavior, and it reflects the uncertainties and ambiguities of love in a society that is characterized by rapid social change.

8. Contemporary Italian Literature and Its Influence Beyond Tuscany

Voices from the Present Day

The literature produced in contemporary Tuscany contains a wide variety of voices and topics that are all tied to love and passion. In a postmodern setting, the difficulties of love have been investigated by authors such as Dacia Maraini, Alessandro Baricco, and Niccol Ammaniti, amongst others. Issues pertaining to gender, sexuality, and the interaction of love with one's identity and the myriad of ethnic backgrounds are frequently brought up in their works.

The Impact on a Global Scale

The everlasting imprint that Tuscan literature has made on the literary landscape of the world can be attributed to the region's unending investigation of love and romance. In particular, Dante, Petrarch, and Boccaccio have served as motivation for a large number of authors and poets all across the world. The motif of love that is not returned, which may be found in Petrarchan sonnets, has found resonance in the works of many authors, including William Shakespeare, John Keats, and a great many more. The manner in which love is portrayed in Tuscan literature has had a global impact and continues to direct the development of literary canons in other parts of the world.

The concepts of love and passion in Tuscan literature have undergone significant development and morphing over the course of several centuries, reflecting the region's shifting social, cultural, and creative landscapes. From the medieval musings of Dante Alighieri to the passionate sonnets of Petrarch, the satirical tales of Boccaccio, the humanism of the Renaissance, the Arcadian ideals of Guarini and Tasso, and the exploration of love in the Enlightenment, Romanticism, and modern periods, Tuscan literature has offered a rich tapestry of emotions, ideas, and perspectives on the human heart. This can be seen in works such as "

The themes of unrequited love, idealized beauty, and the struggle between desire and virtue have lasted over the centuries, but the way in which these themes are portrayed has undergone significant transformation.

Love in Tuscan literature has always been a reflection of the society and ideals of each era, from the traditional courtly love to the satirical and funny depictions in the "Decameron," from the pastoral idylls of the Arcadian movement to the psychological depths of contemporary writing. This can be seen from the courtly love tradition to the satirical and amusing depictions in the "Decameron."

In today's quickly evolving world, where concerns of identity, gender, and cultural variety are at the forefront of the investigation of love and romance, contemporary Tuscan literature continues to wrestle with the complexity of love in all its myriad forms.

The legacy of Tuscan literature's investigation of love has spread well beyond the confines of

the region, with authors such as Dante, Petrarch, and Boccaccio acting as guiding lights for poets and writers all over the world. It is a testimonial to the continuing strength of love and passion as subjects that transcend time and place that their influence has been so significant in the canon of world literature.

8.1 Dante Alighieri's Divine Comedy

The "Divine Comedy" written by Dante Alighieri is widely recognized as one of the most important and significant works in the annals of literary history. This epic poem, which was written around the beginning of the 14th century, examines topics like as sin, salvation, and the journey of the soul through the afterlife. The work is a reflection of Dante's complicated worldview, which is rich with references to various aspects of culture, politics, and religion. In this essay, we will delve into the complexities of Dante's "Divine Comedy," including its historical and cultural setting, its structure, and the enormous impact it has had on art, literature, and theology.

1. Background, Both Historical and Cultural
   In order to get a complete appreciation for Dante's "Divine Comedy," one needs have a solid understanding of the historical and cultural milieu in which it was written. Dante Alighieri was born and raised during a turbulent time in the history of Italy. It was 1265 when he was born in Florence, thus he lived through the political and social upheavals that occurred during the late Middle Ages. The competition for power within Italian city-states, the rise of the Renaissance, and the conflict between the Papacy and the Holy Roman Empire were all defining characteristics of this era.
   Dante was an active participant in the political life of Florence and played a part in the war between the Guelphs and the Ghibellines, two opposed factions in the city. He is most known for writing the epic poem "Divine Comedy."
   In 1302, as a result of his political actions, he was forced to flee Florence, which proved to be a pivotal moment in both his life and his professional career. His exile is notable because it caused him to walk through numerous places in Italy, giving him the opportunity to examine the diverse political and cultural scene of his day. He was able to gain valuable insight as a result of his experiences.
2. The Compositional Outline of the Divine Comedy

The "Divine Comedy" is comprised of three sections: Inferno, Purgatorio, and Paradiso. Each section is comprised of 33 cantos, and Inferno also contains an opening canto, bringing the total number of cantos in the "Divine Comedy" to 100. This split has symbolic significance, with the number 100 standing for fullness and perfection as well as the three-in-one nature of God, which is central to the Christian faith.

1. The Hellfire
   In the first section, titled "Inferno," the author guides the reader on a journey into the bowels of hell. Dante, with the assistance of the Roman poet Virgil, travels through the nine circles of Hell, which are each devoted to a certain kind of sin. The perpetrators of sin inside each circle are made to endure punishments that are proportionate to the seriousness of their transgressions. The journey into Hell is

meant to be interpreted as a metaphorical picture of the human situation as well as the results of sin.

2. Purgatorio

   Dante's journey up Mount Purgatory, as depicted in the second portion of the poem known as Purgatorio, is the subject of the second section. The purpose of these purification and atonement rituals for the sins committed by souls is to prepare them for entry into heaven. The concept of Purgatory, which describes a state of being intermediate between damnation and salvation, played a crucial role in the theology of medieval Christians.

3. Paradiso

Dante arrives at the heavenly realms with the help of his lover Beatrice in the final section, which is titled Paradiso. In this region, he comes across the highest heavens, each of which stands for a different moral quality, and he converses with a variety of saints, angels, and the Blessed Virgin Mary. The Paradiso delves into the philosophical and theological underpinnings of divine love and wisdom, as well as the concept of complete oneness with God.

III. Symbolic Recurrences and Theological Concepts

1. Original Sin and Its Atonement

   The concepts of sin and redemption play a significant role throughout Dante's "Divine Comedy." The trip that Dante takes through Hell and Purgatory acts as a metaphorical and spiritual allegory for the effects of sin as well as the opportunity for atonement. This work places an emphasis on the necessity of turning away from sin and turning to the mercy of God.

2. Three Persons in One

   The "Divine Comedy" places a strong emphasis on the number three for several reasons. It is a symbol of the Holy Trinity, which consists of God the Father, God the Son, and God the Holy Spirit. This theological idea is reflected in the poem's structure, which consists of three parts: the Inferno, which stands for sin and estrangement from God; the Purgatorio, which stands for purification and reconciliation; and the Paradiso, which depicts unity with the divine.

3. The Importance of Virgil and Beatrice in the Story

   The Roman poet Virgil is seen as a symbol of human reason and the quest for the truth in philosophical circles. Dante is able to follow him through Hell and Purgatory, but he is unable to accompany him to Paradise due to the fact that reason cannot lead to divine

revelation. Beatrice, on the other hand, is representative of divine grace and theology, and she is the one who guides Dante to the heavenly realms that are the most elevated. She exemplifies the idea of divine love as well as the significance of faith in one's pursuit of a closer relationship with God.
4. Defining the Function of the Poet

The main character and writer of "The Divine Comedy," Dante, has a one-of-a-kind function in the story. He is not only a participant in the story, but also a witness to the happenings that he relates. Not only is it a literal voyage, but it also serves as a metaphor for the spiritual search that every person does to find God. Dante is able to gain insight into the human condition, the difficulties of a life on earth, and the quest for spiritual salvation as a result of his own experiences.

IV. The Influence on Literature and Culture

1. Language and the Continuity of Italian Identities
   Dante's decision to write the "Divine Comedy" in the Tuscan dialect rather than in Latin had a significant impact on the development of the Italian language over the course of its history.
   His use of vernacular Italian made a great contribution to the development of the language as well as the construction of a single, unified identity for the Italian people. Dante is frequently referred to in this context as the "Father of the Italian Language."
2. The Written Word, Including Poetry
   The "Divine Comedy" was a groundbreaking work that raised the bar for epic poetry and allegorical writing. Petrarch, Chaucer, Milton, and T.S. Eliot are just a few of the poets and writers who have been impacted by it. These authors and poets took their cues from Dante's composition in terms of structure, symbolism, and subject depth.
3. Theology and Philosophy
   The "Divine Comedy" of Dante has had a long-lasting influence on both the philosophical and
   theological thought of Christians as a result of Dante's investigation of various philosophical and religious subjects. His body of work has been extensively researched and cited by philosophers, theologians, and other academics for centuries.
4. Art and the Representation of Visual Experience
   Dante's evocative images of the afterlife in the "Divine Comedy" have influenced a wide variety of artists over the ages, from painters such as Sandro Botticelli and Gustave Doré to filmmakers and

current visual artists. The concepts of Hell, Purgatory, and Paradise have provided a wealth of material for creative interpretation throughout history.

5. Symbolism in Political and Cultural Affair

The "Divine Comedy" is an important historical document due to Dante's comments on the political and social context of his day, which can be found in the poem. His depictions of political officials, such as Popes and emperors, reveal his views on the appropriate functions of secular and religious authority as well as the boundaries that should be respected by each. Those who are interested in the political and cultural history of medieval Italy should continue to find this work helpful.

The "Divine Comedy" written by Dante Alighieri is a literary and theological masterpiece that continues to captivate readers and researchers all over the world. It is also a source of inspiration. It provides profound insights into the human condition and the search for divine salvation through its examination of sin, atonement, and the journey of the soul through Hell, Purgatory, and Paradise. The book is a colossal contribution to the world of letters as a result of its complex structure, religious topics, and enduring impact on literature, theology, and the arts. The enduring legacy that Dante has left behind, both as a poet and as a cultural figure, guarantees that the "Divine Comedy" will continue to serve as a source of illumination for future generations.

8.2 Petrarch's Sonnets to Laura

Petrarch is widely recognized as one of the most important Italian poets of the 14th century. He is most known for his collection of sonnets, which is variously referred to as the "Canzoniere" or the "Rime Sparse." The sequence of sonnets that Petrarch penned to Laura de Noves, a woman whom he admired and idealized, make up the core of this collection. It is common practice to refer to these sonnets as "Sonnets to Laura." They are emblematic of Petrarch's profound and everlasting preoccupation with love and beauty, exemplifying the principles of courtly love and humanism while simultaneously leaving an indelible effect on the development of poetry in Europe. In this essay, we will investigate Petrarch's Sonnets to Laura, diving into its historical and cultural context, as well as their form, topics, and significant influence on subsequent writing. Specifically, we will focus on how Petrarch's sonnets have influenced subsequent writers.

1. Background, Both Historical and Cultural

Petrarch, who was born in 1304, was a resident of Italy during a time that was marked by significant social and political upheaval. A new intellectual and cultural movement known as the Renaissance was just beginning to emerge during the 14th century, and it was at this time that tensions between city-states, the papacy, and the Holy Roman Empire were at their height. The life and work of Petrarch can be found in the intersection of these various historical and cultural movements and transformations.

1. The Tradition of Courtly Love
   The tradition of courtly love, which had its roots in the troubadour poetry of the medieval Occitan region, had a significant influence on Petrarch's understanding of what love entailed. Chivalric devotion to an unreachable lady, who was most commonly a married or noble woman, was the defining characteristic of courtly love. Poetry was written by the lover in this tradition to express his passion and longing for his beloved, who was portrayed as an idealized figure. The effect of courtly love may be seen throughout Petrarch's Sonnets to Laura, in which Laura serves as the unreachable object of Petrarch's adoration.
2. The Humanist Philosophy
   Petrarch was another important person in the humanist movement that emerged during the early Renaissance. The study of history, literature, and philosophy were encouraged under the humanist ideology, which placed an emphasis on reviving classical education and centering attention on the individual. Petrarch's contemplation of love and beauty is connected with humanist principles in the "Canzoniere," which may be found in his collection of poems. In doing so, he reflects a more general humanistic concern in the intellectual and moral potential of individuals and raises Laura to the status of a symbol of beauty and virtue.
3. The Form and Organization of the Sonnets
   Petrarch's Sonnets to Laura are organized as a collection of 366 poems, the most majority of which are sonnets but some canzoni are also included. They are broken up into two sections: the first 263 sonnets are written to Laura while she was alive, and the final 103 were written after she passed away. This split illustrates the significant effect that Laura's presence, followed by her absence, had on Petrarch's emotional and artistic journey.
4. The first sonnet written by Petrarch

The sonnets written by Petrarch adhere to a certain structural form that is referred to as the Petrarchan sonnet or the Italian sonnet. This particular structure is made up of 14 lines, which are broken up into an octave (the first eight lines) and a sestet (the latter six lines). The rhyme pattern for the octave is normally ABBAABBA, whereas the rhyme scheme for the sestet can be somewhat variable and could be, for example, CDCDCD or CDECDE. Because of the structure of the Petrarchan sonnet, the poet is able to pose an issue or question in the octave, and then either provide a solution to the dilemma or reflect on it in the sestet.

II. Themes Explored in Petrarch's Sonnets Addressed to Laura

1. Love in its Ideal Form
   The concept of idealized love plays an important role throughout the Sonnets to Laura. Laura is more than just a woman; she is a representation of the heavenly beauty and goodness. Petrarch lauds her as an airy and unreachable ideal figure in his writings. His love for Laura extends beyond the confines of the physical world and into the realms of the spiritual and the intellectual.
2. Wanting and the Sense That One Cannot Have It
   The sonnets are infused with a great sense of yearning and of being unable to fulfill that want. Petrarch's need grows as Laura continues to reject his advances and maintains her emotional distance from him. This topic is consistent with the courtly love tradition, which holds that the lover's anguish is intimately related to the inability to be united with the beloved.
3. The Petrarchan Paradox, as the third option.
   Petrarch's poetry frequently exemplifies the Petrarchan paradox, which describes a situation in which the anguish of unrequited love paradoxically produces pleasure and acts as a source of inspiration for creative endeavors. Even though he hasn't been able to be with Laura, his love for her continues to inspire his creativity and artistic expression. The tension between the agony of impossible love and the beauty of his poetry lines exemplifies the paradox, which can be seen as an expression of the contradiction.
4. The Unstoppable March of Time
   In his sonnets, Petrarch returns again and again to the subject of the passage of time. He bemoans the ephemeral qualities of beauty and youth, highlighting the fleeting essence of life itself in the process. This topic emphasizes how fleeting life on earth may be as well as how important it is to memorialize the beauty of a beloved in verse before it is lost forever.
5. The Natural World and Its Beauty

Petrarch's sonnets frequently feature imagery related to the natural world. He frequently draws
comparisons between Laura's beauty and aspects of the natural world, such as flowers, stars, and light, when he is attempting to express her attractiveness. The humanist ideal of beauty as a harmonious element of the natural order is reflected here in the relationship between the object of affection and the natural world.

IV. Impact on the Creative Arts and Culture

1. The Tradition of Petrarch and His Followers
   The sonnet written by Petrarch proved to be an important poetry form in the literature of Europe because of the specific structure and topics it covered. Petrarch's investigation of love and beauty had a profound impact on a large number of later poets, including Geoffrey Chaucer, Sir Thomas Wyatt, and William Shakespeare, all of whom modified and expanded upon the Petrarchan tradition in their own sonnets.
2. The Worship of Petrarch and His Cult
   The worship and idealization of the beloved that Petrarch exhibited in his sonnets gave rise to a cultural movement that came to be known as Petrarchism. This movement had an impact not only on the literary world of the Renaissance period but also on the artistic, musical, and courtly cultures of that time.
3. The Effects of Other Languages on the Italian Language
   Petrarch's writings, notably his Sonnets to Laura, had a significant impact on the development of the Italian language during the course of his lifetime. His use of vernacular Italian in his poetry helped to the development of the language as well as the establishment of a unified Italian identity, in a manner that is comparable to the role that Dante Alighieri played in the creation of his "Divine Comedy."
4. The Influence on the Art

The ideas and images presented in Petrarch's sonnets had a significant impact on the development of visual art. Petrarch's romanticized picture of Laura and her beauty served as a source of creativity for many painters, including Sandro Botticelli and Titian, among others. His verse and the subjects it explored frequently found artistic expression in the form of sculpture and painting during the Renaissance.

The Sonnets to Laura are an important and everlasting contribution to the fields of literature and culture that were written by Petrarch. In addition to reflecting the political and cultural climate of Petrarch's period, they offer a glimpse into the complexity of love, beauty, and the human condition. The structure of the Petrarchan sonnet and the ideas of idealized love, longing, and the passage of time have struck a chord with poets and artists for centuries, thereby influencing the development of European literature and art. The evergreen appeal of Petrarch's Sonnets to Laura is attested to by both his enduring legacy as a poet and the influence he has had on generations that came after him.

8.3 Boccaccio's The Decameron

The "Decameron" by Giovanni Boccaccio is a classic piece of Italian literature that was written in the 14th century and is revered for the skill with which it tells stories as well as the insightful social commentary it contains. This collection of one hundred tales, told over the course of ten days by a group of young Florentines who have fled the Black Death, is a monument to Boccaccio's skill as a storyteller, his wit, and his understanding of the character of human beings. In this essay, we will investigate "The Decameron" in great depth, looking at its structure, topics, historical and cultural context, as well as its tremendous impact on literature and society.

1. Background, Both Historical and Cultural

Boccaccio was born and spent his life in Italy amid a time of significant social and political upheaval. He was a witness to the turbulent 14th century, which was defined by wars, political struggles, and the catastrophic Black Death. He was born in 1313 in the town of Certaldo, which is close to Florence. People in Europe throughout the middle of the 14th century were profoundly affected psychologically by the Black Death, which resulted in a preoccupation with death and the hereafter as a result of this effect.

1. The Great Plague of Europe
   The horrific pandemic brought on by the bubonic plague had a significant impact on the social structure of Italy during the time of the "Black Death." It is thought that the plague was responsible for the death of a sizeable proportion of the population throughout Europe. In the novel "The Decameron," the protagonists and other characters leave the horrors of the plague in Florence and seek safety at a villa in the surrounding countryside.
   This location acts as a backdrop for the plot, which allows the characters to briefly escape the harsh reality of the city that is ravaged by the epidemic.

2. The Humanist Philosophy
   Humanism was an intellectual and cultural movement that stressed the rebirth of classical learning and the study of the humanities. It began to flourish around the 14th century, which was also known as the Golden Age of Humanism. Boccaccio was closely affiliated with the humanist movement and had a vital role in promoting the study of ancient literature, which included the works of authors such as Dante and Petrarch.
3. The Uncertainty of Boccaccio

Both Boccaccio's life and his works frequently reflect the ambiguities and paradoxes that were prevalent during his time period. He was concerned with earthly pleasures as well as societal satire, despite the fact that humanism was a major influence on his thinking. This contradiction is made clear in the book "The Decameron," in which the protagonists fabricate stories to amuse themselves and provide a distraction from the harsh reality of their era.

II. Outline of the Plot in "The Decameron"

The anthology known as "The Decameron" is organized as a collection of one hundred short stories, with each of the book's ten days containing ten of those pieces. This hierarchical arrangement is a reflection of the work's title, which can be translated as "The Ten-Day Work." The characters, which include seven women and three men, come to an agreement that they will tell stories over each of the 10 days while keeping to a topic that has been designated for that particular day.

1. The Narrative of the Frame
   The story begins with a depiction of the disastrous effects that the Black Death had on Florence, which prompted the ten young people to seek safety in a villa in the countryside. They come to the conclusion that telling stories will help pass the time. Because of the way the stories are organized around the interactions of the characters, "The Decameron" is an excellent illustration of a frame narrative, which is a literary device in which one story encloses another.
2. The Overarching Ideas of Each Day

The tales that are told on each of the ten days are expected to adhere to the corresponding theme that has been assigned to that day. There are ten days total. Stories revolving around love, fortune, deceit, and the repercussions of sin are some examples of these topics. Boccaccio uses the topics quite frequently as a means to investigate a variety of facets of human nature and the society in which people live.

III. Recurring Ideas Throughout "The Decameron"

1. Love and Carnal Desire
   The concept of love, in both its idealized and sensual forms, appears often throughout "The Decameron." The love and sexual lives of the characters are the subject of many of the tales, which frequently take a lighthearted or ironic tone. Boccaccio illustrates the complexity of love and desire by depicting the characters' internal drives and the acts they take in response to a variety of circumstances.
2. A Commentary on Society and Morality
   The style of a story told by Boccaccio is used to give comments on social, moral, and ethical themes that were prevalent during his day. In the process of criticizing the Church, the nobles, and the clergy, he exposes the moral faults and hypocrisies of these groups. A pointed indictment of Florentine society is provided via Boccaccio's depiction of social hierarchy and vices.
3. The use of Irony and Satire
   The "Decameron" is replete with comedic, satirical, and ironic moments throughout. In many of his works, Boccaccio makes witty and humorous observations about the mistakes and failings of the people he creates. His stories typically include cunning ruses, hilarious reversals of fortune, and other amusing twists and turns of events.
4. The ability to be Redeemed and Forgiven

There are narratives that address themes of redemption and forgiveness interspersed throughout the humorous and frequently risqué anecdotes in the collection. Characters in several of Boccaccio's stories are able to make amends for their wrongdoings or ask forgiveness from Boccaccio for their transgressions, reflecting the author's more humane and optimistic view of human nature.

IV. Impact on the Arts and Culture, as well as Society

1. The Tradition of the Novella
   The manner in which Boccaccio told stories in "The Decameron" served as the prototype for the novella, a more condensed form of storytelling that was common during the Renaissance. The legacy of the novella was taken up by authors such as Geoffrey Chaucer, Marguerite de Navarre, and Giovanni Sercambi, who created collections

of short stories fashioned after the work of Boccaccio. These authors all contributed to the novella genre.

2. **The Impact on Irony and Satire**
The witty and biting satire found throughout "The Decameron" had a significant and enduring influence on later literary satirists. Boccaccio's use of satire and irony to comment on the absurdities of society and the actions of humans served as a source of inspiration for later authors such as Francois Rabelais, Jonathan Swift, and Voltaire.

3. **The Influence on the Visual Arts**
The stories written by Boccaccio were influential to a wide variety of artists, including painters, playwrights, and composers. His stories were turned into musical compositions, dramas, and frescoes after he passed away. Boccaccio's storytelling had a significant cultural impact, and this is seen in the Decameron's influence on the visual arts.

4. **A Commentary on Societal and Cultural Aspects**

The book "The Decameron" is a rich source of information regarding the social and cultural customs of the 14th century. It provides a window into the society and values of the historical period, providing an insightful view on the Church, the nobles, and the complicated moral terrain of the age.

It is widely acknowledged that "The Decameron" by Giovanni Boccaccio is a literary classic that is renowned for its wit, talent in narrative, and social satire. Reflecting the turbulent era of the Black Death, the emergence of humanism, and the intricacies of human nature, it is a work that stands at the crossroads of historical and cultural upheavals. It is a work that stands at the crossroads of historical and cultural transformations. The collection of one hundred tales that Boccaccio recounted over the course of ten days has left an indelible mark on the landscape of literature and the arts. It has influenced future generations of writers, satirists, and painters. Boccaccio's tales were told over the course of ten days. In addition to being a work of storytelling, "The Decameron" is also a mirror that reflects the humor, follies, and vices that are inherent in the human condition.

8.4 Modern Tuscan Writers and Poets

The modern literature of Tuscany is distinguished by its wide-ranging and dynamic collection of authors and poets, all of whom have made significant contributions to the intricate web that is the rich literary tradition of Italy. Since the late 19th century to the present day, authors from Tuscany have investigated a diverse range of topics, literary techniques, and genres. These explorations are reflective of the social, cultural, and political shifts that have occurred in contemporary Italy. In this essay, we will investigate the works and contributions of several well-known modern writers and poets from Tuscany, focusing on their distinctive points of view and the literary accomplishments they have attained.

1. Giovanni Verga

    Giovanni Verga, an important character in Italian verismo, was born in Sicily but lived a considerable portion of his life in Tuscany. Although he was born in Sicily, he is most known for his contributions to Italian verismo. His works, such as "I Malavoglia" and "Mastro-Don Gesualdo," are distinguished by the fact that they present a life in the countryside and the problems of the working class in an accurate and convincing manner. The author Verga uses a style of writing that is reminiscent of the naturalist movement, with an emphasis on the harsh realities of poverty, social injustice, and the intricacies of human relationships. Because of his acute observations of ordinary life and his ability to capture the core of the human experience, he is regarded as one of the most prominent naturalist authors in Italian literature.

2. Italo Calvino is up next

    Italo Calvino was an important character in 20th-century Italian literature. Although he was born in Cuba, he was raised in Italy. His writings feature a singular synthesis of existentialist, fantasy, and postmodernism in their various iterations. Early works by Calvino, such as "Il sentiero dei nidi di ragno" and "Il visconte dimezzato," are excellent examples of the author's propensity for experimenting with the narrative structure and genre of his writing. His later works, such as "Le città invisibili" and "Se una notte d'inverno un viaggiatore," demonstrate his preoccupation with metafiction and the literary spirit of humor. The contributions to contemporary Tuscan literature that Calvino has made are a reflection of his original spirit and his ability to captivate readers with stories that are rich in imagination and intellectual depth.

3. The Dacia Maraini

    Contemporary writer and dramatist from Tuscany Dacia Maraini has made significant contributions to Italian writing, particularly in the fields of feminism and social commentary. Maraini is known for her work in Tuscany. Her writing frequently addresses issues pertaining to gender, identity, and the struggles that women confront in Italian culture and society. The female protagonists in Maraini's books, such as "La lunga vita di Marianna Ucr" and "La bambola," as well as the protagonists in her plays, such as "Maria Stuarda" and "Isolina," are shown in a nuanced manner throughout her works. These works include plays such as "Maria Stuarda" and "Isolina." Maraini's status as a key voice in contemporary Italian literature has been cemented thanks to the audacious and thought-provoking storylines she has written.

4. Alessandro Baricco

   Alessandro Baricco is widely regarded as one of the most important modern writers to come out of Tuscany. He is most recognized for the experimental and lyrical writing that he writes. Metafiction, historical fiction, and magical realism are just a few of the genres that may be found in his writings, which frequently blur the borders between them. Poetic language, vivid imagery, and philosophical observations on the human condition may be found throughout Baricco's novels, such as "Ocean Sea" and "Silk," which are defined by these qualities.

   In addition to writing novels and short stories, he has also penned plays, essays, and works of nonfiction, demonstrating both his versatility as a writer and his dedication to expanding the bounds of conventional story telling.

5. Niccolo Ammaniti. Ammaniti

   Niccol Ammaniti is a well-known contemporary Tuscan author who is noted for writing narratives that are both engaging and often hilarious in a dark way. His novels, such as "I'm Not Scared" (which translates to "I Have No Fear") and "Che la festa cominci" (which translates to "Let the Games Begin"), usually investigate topics related to childhood, coming of age, and the influence that social and political changes have on individual lives. The works of Ammaniti are recognizable by their vivid characterizations, harsh realism, and investigation of the human mind as it relates to adversity. Critical acclaim has been showered upon him in Italy as well as on an international scale for his ability to convey the nuances of human feelings and interpersonal connections.

6. The Influence on Culture and the Arts

   The writings and poetry of modern authors and poets from Tuscany have had a great influence not only on the cultural and creative landscape of Italy but also on that of the rest of the world. Their contributions have had an impact not just on the literary world but also on a wide range of artistic practices and cultural debates. These authors have made significant contributions to the canon of contemporary Italian literature by tackling urgent societal problems and testing the boundaries of traditional literary conventions, as well as playing an important part in constructing the story of contemporary Italian literature. Their investigations into topics such as identity, society, and the human experience continue to reverberate with readers and academics all over the world, therefore securing their position in the canon of modern Tuscan literature.

7. Contemporary Themes and Perspectives

The complexity of modern society is reflected in the varied topics and points of view that are included in modern Tuscan literature. When writing their works, authors frequently investigate topics such as globalization, identity, immigration, and the influence of technology on human interactions. Their narratives cope with the difficulties posed by a world that is changing at an accelerated rate, providing deep insights into the experience of being human and the intricacies of contemporary living. Writers and poets in contemporary Tuscan literature continue to push the frontiers of literary expression and engage with a variety of different cultural and social situations, making the field of contemporary Tuscan literature a vibrant and ever-changing one.

8. The Literary Heritage and Directions for the Future

The literary legacy left behind by modern writers and poets from Tuscany continues to have a significant impact on the development of Italian literature.Their creative approaches to telling stories, profound subject matter, and unwavering dedication to making social and cultural criticism have served as a model for succeeding generations of authors and artists. To ensure that the rich tradition of modern Tuscan literature continues to thrive in the global literary environment, contemporary authors remain devoted to exploring new narrative forms and addressing rising socioeconomic challenges as the landscape of Tuscan writing continues to evolve.

Chapter 9

Tuscany's Hidden Romantic Gems

Tuscany is an area that reeks of romance and allure thanks to its picture-perfect scenery, illustrious history, and artistic legacy. The region is known as Tuscany. While Florence, Siena, and Pisa are well-known for their cultural riches, Tuscany is also home to a number of hidden romantic gems that provide visitors looking to immerse themselves in the region's romantic charm with a more personal and genuine experience than can be found in the more well-known cultural attractions. A mesmerizing journey through the heart of Italy's most treasured region may be had by exploring Tuscany's lesser-known historical landmarks and natural wonders, as well as its lonely villages and picturesque countryside. Tuscany's hidden romantic jewels provide this type of experience. In this in-depth tour, we will investigate some of Tuscany's less well-known romantic places, focusing on the region's lesser-known gems in terms of their natural beauty, cultural allure, and historical import.

1. **The Opening Statements**
   The romantic allure of Tuscany is frequently connected with the region's famed cities and landmarks, but the region's lesser-known treasures provide a more private and secluded experience for couples and visitors looking for a calmer and more entrancing getaway. Tuscany is filled with hidden romantic places that inspire visitors to discover the region's lesser-known secrets. These hidden romantic destinations range from gorgeous hilltop villages and vineyard-dotted landscapes to secret gardens and lesser-known historical landmarks. This travel book will provide an in-depth examination of the romantic gems that are tucked away in Tuscany. It will reveal the region's most closely guarded secrets and shine a spotlight on the

one-of-a-kind experiences that are waiting for tourists who are looking for an up-close and personal excursion through one of Italy's most entrancing regions.

2. Picturesque Towns Perched Atop Hills

   The Montepulciano wine

   The hilltop town of Montepulciano in the southern region of Tuscany is a little-known treasure that is renowned for the medieval allure, Renaissance architecture, and breathtaking vistas that it offers of the surrounding countryside. The town's meandering, tiny alleys lead to secret piazzas, antique churches, and quaint cafes, giving an intimate setting in which couples may explore and appreciate the genuine atmosphere of Tuscany's rural life.

   San Gimignano in Italy

   San Gimignano, which is famous for the ancient towers that dot the skyline, provides a romantic escape that is defined by its well-preserved architecture, artisan stores, and local culinary pleasures. In addition, the town is famous for its towers. Couples who are looking for a romantic getaway in a location that seems frozen in time will find the tranquil atmosphere of the town, which is framed by its historic walls and cobblestone streets, to be the ideal backdrop for their getaway.

   Pienza (Penza)

   The town of Pienza, which is located in the Val d'Orcia and is a UNESCO World Heritage Site, is renowned for the Renaissance architecture that can be found there, as well as the quaint streets and breathtaking views of the Tuscan countryside. The tranquil environment, attractive gardens, and breathtaking vistas of rolling hills and vineyards give the town its romantic charm. As a result, it is a great location for couples who want to immerse themselves in Tuscany's natural beauty and cultural legacy.

3. Charming Getaways Located in the Countryside

   The Valley of Orcia

   The rolling hills, cypress-lined roads, and golden wheat fields that characterize the UNESCO World Heritage Site known as the Val d'Orcia make it one of the most beautiful valleys in all of Italy. This location provides couples with the opportunity to engage in leisurely strolls, wine tastings, and panoramic picnics amidst Tuscany's most beautiful natural panoramas. It is defined by its picture-postcard ideal scenery, vineyards, and medieval villages.

   Chianti wine

   The Chianti region of Tuscany is well-known for its olive groves, vineyards, and picturesque rural landscapes; yet, it is also a well-kept secret that it is a hidden romantic gem that welcomes couples to explore its lovely villages, medieval castles, and renowned wineries. The area's meandering roads and verdant hills provide a calm and picturesque environment for wine tastings, gastronomic experiences, and secluded countryside retreats, allowing couples to appreciate the true flavors and romance of Tuscany's world-famous wine country in a setting that is perfect for the two of them.

4. Historical Relics Found in Remote Areas

   Tombs of the Etruscans in Sovana

   The Etruscan Tombs of Sovana, which can be found in the Maremma region of Tuscany, provide an intriguing look into the history of the region of Tuscany. These ancient burial sites, which date back to the sixth century BCE and are buried within the rolling hills and meadows, provide couples with an off-the-beaten-path experience and a unique opportunity to explore Tuscany's rich Etruscan legacy in a calm and private setting. They date back to the sixth century BCE.

   Italo Pitigliano

   Pitigliano is a historic town constructed on a tufa ridge that offers a captivating blend of Etruscan, Roman, and Jewish heritage. It is also known as the "Little Jerusalem" of Tuscany. Pitigliano is also known as the "Little Jerusalem" of Tuscany. An intimate and romantic atmosphere is created by the town's secret synagogues, ancient cellars, and convoluted lanes, which provide couples with a cultural and historical tour through Tuscany's less well-known yet charming past.

5. Calming Attractions Found in Nature

   Natural Park of the Maremma

   The Maremma Natural Park is a little-known natural treasure that may be found along the coast of southern Tuscany. It is famous for its unspoiled beaches, coastal pine woods, and diversified animal population. This unspoiled and peaceful refuge allows couples the opportunity to explore nature paths, relax on isolated beaches, and immerse themselves in the region's rich biodiversity. This sanctuary provides a tranquil and romantic vacation for couples amidst Tuscany's beautiful coastal scenery.

   The Alps of the Apuan

   The Apuan Alps are a magnificent mountain range in northern Tuscany that provide a spectacular and secluded natural refuge. The Apuan Alps are known for their rocky peaks, marble quarries, and panoramic hiking trails. This hidden jewel provides the opportunity for couples to embark on spectacular mountain expeditions, find hidden caves and waterfalls, and enjoy breathtaking views of

Tuscany's alpine landscapes, so creating an intimate and adventurous experience in the middle of nature.

6. Experiences in the Culinary Arts

    Classes on Cooking Offered in Rural Towns and Villages

    Couples can take advantage of one-of-a-kind opportunities to engage in real cooking workshops offered in Tuscany's off-the-beaten-path rural towns. These classes teach participants how to prepare classic Tuscan recipes using ingredients sourced from the immediate area. These culinary experiences offer a hands-on and personal investigation of the gastronomic legacy of Tuscany. They give couples the opportunity to appreciate the delicacies of the region while building memories that will last a lifetime in a setting that is charming and hospitable.

    Dinners Served Straight from the Farm to Your Table

    It is possible for couples to enjoy farm-to-table dining experiences in Tuscany's hidden agriturismi and farmsteads, which allow them to dine on fresh, organic cuisine while being surrounded by the region's pastoral surroundings. Traditional Tuscan cuisine, locally made wines, and olive oils can be enjoyed by couples in the cozy settings of these eating establishments, which encourage a stronger connection to the region's gastronomic customs and rural way of life.

7. Celebrations and Gatherings of Diverse Cultures

    Pageants and Festivals Celebrating the Past

    Throughout the course of the year, numerous cultural celebrations and historical pageants are held in the Tuscan countryside's lesser-known towns and villages. Couples have the opportunity to become fully immersed in the customs, folklore, and historical reenactments of the region through the participation in these events. Couples have the opportunity to see and take part in Tuscany's living history thanks to the fact that the atmosphere at these festivals is both personal and genuine.

    Concerts Including Both Opera and Chamber Music

    Chamber music and opera performances are frequently held in Tuscany's secret theaters and historic venues; these events provide couples with the opportunity to experience nights that are both intimate and culturally fulfilling. Couples can enjoy a night of romance at these events by appreciating the elegance of opera and classical music while being surrounded by the creative legacy of the region.

8. Hidden Gardens and Distant Hideaways

    The Gardens of the Boboli

    Even though the Boboli Gardens in Florence are one of the most famous gardens in the world, Tuscany is home to a large number of other hidden gardens and hidden getaways. These hidden oases provide a serene and romantic hideaway for couples, with features such as lush foliage, sculpted hedges, and tranquil fountains. Discovering these hidden gardens offers couples the opportunity to have intimate moments of peace and quiet while surrounded by the splendor of nature.

The Gamberaia Villa

The Villa Gamberaia is a well-kept secret that can be found in the hills just outside of Florence. It is noted for its beautiful gardens as well as its medieval architecture. The charming grounds of the villa provide a peaceful and enchanting setting for couples to explore, making it a great site for calm walks and intimate moments amidst the backdrop of the Italian Renaissance grandeur.

9. A Tasting of Wines from Lesser-Well-Recognized Wineries

The Principality of Monaco

The small hilltop village of Monte Carlo in the province of Lucca is home to a number of specialized boutique wineries that are known for their outstanding wine production. This hidden gem offers couples an intimate wine tasting experience, enabling them to sample local types, such as the reds and whites produced in Monte Carlo, in an atmosphere that is laid back and genuine. Couples will have a one-of-a-kind opportunity to experience the aromas of Tuscany's hidden wine area if they take the time to explore the Monte Carlo vineyards that are not as well known.

The Wine Road of the Maremma

The Maremma region, which is sometimes passed over in favor of more well-known wine
destinations, is home to an increasing number of secluded vineyards and wineries that provide visitors with individualized opportunities to taste wine. The Maremma Wine Route is a great adventure for couples, since it takes visitors through some of the region's most charming and traditional wineries. Couples looking to explore the unique and rich wine legacy of Tuscany's coastline region will find that these less well-known vineyards offer an intimate atmosphere in which to do so.

10. Museums and Galleries Slightly Off the Beaten Path

The Pinacoteca Civica di Volterra is located in Volterra.

The Pinacoteca Civica di Volterra is a well-kept secret that has one of the most extensive collections of Etruscan, Roman, and Renaissance artwork in all of Italy. It can be found in the ancient town of Volterra. Due to the small size of the museum, visitors are able to avoid the crowds that are typically present in larger establishments while yet experiencing the rich artistic history of Tuscany. The calm and cozy ambiance of the museum makes it the perfect location for romantic encounters between two people who share an appreciation for the cultural tradition of the region.

The Town and County Art Gallery of San Gimignano

Located in the middle of San Gimignano, the Pinacoteca Comunale di San Gimignano is a museum that not many people are familiar with. This hidden gem is home to an impressive collection of medieval and Renaissance art, and it gives couples the opportunity to learn about the artistic history of the area while enjoying the serenity and closeness of the surrounding environment. Couples will find the tranquil atmosphere of the museum to be the ideal setting in which to enjoy the region's many artistic wonders.

Couples and solo travelers alike can enjoy an intimate and genuine escape into the heart of one of Italy's most lovely areas by visiting some of Tuscany's lesser-known romantic jewels. These lesser-known attractions, which are characterized by charming hilltop villages, appealing countryside landscapes, secluded historical monuments, and serene natural wonders, allow visitors to explore the region's hidden treasures and immerse themselves in the romantic allure of Tuscany. Among the region's hidden treasures are a number of ancient sites that date back to the Etruscan civilization. Tuscany's hidden jewels provide a multitude of chances for couples wishing to make lasting memories in an atmosphere of calm, romance, and authenticity. These opportunities include gastronomic experiences, cultural events, secret gardens, and off-the-beaten-path art. Tuscany's hidden gems may be found throughout the region. Couples can unearth the hidden riches of Tuscany and discover the region's enduring beauty and attractiveness by deviating from the well-trodden road and seeking out less traveled routes.

9.1 Exploring Lesser-Known Tuscan Destinations

Tuscany is renowned for its extensive cultural history, breathtaking scenery, and world-famous towns such as Florence, Siena, and Pisa. It is sometimes referred to as one of the most recognizable and popular areas in all of Italy. However, beyond the well-trodden tourist trails, Tuscany is home to a variety of hidden gems that are still, for the most part, unknown to the majority of tourists who visit the region. These less well-known locations in Tuscany provide a one-of-a-kind opportunity to experience the genuine allure of the region, to submerge oneself in the culture of the locals, and to get away from the masses.

THE ROMANCE OF TUSCANY, ITALY ~ 169

In this extensive book, we will set out on a journey to discover some of the lesser-known locations in Tuscany, illuminating their historical significance, natural beauty, and cultural richness along the way.

1. **The Opening Statements**
   Travelers from all over the world have long flocked to Tuscany to experience its famed art and culture, as well as its picturesque landscape of rolling hills and old cities. However, the popularity of renowned cities like Florence and the draw of famous sites like the Leaning Tower of Pisa have sometimes obscured the hidden treasures that Tuscany has to offer. Florence in particular is one of the most visited cities in the world. Beyond the bustling streets of the region's well-known tourist hotspots lies a universe of lesser-known attractions, each of which possesses its own distinctive personality and allure in its own right. These little-known treasures encourage tourists to go off the beaten road, explore pristine landscapes, and get in touch with the genuine spirit of Tuscany by allowing them to discover unspoiled areas. In this travel guide, we will go on an adventure to discover some of the lesser-known locations in Tuscany, throwing light on their rich histories, significant cultural contributions, and the enthralling experiences they have to offer.
2. **Revealing Secluded Towns and Communities**
   The "Little Jerusalem" of Tuscany is the town of Pitigliano
   The charming and secluded village of Pitigliano can be found in the Maremma area of Tuscany. Pitigliano is sometimes referred to as the "Little Jerusalem" of Tuscany. The historical significance of the town, which is perched on top of a tufa ridge, is inextricably bound up with the fact that it served as a haven for Jewish populations during the Renaissance. Pitigliano's beautiful convoluted streets will lead you to hidden synagogues, ancient cellars, and a delightful atmosphere that conjures a sense of timelessness as you go through them. The Etruscan, Roman, and Jewish heritages of the hamlet come together in a way that is harmonious, resulting in the creation of a one-of-a-kind cultural tapestry that invites tourists to delve into the region's history and experience the real flavors of the area.
   Anghiari: The Jewel of the Middle Ages
   Anghiari, a medieval village tucked away in the province of Arezzo, continues to be one of the most well-guarded secrets in all of Tuscany. The historical significance of the town is connected to the great war known as the Battle of Anghiari, which is featured in Leonardo da Vinci's lost fresco, as well as the Palazzo Taglieschi, which is home to an art and cultural center. Visitors who are looking for

a tranquil and genuine Tuscan experience will find Anghiari's well-preserved medieval architecture, its streets paved with cobblestones, and its panoramic vistas to be the ideal setting for their vacation. The town's quaint ambiance, along with the yearly medieval festival it hosts, perfectly reflects the spirit of Tuscany's extensive historical and cultural legacy.

The Scottish version of a Tuscan village is known as Barga

Barga is a little-known village that can be found in the Garfagnana area of Tuscany. It is

renowned for its singular cultural synthesis. Barga is a town in Italy that is well-known for its link to the Scottish diaspora in Italy. It is also the location of a thriving Scottish-Italian community that has managed to keep its legacy alive via the use of festivals and cultural exchanges. The quiet and engrossing experience provided by the village's quaint alleyways, historic cathedral, and panoramic views of the Serchio Valley can be found throughout the village. Barga is a lesser-known but culturally rich location in the heart of Tuscany. Visitors may experience traditional Scottish-Italian food as well as the town's rich history, making Barga a destination that is rich in both history and culture.

3. Secret Locations of Historical Importance

   ### The Etruscan Tombs of Sovana are important archaeological sites

   The Etruscan Tombs of Sovana, which can be found in the Maremma district of Tuscany, offer a fascinating look into the history of the region known today as Tuscany. These burial sites, which date back to the sixth century BCE and are concealed among the undulating hills and meadows, provide visitors with a one-of-a-kind opportunity to explore the Etruscan legacy that is so prevalent in Tuscany. Those who are interested in history and want to feel more connected to Tuscany's early civilizations can have a peaceful and engaging experience by exploring the carved facades and intricate chambers of the tombs, as well as learning about the tombs' archeological value.

   ### Massa Marittima: A Precious Relic from the Middle Ages

   The town of Massa Marittima, which can be found in the middle of the Maremma region of Tuscany, is a medieval jewel that has managed to keep its historical authenticity. The beautiful cathedral of the town, named the Cathedral of San Cerbone, dates back to the 13th century and includes an amazing exterior that is decorated with exquisite sculptures. The picturesque Piazza Garibaldi is waiting to be discovered by guests, as are the city's historic fortifications, and the towering Candeliere Watchtower, which offers breathtaking vistas. Those who are interested in immersing themselves in Tuscany's medieval past will find a peaceful and genuine retreat in the town of Massa Marittima thanks to its extensive history and well-preserved architecture.

4. Marvels of the Natural World

   The Alpi Apuane Is a Secluded Mountain Hideaway

   A tranquil and attractive natural hideaway may be found in the Alpi Apuane, which is a mountain range that dominates the northern part of Tuscany. This undiscovered treasure is a haven for people who adore the outdoors and are always looking for new challenges.

   It is renowned for its craggy peaks, marble quarries, and picturesque alpine vistas. Visitors can enjoy spectacular views of Tuscany's alpine scenery while hiking through scenic trails, discovering hidden caverns and waterfalls, and exploring hidden caves. The Alpi Apuane is the perfect place to visit for individuals who are looking for a serene environment and natural beauty that has not been altered because it is located in the heart of nature.

   The Garfagnana is known for its pristine wilderness.

   The Garfagnana region of Tuscany is a wild region that is defined by its unspoiled landscapes, old forests, and hidden settlements. It is located in the northern section of the region that is known as Tuscany. This less well-known resort is the ideal getaway for vacationers looking to get away from it all and find some peace and quiet. Visitors are able to discover the Garfagnana's rough beauty and immerse themselves in Tuscany's unspoiled landscapes by participating in a variety of outdoor activities, such as hiking, mountain biking, and horseback riding. These activities are offered in the Garfagnana.

5. Hidden Delights in the Gastronomic World

   Montescudaio is often referred to as "The Wine Road Less Traveled"

   A hidden Tuscan wine road may be found in the town of Montescudaio, which is found in the province of Pisa. This route is frequently ignored in favor of more well-known wine destinations. The town and the areas immediately around it are home to a number of quaint wineries that are responsible for the creation of outstanding wines, such as the world-famous reds and whites from Montescudaio. Travelers can indulge in private wine tastings and sample the aromas of Montescudaio's wine country while taking in the territory's serene atmosphere and rustic allure. These activities can be enjoyed while visiting the region.

   The Gastronomic Jewel That Is Volterra

   Volterra, a medieval village in the middle of Tuscany, is a hidden culinary jewel that welcomes tourists to experience traditional Tuscan delicacies. Volterra is a Unesco World Heritage Site. Traditional osterie and trattorie in the town are great places to sample regional delicacies like the highly valued alabaster truffles, hearty soups, and delectable pastries. Those who are eager to really submerge themselves in the traditional Tuscan cuisine will find that Volterra's less well-known culinary scene offers an experience that is both personal and savory.

6. Calming Galleries of Art and Museums

    The Pinacoteca Civica di Volterra: An Artistic Gem Hiding in Plain Sight

    An amazing collection of Etruscan, Roman, and Renaissance artwork may be seen within the walls of the Pinacoteca Civica di Volterra, which is located in the center of the town of Volterra. Discover the region's rich artistic tradition in the secluded and cozy setting of this well-kept secret, which provides art fans an intimate setting. Travelers are able to appreciate the treasures of Tuscan art in a quiet environment away from the throngs that are typically found in larger museums, which allows for a deeper connection with Tuscany's cultural past.

    A Hidden Art Gem Within the City of San Matteo: The Museum of San Matteo

    Pisa's Museum of San Matteo is a hidden gem that is frequently ignored by tourists that come to the city to see the Leaning Tower of Pisa. This museum is not as well-known as others, but it is home to an impressive collection of works of art from the Middle Ages and the Renaissance, including sculptures, paintings, and religious objects. Travelers can completely submerge themselves in the artistic legacy of Tuscany while appreciating the tranquil environment of the museum and engaging in an in-depth examination of the cultural bounty of the region.

7. Remote and Beautiful Natural Getaways

    Sanctuary on the Coast: The Natural Park of the Maremma

    The Maremma Natural Park is a well-kept secret that can be found tucked away on the coast of southern Tuscany. It is renowned for the untouched beaches, coastal pine woods, and abundant wildlife that can be found there. This pristine natural wonder gives visitors the opportunity to go along nature trails, unwind on secluded beaches, and experience the region's diverse array of plant and animal life by immersing themselves in the environment. In the middle of Tuscany's mesmerizing coastline vistas, the Maremma Natural Park provides a haven that is peaceful and ideal for couples.

    The Monte Argentario Peninsula: An Area of Stunningly Beautiful

Coastline

The Monte Argentario Peninsula, which can be found in the Maremma region, is home to a stunning stretch of coastline that is often overlooked due to its rugged cliffs, clean waters, and picturesque fishing communities. Visitors can enjoy fresh seafood at local trattorie as they explore the quiet coves, hiking trails, and historic strongholds that dot the peninsula. Those who are looking for a peaceful coastal hideaway in Tuscany will find that the Monte Argentario Peninsula offers a secluded and picture-perfect place to go.

8. Unknown Celebrations and Gatherings of the Cultural

Pisa's Luminara di San Ranieri: A Tradition That's Been Kept in the Shadows

Despite the fact that it is conducted annually in Pisa, the Luminara di San Ranieri celebration is still largely unknown to the general public despite its importance historically. On the 16th of June, a magical event that will light up the city with thousands of candles will take place along the Arno River. The ancient city of Pisa is illuminated by candlelight, creating a stunning spectacle that visitors can view while also participating in the original customs of this less well-known celebration.

The Antique Market Extravaganza That Is the Fiera Antiquaria di Arezzo

Fiera Antiquaria di Arezzo is one of the oldest and largest antique markets in Italy. It offers visitors who have an interest in history and craftsmanship the opportunity to partake in a cultural experience that is relatively unknown. The market is held on the first Sunday of each month in addition to the Saturday that comes before it, and it contains a wide variety of antiques, including furniture, artwork, and collectibles. Visitors have the opportunity to investigate the diverse cultural traditions of Tuscany and to search for buried riches among the stalls that make up the Arezzo antique market.

9. Inaccessible Gardens and Confidential Retreats

The Hidden Garden Paradise That Is the Villa Reale di Marlia

The hidden garden paradise that is the Villa Reale di Marlia has, for the most part, eluded the discovery of typical vacationers, despite its proximity to the city of Lucca. The serene and romantic atmosphere created by the villa's beautiful gardens, fountains, and elegant statues welcomes guests to enjoy leisurely strolls, rest among the luscious greenery, and immerse themselves in the tranquility of Tuscany's hidden garden jewel.

A Secret Paradise in the Heart of Tuscany: Villa Grabau

Another garden oasis that provides a tranquil and idyllic refuge is

Villa Grabau, which can be found in the Lucca region of Italy. Villa Grabau is a lesser-known garden oasis. Away from the hustle and bustle of the main tourist routes, the villa's gardens offer visitors an intimate setting in which to discover hidden pathways, take in breathtaking panoramas, and appreciate moments of peace and quiet. The grounds have an extensive variety of plant species and exquisite architecture.

10. Unusual and Useful Learning Opportunities

Vinci has the Leonardo Interactive Museum, which is located there.

A less well-known educational opportunity that dives into the life and work of the renowned Renaissance genius Leonardo da Vinci may be found at the Leonardo Interactive Museum, which is located in Vinci, the city where Leonardo da Vinci was born. This undiscovered treasure gives visitors the opportunity to explore interactive displays, learn about the scientific advancements made by Leonardo, and get a glimpse into the mind of one of the most creative brains in the annals of human history.

The Baratti and Populonia Archaeological Park

The Archaeological Park of Baratti and Populonia is a hidden educational treasure that unveils the ancient history of Tuscany. It may be found in the province of Livorno. The park is home to Etruscan remains, as well as necropolises and a museum, all of which contribute to a more in-depth examination of the Etruscan culture and the role it played in the history of Tuscany. Visitors get the opportunity to explore the region's archeological legacy and gain exposure to a facet of Tuscany's past that is not as well known.

Travelers from all over the world can't seem to get enough of Tuscany's world-famous cities and attractions thanks to the region's undeniable charm. However, the region's hidden treasures offer a richer and more genuine understanding of Tuscany's culture, history, and natural beauty than other tourist attractions in the region. These lesser-known destinations in Tuscany provide one-of-a-kind opportunities to escape the crowds and start on a voyage of discovery. From entrancing villages and historical buildings to natural wonders and gastronomic pleasures, these destinations offer something for everyone. Travelers can develop a deeper connection with the region of Tuscany, taste the region's unique charm, and make memories that will last a lifetime by stepping off the beaten road and discovering the region's hidden gems. These experiences go beyond the conventional tourist experience. Those who are prepared to explore Tuscany's lesser-known places are rewarded with a richer tapestry of history, culture, and natural grandeur than the region's most well-known attractions.

9.2 Secret Gardens and Hidden Courtyards

A haven of peace amidst the commotion of city life, hidden gardens and courtyards can be found tucked away in the middle of busy cities, disguised behind centuries-old walls, and tucked away within sprawling historic estates. These charming getaways, which are frequently hidden from public view, exemplify a sense of solitude and seclusion, encouraging guests to escape into a world of natural beauty and peace. Secret gardens and hidden courtyards have always held a certain attraction, acting as havens of serenity and inspiration in a variety of architectural settings, including historic castles and monasteries, private dwellings, and public institutions.

In the course of this investigation, we will reveal the mystery and attraction of these hidden paradises by diving into their cultural importance, architectural achievements, and the entrancing sensations they provide to those who are fortunate enough to find them.

1. The Opening Statements

   The imaginations of poets, painters, and dreamers have long been captivated by hidden gardens and courtyards, which often serve as the backdrop for love stories, spiritual reflection, and periods of calm meditation. These quiet oases, which are tucked away from the bustling thoroughfares and the prying eyes of the world, provide visitors with a glimpse into the unseen beauties of both nature and the human soul. In this article, we will embark on a journey to discover the entrancing universe of hidden courtyards and secret gardens, unearthing their historical legacies, architectural marvels, and the ageless beauty that continues to fascinate people who seek solitude and inspiration inside its verdant embrace. Throughout our travels, we will uncover their historical legacies, architectural marvels, and the beauty that has stood the test of time.

2. The Importance of Hidden Gardens to the Course of History
   Monastic Gardens from the Middle Ages
   Monastic gardens throughout the middle ages were important places for spiritual reflection as well as horticultural experimentation. These gardens were frequently concealed within the walls of ancient monasteries and convents. These secluded gardens, which were encompassed by high walls and decorated with medicinal herbs, aromatic flowers, and symbolic plants, provided a calm refuge for monks and nuns, allowing them to nurture their spiritual connection with nature and the divine in a serene environment. The significant

effect of spirituality on the design and function of these hidden sanctuaries can be seen in the exquisite layouts of these gardens, which feature meticulously constructed walkways, water features, and sacred symbols.

Gardens of the Renaissance Palazzo

The Italian aristocracy throughout the Renaissance period was known for commissioning extravagant palazzo gardens as a way to display their riches and rank as well as their respect for art and nature. These mysterious gardens, which were kept hidden within the expansive estates of aristocratic families, were filled with magnificent statues, extravagant fountains, and precisely tended flora. The gardens of Renaissance palazzos were emblems of prestige and cultural refinement as a result of their adherence to the aesthetic principles of symmetry, harmony, and classical aesthetics. These gardens also served as private havens for the elite to meet for leisurely strolls, social gatherings, and intellectual talks.

3. ## The Architectural Wonders Concealed Within Secret Courtyards

   ### The Andalusian Moorish Patios and Courtyards

   The core of Islamic architecture and style may be found in the Moorish courtyards of Andalusia. These courtyards are distinguished by their beautiful tile work, abundant flora, and peaceful water elements. These secret courtyards were found tucked away within the lavish palaces and private mansions of Spain. They were used as gathering places for friends and family, as well as for personal reflection and relaxation. The mix of geometric designs, fragrant blooms, and the lulling sound of fountains produced an atmosphere of peace and sensory delight, offering a relief from the dry landscapes and hectic towns that are found across the region.

   ### Istanbul's Historic Ottoman Courtyards

   The memory of the Ottoman Empire has been preserved throughout the centuries-old city of Istanbul by being kept in the secret courtyards of historical mosques, palaces, and traditional dwellings. The cultural blending of Eastern and Western influences can be seen in these tranquil havens, which are embellished with artistically constructed archways, mosaic tile work, and lush gardens. inside the hustling and bustling urban scene of Istanbul, the courtyards functioned as common areas for prayer, meditation, and social meetings. This helped to build a sense of community as well as a spiritual commitment inside the city.

4. ## Enchanting Adventures in Hidden Gardens and Places

   ### Hidden courtyards offer secluded spots for romantic getaways

   Hidden courtyards, with their hidden atmosphere and charming appeal, serve as exquisite locations for romantic exploits and personal encounters. Hidden courtyards may be found in a variety of different architectural styles. The mix of soft candlelight, fragrant blossoms, and the soothing murmur of water features creates an environment of intimacy and romance, allowing couples a quiet hideaway in which they may celebrate their love and make memories that will last a lifetime. These hidden courtyards, whether they are located within a historic inn, a boutique hotel, or a private estate, provide an appealing setting for memorable moments and quiet gatherings.

Inspiration for the Arts Found in Secret Gardens

Poets, painters, and creative minds throughout history have been inspired to create beautiful works of art by the harmonious balance of natural beauty and artistic design found in secret gardens. The dynamic interplay of nature's vivid hues, fragrant scents, and ever-shifting rhythms ignites the imagination and cultivates a profound connection with the creative spirit.

Artists are able to find peace and inspiration in the isolated walkways, hidden alcoves, and blooming flowers of these secret gardens, which allows their artistic visions to flourish in harmony with the beauty of the natural world that is all around them.

5. **Efforts Made in the Areas of Preservation and Restoration**

Initiatives for the Preservation of Cultural Resources

In recent years, there has been a rising understanding of the historical and cultural significance of hidden courtyards and secret gardens, leading to conservation programs that strive to preserve these priceless cultural legacies. These initiatives aim to preserve these cultural legacies since they are an invaluable cultural legacy. Collaborations between historians, architects, and preservationists are necessary in order to safeguard and repair these secret sanctuaries. These individuals put in a lot of hard work to ensure that the architectural characteristics, horticultural diversity, and historical narratives of these spaces are preserved in their entirety. Cultural conservation activities ensure that future generations will be able to continue appreciating the beauty and relevance of beautiful retreats by protecting these hidden gems and so preserving them for future generations.

Practicing Permaculture in the Garden

Many hidden gardens and courtyards have embraced environmentally friendly horticulture practices and sustainable architectural ideas as a response to the global need for environmental sustainability. This call was made in response to the global demand for sustainable development. These hidden sanctuaries are leading the way in promoting environmental consciousness and responsible management of the natural world. From water conservation measures and organic gardening techniques to the integration of native plant species and renewable energy sources, these hidden sanctuaries are leading the way in promoting environmental consciousness. These hidden oasis serve as models for encouraging biodiversity, ecological balance, and the preservation of natural resources inside urban settings because they prioritize sustainable garden techniques.

6. The Importance of Secret Gardens and Intimate Courtyards in Today's Society

Sanctuaries in the Heart of Contemporary Cities

Hidden gardens and courtyards play an important part in giving urban people with a sense of serenity, balance, and connection to nature in the setting of constantly increasing metropolitan centers and the challenges of modern living. These hidden sanctuaries offer a haven for relaxation, meditation, and community gatherings amidst the concrete jungles and bustling streets of contemporary cities. They cultivate a sense of well-being and environmental sensitivity within the fast-paced rhythms of metropolitan life.

Centers for Cultural Expression and Educational Purposes

Many secret gardens and courtyards have been transformed into cultural and educational institutions, and they now host a wide variety of classes, workshops, and other events that encourage community involvement, artistic expression, and the cultivation of horticultural knowledge. These restored places serve as platforms for promoting cultural variety, artistic discovery, and environmental awareness within local communities, which helps to build a sense of inclusivity and social cohesion. Hidden gardens and courtyards will undoubtedly continue to motivate upcoming generations of artists, academics, and environmental activists so long as they continue to embrace their roles as centers of culture and learning.

7. The Everlasting Charm of Secret Hideaways

Hidden gardens and courtyards are still treasured havens because of their enduring charm and entrancing beauty. These spaces encapsulate the spirit of natural harmony, cultural legacy, and artistic expression. These hidden retreats are a reminder of the human desire for tranquility, contemplation, and connection to the natural world. They can be found tucked away within the walls of historic monasteries, vast palaces, or contemporary urban environments. As we continue to uncover their hidden wonders, we are reminded of the everlasting magic that hidden courtyards and secret gardens bring to those who seek refuge and inspiration within their solitary embrace. This is especially true as we continue to uncover their hidden beauties. These exquisite retreats are ageless testaments to the enduring power of nature, culture, and artistic expression to transcend the constraints of time and space, and they provide a look into the hidden mysteries of the human soul.

9.3 Romantic Strolls and Off-the-Beaten-Path Adventures

The unexpected, the unplanned, and the off-the-beaten-path events that lead to moments of connection, intimacy, and adventure are frequently at the heart of the fascination of romance. There is a universe of hidden treasures and less well-known adventures just waiting to be discovered by couples who are looking to reignite or rekindle their love. Iconic locations such as Paris and Venice have long been associated with romantic strolls and passionate encounters. In this investigation, we will embark on a trip to explore the charm of romantic strolls and off-the-beaten-path adventures. Along the way, we will shine light on the hidden treasures, cultural marvels, and one-of-a-kind experiences that await those who are courageous enough to walk off the well-trodden path and embrace the unexpected.

1. The Opening Statements

    Couples have the opportunity to establish profound relationships with one another, make memories that will last a lifetime, and experience the transformational power of love when they embark on romantic strolls or off-the-beaten-path activities. When it comes to matters of romance, well-known locations frequently steal the show. However, there is a variety of hidden gems and unknown adventures that have the potential to stoke the fires of passion.

    In this article, we will embark on a journey to explore the charm of romantic strolls and off-the-beaten-path excursions, revealing the stories, sceneries, and experiences that await those who venture beyond the ordinary and discover the extraordinary. This voyage will take us all over the world.

2. The Secret Gems That Can Be Found on Romantic Walks

    The Philosopher's Path in Kyoto: A Wonderland of Cherry Blossoms in Japan

    The Philosopher's Path in Kyoto, Japan, is a well-kept secret that provides the opportunity for couples to take a romantic stroll along a canal that is surrounded by a forest of hundreds of cherry trees. During the time of year when cherry trees are in bloom, the pathway transforms into an enchanted tunnel of pink and white blossoms, resulting in an ambiance that is peaceful and beautiful. During the course of this secretly romantic journey, engaged couples have the opportunity to investigate the local temples, contemplate the splendor of nature, and participate in the numerous cultural customs of Japan.

The Minnewater Lake in Bruges, often known as the Lake of Love
The city of Bruges, which is frequently referred to as the "Venice of the North," is renowned for its charming alleys and picture-perfect canals. The Minnewater Lake, commonly referred to as the "Lake of Love," is a well-kept secret that attracts couples to its placid waters, graceful swans, and picturesque medieval bridge. The tragic story of Minna, a young woman who passed away from a broken heart, contributes to the already lovely atmosphere of this location. Couples can write their own love stories in this hidden nook of Bruges by taking a romantic stroll along the lake's banks and over the Lover's Bridge.

The Montmartre Artists' Colony was Known as "The Paris of Artists"
A secret vineyard that provides a secluded and romantic retreat from the hustle and bustle of the city's streets can be found right in the middle of Paris's historic Montmartre neighborhood. The Clos Montmartre, the last working vineyard in Paris, is a living tribute to the area's creative past and enthusiasm for wine. The vineyard is located in the Montmartre neighborhood. Couples can enjoy a leisurely stroll through the rows of the vineyard, uncover artistic treasures, and appreciate the genuine beauty of Montmartre while sipping on the world-famous wine produced in the region.

3. **Cultural Wonders to Be Discovered on Off-the-Beaten-Path Journeys**

   Bagan's Temples Reveal Myanmar's Mysterious Side
   Bagan, in Myanmar, is a cultural wonder that few people know about. It is home to hundreds of old temples and pagodas that are spread out across the terrain. Bagan provides a more personal and uplifting experience than Angkor Wat in Cambodia, which is known for its popularity among tourists. The spiritual and historical wealth of this one-of-a-kind place can be experienced by couples as they discover these ancient wonders, see the golden light of sunrise or sunset, and immerse themselves in the region's rich culture.

   Lalibela's Rock-Cut Churches: A Sacred Space in Ethiopia's Past and Present
   The remarkable Rock-Hewn Churches are located in the town of Lalibela in Ethiopia. They are a network of underground churches that

were carved from solid rock. These unseen wonders are a testimony to human creativity and commitment, and they provide an immersive cultural experience for couples who are up for an adventure. Couples get the opportunity to engage with Ethiopia's profound spiritual traditions by traversing these ancient corridors, visiting the hidden rooms, and observing the complicated religious events.

4. One-of-a-Kind Experiences Obtained Through Off-the-Beaten-Path Travel

   Discovering Myanmar's Undiscovered Paradise While Sailing the Mergui Archipelago

   The Mergui Archipelago in Myanmar is a secret paradise with untouched beaches, clear waters, and isolated coves to explore. The Mergui Archipelago is still relatively unknown among travelers, in contrast to the popular islands of Thailand, which bring in large numbers of visitors every year. It is possible for couples to embark on a sailing journey together, during which they can explore uninhabited islands, snorkel in coral reefs that have not been disturbed, and indulge in the ultimate romantic experience in one of the world's last unspoiled paradises.

   The Romance of the Arctic: Dog Sledding in Lapland

   The undiscovered wonder that is Lapland, located in northern Europe, is just waiting to be discovered. Rather than the typical outings that take place during the warmer months, couples can consider braving the cold and going on a dog sledding excursion. Couples may share the pleasure of mushing their own team of dogs through snow-covered forests in Lapland, which is surrounded by the wilderness of the Arctic, while also enjoying the other one-of-a-kind activities that Lapland has to offer.

5. Experiencing a Deeper Connection with Nature Through Off-the-Beaten-Path Travel

   The Faroe Islands are a natural paradise that few people know about

   The Faroe Islands, which are located in the North Atlantic Ocean between Iceland and Norway, are still largely unknown to tourists. The stunning vistas, steep cliffs, and lush valleys of these rough and secluded islands are sure to take your breath away. Hiking expeditions, the discovery of secluded waterfalls, and the awe-inspiring natural splendor of this one-of-a-kind location are all possibilities for romantic couples. A personal and unforgettable experience with nature can be had on the Faroe Islands thanks to the pristine nature that still exists there.

   The Bornean Rainforest is a Wildlife Wonderland for the Country of Malaysia

One of the world's most ancient rainforests may be found on the island of Borneo, which is the third-largest island in the planet. Borneo continues to be a well-kept secret for travelers who are interested in having close interactions with a wide variety of unusual animals, despite the fact that tourists rush to other popular wildlife destinations. It is possible for couples to go on forest excursions, explore riverways, and look for unusual animals such as pygmy elephants and orangutans. This journey off the beaten route will instill in you a greater respect for the natural environment and help you form a connection with the astonishing variety of life that exists on our planet.

6. Participating in Off-the-Beaten-Path Activities While Honoring the Local Culture

The Marvels of Matera, the Undiscovered Jewel of Italy

It is common to refer to Matera, which is located in the southern part of the region of Basilicata, as the "City of Stones." Its ancient cave houses, which are known as Sassi, are a UNESCO World Heritage site and provide a one-of-a-kind opportunity to immerse oneself in the history and culture of the local area. Couples can connect with the friendly and inviting residents who call this hidden jewel home while discovering hidden courtyards, dining in cave eateries, and experiencing the timeless beauty that Matera has to offer all at the same time.

Petra, often known as the Lost City, is a historical marvel located in Jordan

Petra, the archaeological wonder of Jordan, continues to be a place that is drenched in history and shrouded in mystery. Petra's distant position makes for a more personal and awe-inspiring experience than can be had at other well-known archaeological sites, which are typically overrun with visitors. Visitors can take their sweethearts on a romantic stroll through the mysterious Siq, take in the breathtaking views of the Treasury, and discover the city's many secret tombs and rooms.

This off-the-beaten-path excursion provides couples with the opportunity to interact with the eons-old history of Petra as well as the Bedouin culture of the surrounding area.

7. Establishing Memories That Will Last A Lifetime

The Influence of Things That Are Not Anticipated

THE ROMANCE OF TUSCANY, ITALY ~ 183

The unexpected moments, the surprises, and the one-of-a-kind experiences that can only be found while straying off the well-trodden road are what give romantic strolls and off-the-beaten-path adventures their enchantment. This is also true of off-the-beaten-path adventures in general. These unplanned meetings become cherished memories that define a relationship and deepen the bond between couples. For example, during a jungle trek in Borneo, stumbling upon a hidden waterfall; discovering a secluded beach in the Mergui Archipelago; or spending a quiet moment beneath the cherry blossoms of Kyoto.

The Value of Maintaining Connections

Couples have the opportunity to connect not only with each other but also with the world around them when they go on outings together that involve romantic strolls and off-the-beaten-path excursions. Together, a couple can produce memories that will last a lifetime and enhance the emotional bonds that bind them together via shared experiences of the wonders of nature, the richness of culture, and the depth of history. These experiences enable open communication, shared laughter, and mutual support; as a result, they build a greater sense of unity among the participants.

Couples have the opportunity to find love in unexpected places, make memories that will last a lifetime, and recognize the transformational power of engaging in activities together through activities such as romantic strolls and off-the-beaten-path adventures. Hidden treasures and less well-known adventures offer a one-of-a-kind and personal canvas on which love can blossom. While well-known locations will always have their own allure, these types of trips are ideal for couples. Couples that venture beyond the ordinary frequently find that they are rewarded with a deeper connection, stronger bonds, and the eternal magic of love. This can occur through activities such as exploring remote landscapes, interacting with the culture of the local community, or embarking on remarkable travels. These events serve to remind us that the journey, the times spent together, and the beauty that can be discovered in the unexpected are all essential components of a loving relationship. In the end, the love tales that are the most meaningful and enduring are frequently those that are written on the pages of off-the-beaten-path adventures and undiscovered treasures.

Chapter 10

Practical Tips for a Romantic Getaway

The unexpected, the unplanned, and the off-the-beaten-path events that lead to moments of connection, intimacy, and adventure are frequently at the heart of the fascination of romance. There is a universe of hidden treasures and less well-known adventures just waiting to be discovered by couples who are looking to reignite or rekindle their love. Iconic locations such as Paris and Venice have long been associated with romantic strolls and passionate encounters. In this investigation, we will embark on a trip to explore the charm of romantic strolls and off-the-beaten-path adventures. Along the way, we will shine light on the hidden treasures, cultural marvels, and one-of-a-kind experiences that await those who are courageous enough to walk off the well-trodden path and embrace the unexpected.

1. The Opening Statements

    Couples have the opportunity to establish profound relationships with one another, make memories that will last a lifetime, and experience the transformational power of love when they embark on romantic strolls or off-the-beaten-path activities. When it comes to matters of romance, well-known locations frequently steal the show. However, there is a variety of hidden gems and unknown adventures that have the potential to stoke the fires of passion. In this article, we will embark on a journey to explore the charm of romantic strolls and off-the-beaten-path excursions, revealing the stories, sceneries, and experiences that await those who venture beyond the ordinary and discover the extraordinary. This voyage will take us all over the world.

2. The Secret Gems That Can Be Found on Romantic Walks
   The Philosopher's Path in Kyoto: A Wonderland of Cherry Blossoms in Japan
   The Philosopher's Path in Kyoto, Japan, is a well-kept secret that provides the opportunity for couples to take a romantic stroll along a canal that is surrounded by a forest of hundreds of cherry trees. During the time of year when cherry trees are in bloom, the pathway transforms into an enchanted tunnel of pink and white blossoms, resulting in an ambiance that is peaceful and beautiful. During the course of this secretly romantic journey, engaged couples have the opportunity to investigate the local temples, contemplate the splendor of nature, and participate in the numerous cultural customs of Japan.
   The Minnewater Lake in Bruges, often known as the Lake of Love
   The city of Bruges, which is frequently referred to as the "Venice of the North," is renowned for its charming alleys and picture-perfect canals. The Minnewater Lake, commonly referred to as the "Lake of Love," is a well-kept secret that attracts couples to its placid waters, graceful swans, and picturesque medieval bridge. The tragic story of Minna, a young woman who passed away from a broken heart, contributes to the already lovely atmosphere of this location. Couples can write their own love stories in this hidden nook of Bruges by taking a romantic stroll along the lake's banks and over the Lover's Bridge.
   The Montmartre Artists' Colony was Known as "The Paris of Artists"
   A secret vineyard that provides a secluded and romantic retreat from the hustle and bustle of the city's streets can be found right in the middle of Paris's historic Montmartre neighborhood. The Clos Montmartre, the last working vineyard in Paris, is a living tribute to the area's creative past and enthusiasm for wine. The vineyard is located in the Montmartre neighborhood. Couples can enjoy a leisurely stroll through the rows of the vineyard, uncover artistic treasures, and appreciate the genuine beauty of Montmartre while sipping on the world-famous wine produced in the region.
3. Cultural Wonders to Be Discovered on Off-the-Beaten-Path Journeys
   Bagan's Temples Reveal Myanmar's Mysterious Side
   Bagan, in Myanmar, is a cultural wonder that few people know about. It is home to hundreds of old temples and pagodas that are spread out across the terrain. Bagan provides a more personal and uplifting experience than Angkor Wat in Cambodia, which is known for its

popularity among tourists. The spiritual and historical wealth of this one-of-a-kind place can be experienced by couples as they discover these ancient wonders, see the golden light of sunrise or sunset, and immerse themselves in the region's rich culture.

Lalibela's Rock-Cut Churches: A Sacred Space in Ethiopia's Past and Present

The remarkable Rock-Hewn Churches are located in the town of Lalibela in Ethiopia. They are a network of underground churches that were carved from solid rock. These unseen wonders are a testimony to human creativity and commitment, and they provide an immersive cultural experience for couples who are up for an adventure. Couples get the opportunity to engage with Ethiopia's profound spiritual traditions by traversing these ancient corridors, visiting the hidden rooms, and observing the complicated religious events.

4. **One-of-a-Kind Experiences Obtained Through Off-the-Beaten-Path Travel**

Discovering Myanmar's Undiscovered Paradise While Sailing the Mergui Archipelago

The Mergui Archipelago in Myanmar is a secret paradise with untouched beaches, clear waters, and isolated coves to explore. The Mergui Archipelago is still relatively unknown among travelers, in contrast to the popular islands of Thailand, which bring in large numbers of visitors every year. It is possible for couples to embark on a sailing journey together, during which they can explore uninhabited islands, snorkel in coral reefs that have not been disturbed, and indulge in the ultimate romantic experience in one of the world's last unspoiled paradises.

The Romance of the Arctic: Dog Sledding in Lapland

The undiscovered wonder that is Lapland, located in northern Europe, is just waiting to be discovered. Rather than the typical outings that take place during the warmer months, couples can consider braving the cold and going on a dog sledding excursion. Couples may share the pleasure of mushing their own team of dogs through snow-covered forests in Lapland, which is surrounded by the wilderness of the Arctic, while also enjoying the other one-of-a-kind activities that Lapland has to offer.

5. **Experiencing a Deeper Connection with Nature Through Off-the-Beaten-Path Travel**

The Faroe Islands are a natural paradise that few people know about

The Faroe Islands, which are located in the North Atlantic Ocean between Iceland and Norway, are still largely unknown to tourists.

THE ROMANCE OF TUSCANY, ITALY ~ 187

The stunning vistas, steep cliffs, and lush valleys of these rough and secluded islands are sure to take your breath away. Hiking expeditions, the discovery of secluded waterfalls, and the awe-inspiring natural splendor of this one-of-a-kind location are all possibilities for romantic couples. A personal and unforgettable experience with nature can be had on the Faroe Islands thanks to the pristine nature that still exists there.

The Bornean Rainforest is a Wildlife Wonderland for the Country of Malaysia.

One of the world's most ancient rainforests may be found on the island of Borneo, which is the third-largest island in the planet. Borneo continues to be a well-kept secret for travelers who are interested in having close interactions with a wide variety of unusual animals, despite the fact that tourists rush to other popular wildlife destinations. It is possible for couples to go on forest excursions, explore riverways, and look for unusual animals such as pygmy elephants and orangutans. This journey off the beaten route will instill in you a greater respect for the natural environment and help you form a connection with the astonishing variety of life that exists on our planet.

6. **Participating in Off-the-Beaten-Path Activities While Honoring the Local Culture**

   The Marvels of Matera, the Undiscovered Jewel of Italy

   It is common to refer to Matera, which is located in the southern part of the region of Basilicata, as the "City of Stones." Its ancient cave houses, which are known as Sassi, are a UNESCO World Heritage site and provide a one-of-a-kind opportunity to immerse oneself in the history and culture of the local area. Couples can connect with the friendly and inviting residents who call this hidden jewel home while discovering hidden courtyards, dining in cave eateries, and experiencing the timeless beauty that Matera has to offer all at the same time.

   Petra, often known as the Lost City, is a historical marvel located in Jordan.

   Petra, the archaeological wonder of Jordan, continues to be a place that is drenched in history and shrouded in mystery. Petra's distant position makes for a more personal and awe-inspiring experience than can be had at other well-known archaeological sites, which are typically overrun with visitors. Visitors can take their sweethearts on a romantic stroll through the mysterious Siq, take in the breathtaking views of the Treasury, and discover the city's many secret tombs and rooms. This off-the-beaten-path excursion provides couples with the opportunity to interact with the eons-old history of Petra as well as the Bedouin culture of the surrounding area.

7. Establishing Memories That Will Last A Lifetime

The Influence of Things That Are Not Anticipated

The unexpected moments, the surprises, and the one-of-a-kind experiences that can only be found while straying off the well-trodden road are what give romantic strolls and off-the-beaten-path adventures their enchantment. This is also true of off-the-beaten-path adventures in general. These unplanned meetings become cherished memories that define a relationship and deepen the bond between couples. For example, during a jungle trek in Borneo, stumbling upon a hidden waterfall; discovering a secluded beach in the Mergui Archipelago; or spending a quiet moment beneath the cherry blossoms of Kyoto.

The Value of Maintaining Connections

Couples have the opportunity to connect not only with each other but also with the world around them when they go on outings together that involve romantic strolls and off-the-beaten-path excursions. Together, a couple can produce memories that will last a lifetime and enhance the emotional bonds that bind them together via shared experiences of the wonders of nature, the richness of culture, and the depth of history. These experiences enable open communication, shared laughter, and mutual support; as a result, they build a greater sense of unity among the participants.

Couples have the opportunity to find love in unexpected places, make memories that will last a lifetime, and recognize the transformational power of engaging in activities together through activities such as romantic strolls and off-the-beaten-path adventures. Hidden treasures and less well-known adventures offer a one-of-a-kind and personal canvas on which love can blossom. While well-known locations will always have their own allure, these types of trips are ideal for couples. Couples that venture beyond the ordinary frequently find that they are rewarded with a deeper connection, stronger bonds, and the eternal magic of love. This can occur through activities such as exploring remote landscapes, interacting with the culture of the local community, or embarking on remarkable travels. These events serve to remind us that the journey, the times spent together, and the beauty that can be discovered in the unexpected are all essential components of a loving relationship. In the end, the love tales that are the most meaningful and enduring are frequently those that are written on the pages of off-the-beaten-path adventures and undiscovered treasures.

10.1 Planning Your Romantic Tuscany Trip

Since ancient times, Tuscany has been regarded as one of the most romantic locations on the planet due to the region's breathtaking scenery, extensive cultural history, and mouthwatering culinary specialties. For couples looking for a romantic trip, Tuscany provides a multitude of experiences that are guaranteed to ignite passion, develop friendships, and create lasting memories. From the rolling hills of the Chianti region to the historic streets of Florence, Tuscany is home to a variety of destinations that are perfect for couples. In this extensive travel guide, we will delve into the vital parts of organizing a romantic vacation to Tuscany. We will highlight the region's fascinating sights, cultural treasures, and gastronomic delights that are certain to make your visit an amazing celebration of love and romance.

1. The Opening Statements

   A trip to Tuscany with your significant other is like going on a journey of discovery. Here, you and your partner can lose yourselves in the region's ageless beauty, its illustrious history, and its captivating culture. Travelers are bound to be captivated by Tuscany's combination of natural beauty and cultural depth, which can be seen throughout the region, from the rolling hills of the countryside that are covered in vineyards to the bustling piazzas of cities that date back to the middle ages. In this travel guide, we will discuss the most important aspects of organizing a romantic vacation in Tuscany, such as choosing the best places to visit, indulging in the gastronomic specialties of the region, and appreciating its artistic and cultural traditions.

2. Deciding Which Location Is Best for You

   The Romantic Capital of the Renaissance is Florence.

   The city of Florence, which serves as the region's capital, is often regarded as the ideal vacation spot for married individuals who wish to experience Tuscany's rich artistic and cultural heritage. Florence is home to a plethora of ancient landmarks, art treasures, and architectural marvels that recall the spirit of the Renaissance. Some of these attractions include the world-famous Duomo and the Uffizi Gallery, as well as the charming Ponte Vecchio. Walking hand in hand down the Arno River, indulging in traditional Tuscan cuisine at one of the city's trattorias, and basking in the city's pulsating atmosphere, which is rich in artistic heritage and ageless romance, are all options for couples visiting Florence.

   Siena is known as the "Middle Ages Jewel" of Tuscany

   Couples looking for a romantic getaway into the past will find Siena, with its well-preserved ancient buildings and rich cultural traditions, to be an ideal destination. The romantic charm of the city is mostly due to the majestic Piazza del Campo, the breathtaking Siena Cathedral, and the long-standing Palio horse race. Immersing themselves in Siena's original medieval charm and dynamic local culture can be done by couples through activities such as strolling the winding alleyways, paying a visit to local artisan workshops, and indulging in traditional Tuscan specialties.

Chianti is considered to be the center of the Tuscan wine region
An idyllic getaway into the Tuscan countryside can be found in the Chianti region, which is famed for its extensive vineyards, charming villages, and renowned wineries. Chianti provides a tranquil and romantic setting for couples to relax, unwind, and taste the flavors of Tuscan wine country. This may be experienced through the stunning vineyard tours and wine tastings, as well as through the attractive hilltop towns and olive groves in Chianti. A vacation spent in the company of a loved one in an idyllic agritourismo, surrounded by the breathtaking scenery and delectable specialties of the local area, is certain to produce cherished memories that will last a lifetime.

3. Participating in Diverse Cultural Activities

   Masterpieces of Art and Architecture to be Discovered in Tuscany
   Couples have the extraordinary opportunity to immerse themselves in the region's unrivaled cultural inheritance thanks to Tuscany's rich artistic tradition, which is expressed in the works of renowned masters such as Michelangelo, Leonardo da Vinci, and Botticelli. This presents a once-in-a-lifetime experience for these couples. Couples can embark on a journey through time, exploring the artistic marvels that have shaped Tuscany's identity as a cradle of the Renaissance, while visiting Florence's historic churches and palaces. The awe-inspiring masterpieces of the Uffizi Gallery and the Accademia Gallery, as well as the architectural wonders of Florence's historic churches and palaces, can be found in Florence.

   Appreciating Music and Performance While Attending Traditional Tuscan Cultural Events
   Couples have the opportunity to interact with Tuscany's thriving artistic community by participating in the region's bustling cultural scene, which is defined by its music festivals, opera performances, and traditional folk activities. Couples will gain a deeper understanding of Tuscany's rich cultural heritage and a one-of-a-kind opportunity to embrace the region's artistic and musical traditions by going to a classical concert held in an ancient church, witnessing a local opera production, or participating in a traditional folk festival. These activities all take place in the region.

4. Participating in the Pleasures of Gastronomy

   Cuisine of Tuscany: A Gastronomic Journey Through the Flavors of Tuscany

   An unforgettable gourmet experience may be had by couples thanks to the culinary traditions of Tuscany, which are lauded for the simplicity, freshness, and robustness of their flavors. Couples can embark on a gastronomic trip that captures the essence of Tuscan food by indulging in the region's famous Chianina steaks and traditional ribollita, as well as tasting the exquisite flavors of locally produced olive oil and pecorino cheese. This type of excursion is perfect for those who want to learn more about Tuscan cuisine. Couples that visit Tuscany and participate in hands-on activities such as shopping at the regional markets, dining at trattorias that are owned and operated by families, and taking cooking classes come away with a greater appreciation for the region's illustrious culinary history.

   Exploring Tuscan Wine Country Through Tastings of Local Wine and Visits to Vineyards

   Tuscany's world-famous wine culture, which is distinguished by its rich reds, crisp whites, and
   aromatic varietals, gives couples an immersive trip into the region's vineyard-dotted landscapes and historic wineries. Tuscany is known for its rich reds, crisp whites, and aromatic varietals. Couples can indulge in the romance of Tuscan wine country and savor the region's finest vintages in a picturesque setting that embodies the essence of 'la dolce vita' by doing activities such as sampling the bold flavors of Chianti Classico and Brunello di Montalcino, exploring the wine cellars of local vintners, and participating in vineyard tours. Other activities include tasting the region's most famous wines, such as Chianti Classico and Brunello di Montalcino.

5. Creating Intimate and Romantic Moments

   Embracing the Romance of Tuscany with Evening Walks and Beautiful Views of the Sunset

   The stunning landscapes of Tuscany, which are distinguished by its rolling hills, picturesque vineyards, and old towns, provide couples with the ideal setting for private and passionate moments to share together.

   Couples may embrace the natural beauty of Tuscany and create cherished memories that capture the essence of romance and enchantment in this exquisite setting by doing things such as taking leisurely strolls in the countryside at dusk or enjoying panoramic views from medieval towers and hilltop villages.

   Spa Resorts & Health Vacation Getaways: Unwinding in the

Peaceful Countryside of Tuscany

Couples looking for the perfect getaway for relaxation, regeneration, and overall wellness can find it in Tuscany's magnificent spa resorts, which are hidden away in the region's peaceful landscapes and attractive vineyards. Couples can immerse themselves in the calming atmosphere of Tuscany and nurture their sense of well-being in a setting that promotes harmony, balance, and intimacy by indulging in couples' massages and thermal baths, as well as experiencing holistic treatments inspired by local ingredients and ancient traditions. Other options include pampering themselves with holistic treatments inspired by local ingredients and ancient traditions.

6. Planning an Experience That Will Live Long in the Memory

Cultural and Gastronomic Explorations: Striking a Balance Between Action and Relaxation

It is vital to develop a schedule for a romantic trip to Tuscany that strikes a balance between cultural exploration and culinary indulgence, times of relaxation and closeness, and other opportunities for indulgence. Couples are able to fully immerse themselves in the region's rich heritage and vibrant culture by planning their vacations to include visits to historic sites, art galleries, and vineyards, as well as leisurely walks, spa treatments, and intimate dining experiences. This helps couples form a deeper connection with one another and develop a shared appreciation for the beauty and romance of Tuscany.

Discovering Local Treasures and Unforgettable Adventures While Embracing the Authentic Tuscan Charm

Couples have a one-of-a-kind opportunity to connect with the region's genuine allure and the culture of the locals when they travel to Tuscany and explore the region's hidden gems, such as quiet villages, family-owned vineyards, and off-the-beaten-path trattorias. Couples can create original and unforgettable experiences that go beyond the standard tourist schedule and celebrate the heart and spirit of Tuscany by venturing beyond the tourist routes and embracing encounters with warm and inviting people.

The voyage of love, culture, and enchantment that is a trip to Tuscany is one in which couples may immerse themselves in the region's timeless beauty, artistic heritage, and gastronomic delights. Tuscany is a journey of love, culture, and magic. Tuscany has a plethora of experiences that celebrate the essence of love and passion, such as wandering the historic streets of Florence, savoring the flavors of Tuscan food, and indulging in the romanticism of wine country. All of these activities can be found in Tuscany. Couples can create a memorable journey that captures the heart and soul of Tuscany by carefully planning an itinerary that balances cultural exploration, culinary indulgence, and intimate moments. This allows couples to forge deep connections, ignite passion, and celebrate the transformative power of love in this idyllic and enchanting setting.

10.2 Traveling in Tuscany: Transportation and Accommodation

Tuscany, with its undulating hills, medieval cities, and attractive vineyards, is a region that attracts tourists from all over the world who come to explore its extensive cultural history and enchanting scenery. When organizing a vacation to Tuscany, it is critical to have a thorough awareness of the various modes of transportation and to choose the most suitable lodging options in order to have a trip that is both enjoyable and memorable. In this extensive guide, we will delve into the various transportation options that are available for exploring the diverse regions that make up Tuscany. We will also highlight the range of accommodation choices that cater to different preferences and budgets, which will enable travelers to navigate the region with ease and find the ideal place to call home while they are exploring Tuscany.

1. The Opening Statements
   Traveling through Tuscany is like going on a journey of discovery because tourists may completely submerge themselves in the region's illustrious past, renowned artists, and delectable cuisine. There is a wide variety of activities and sights to see in Tuscany, ranging from the historic alleyways of Siena to the vineyard-covered hills of Chianti. These activities and sights appeal to the preferences and interests of each individual traveler. In this travel guide, we will delve into the fundamentals of what it takes to have a successful trip to Tuscany. We will discuss the many modes of transportation that are at your disposal as well as provide advice on how to pick the lodging that is best suited to meet the requirements and whims of each individual traveler.
2. Available Methods of Transportation in Tuscany
   Car rental provides both independence and adaptability
   Travelers have the flexibility to explore the region at their own leisure and go off the beaten route to find hidden treasures and stunning vistas when they rent a car in Tuscany. Driving gives you the flexibility to explore remote towns, scenic vistas, and historic sites that may not be easily accessible by using public transit.
   Tuscany's major cities and rural areas are connected by highways that are kept in good condition, and these roads link to each other. In addition, there is an abundance of car rental firms at major airports

and in urban centers, each of which provides a variety of vehicle choices to cater to different travelers' requirements and tastes when they are on the road.

Train Travel: Convenient and Beautiful Routes to Explore

Travelers interested in discovering the various cities and landscapes that Tuscany has to offer can do so in comfort and style by taking use of the region's extensive and well-maintained rail network. Travelers are able to appreciate pleasant and hassle-free journeys while appreciating the magnificent vistas of the Tuscan countryside thanks to the regular train services that connect major cities such as Florence, Pisa, and Siena to one another. Because the train network also provides high-speed connections to other major towns in Italy, it is an excellent choice for tourists who prefer to visit Tuscany as part of a larger itinerary that also includes other destinations in Italy.

Traveling is Made Easier and More Affordable Thanks to Bus Services

Travelers have a variety of transportation alternatives that are both accessible and affordable thanks to Tuscany's extensive bus services, which allow them to reach a variety of locations within the area. Tuscany's metropolitan centers, rural towns, and popular tourist attractions are all connected by local and regional bus routes, giving visitors the opportunity to see the region's cultural and natural beauties while also benefiting from the convenience of economical and dependable public transit. In addition, tourists who favor planned and educational adventures that are led by experienced local guides might opt to take a guided bus tour or excursion during their time in the area.

Rental Bicycles Offer Eco-Friendly and Beautiful Ways to Explore the Area

Travelers looking for an eco-friendly and engaging approach to discover the picturesque vineyards, rolling hills, and quaint villages of Tuscany may find that exploring the region by bicycle is the way to go. It is possible for tourists to embark on self-directed or guided bicycle tours in major towns and hubs of tourism thanks to the availability of a large number of bike rental shops and tour operators. These excursions can accommodate to a variety of skill levels and preferences. Cycling across Tuscany's stunning landscapes provides tourists with the opportunity to take in the region's natural beauty, gain an intimate understanding of the culture of the locals, and appreciate a means of transportation that is both leisurely and kind to the environment.

3. **Various Options Available for Lodging in Tuscany**

The Finest in Comfort and Hospitality Can Be Found in Luxurious Hotels and Resorts

Luxury hotels and resorts in Tuscany provide a refined and sumptuous escape for discerning guests, one that is distinguished by magnificent rooms, exceptional service, and world-class amenities. These high-end institutions, which can be found tucked away within the region's picturesque landscapes and historic cities, offer a luxurious and all-encompassing experience that captures the spirit of Tuscany's renowned hospitality and refined style. Luxury hotels and resorts in Tuscany cater to the demanding needs of guests who are looking for a unique and memorable stay in the heart of this gorgeous region. Amenities such as opulent spas, gourmet dining options, and personalized concierge services are just some of the amenities offered by these establishments.

Intimate enchantment and genuineness can be found in boutique hotels and historic villas

Travelers can have a more personal and genuine lodging experience in Tuscany by staying in one of the region's many charming boutique hotels or historic homes, which pay homage to the region's long and illustrious history. These boutique businesses offer a combination of rustic elegance, personalized care, and a genuine connection to Tuscany's local culture and customs. They are located in historic buildings that have been renovated, as well as villas that date back centuries and traditional farmhouses. Boutique hotels and historic villas in Tuscany offer a one-of-a-kind and immersive stay that captures the essence of the region's enduring fascination. Guests can expect to find rooms that have been individually created, lovely courtyards, and culinary options that are locally inspired at these properties.

Tranquility in the countryside and genuine experiences can be found in agriturismos and farmstays

Agriturismos and farmstays in Tuscany offer visitors an authentic and immersive lodging experience that pays homage to the region's agricultural past and the calm of rural life. These working farms and rural retreats offer visitors the chance to experience the slower pace of rural life, indulge in farm-to-table cuisine, and participate in agritourism activities that highlight the region's agricultural traditions and sustainable farming practices. They are set amongst the picturesque countryside and landscapes dotted with vineyards. Agritourismos and farmstays give a true and enriching stay for tourists who are looking for an authentic connection to the agricultural roots of the region. Agriturismos and farmstays offer comfortable guest lodgings, farm-fresh meals, and panoramic views of Tuscany's natural splendor.

Apartments for Self-Contained Living and Vacation Rentals: Your Home Away From Home

Travelers can experience the comfort, convenience, and privacy of a fully equipped living space in Tuscany by staying in one of the region's vacation rentals or self-catering flats. These accommodations can be found throughout the region's bustling cities as well as its peaceful countryside. Travelers who are looking for a personalized and independent experience during their time in Tuscany can choose from a wide variety of vacation rental properties, ranging from quaint flats in the heart of ancient city centers to spacious villas in the midst of remote rural settings. Vacation rentals respond to the various requirements and tastes of these kinds of visitors. Vacation rentals and self-catering apartments provide guests the option to create their own one-of-a-kind and unforgettable experiences while enjoying the luxuries of a private property in the heart of Tuscany. Amenities found in vacation rentals and self-catering apartments include modern conveniences, fully equipped kitchens, and extensive living rooms.

VI. Organizing Your Trip Schedule and Itinerary

Developing an Itinerary That Strikes the Right Balance Between Comfort and Exploration

It is crucial to construct a balanced timetable that allows for both comfortable relaxation and immersive exploration of the region's different attractions and landscapes while you are organizing your trip itinerary in Tuscany. Travelers can enjoy a seamless and enriching travel experience by incorporating a mix of transportation options, such as car rentals for scenic drives, train travel for city-to-city journeys, and guided tours for cultural excursions. This allows travelers to combine the convenience of modern transportation with the authenticity of local discoveries and experiences.

Choosing a Lodging Option That Suits Your Needs While Staying Within Your Means

The preparation of your trip relies heavily on carefully selecting the most suitable lodging options available in Tuscany. When choose a place to stay in this diverse region, visitors should give some thought to their individual preferences, particular interests, and financial constraints. There are a variety of options available in Tuscany that can satisfy a variety of travel preferences and types, including those wanting luxury, authenticity, or independence. Explore a variety of lodging alternatives that are in line with your concept of a memorable and comfortable stay in the middle of this engaging region after you have determined the amenities, location, and atmosphere that are most important to you during your time here.

Traveling in Tuscany provides visitors with a plethora of alternatives for modes of transportation and places to stay, all of which are tailored to meet the varied requirements and tastes of tourists who are interested in seeing this wonderful region. Tuscany offers a diverse range of experiences that capture the essence of its rich culture, natural beauty, and historic charm.

Whether you choose to embark on scenic drives through the countryside, indulge in luxurious stays at upscale hotels and resorts, or immerse yourself in the rural tranquility of agriturismos and farmstays, Tuscany provides a variety of opportunities for you to enjoy these aspects of the region. You can embark on a flawless and memorable journey across Tuscany by carefully preparing your transportation and hotel arrangements. This will allow you to forge a deeper connection with the region's timeless allure and create memories that will last a lifetime that celebrate the heart and soul of this fascinating place.

10.3 Romantic Gestures and Activities

Romance is a language that is understood by people all across the world and throughout all of time. It is the element that binds love stories together and strengthens the connection between partners in a relationship. It doesn't matter if you're in a brand-new relationship, celebrating decades together, or trying to reignite the flame of a long-term partnership: romantic gestures and activities are an essential component in the process of cultivating love and connection. In this article, we will delve into the world of romantic gestures and activities, covering everything from straightforward and sincere demonstrations of love to thrilling experiences that might rekindle the flame that once existed between a couple.

1. The Opening Statements

    Making romantic gestures and participating in romantic activities together is the foundation of a loving relationship. They deepen the tie between spouses by creating moments of intimacy, desire, and connection between themselves and their partners. It is crucial to have the understanding that romance is not simply a one-time event but rather a continuous effort to keep the flame of love alive. Although the idea of romance is extremely personal and might differ from one relationship to another, it is essential to have this understanding. The purpose of this guide is to encourage couples to infuse their relationships with love, passion, and deep connections by examining a wide variety of romantic gestures and activities that range from the traditional to the unexpected.

2. Insignificant Acts That Have a Substantial Effect
   The expression of affection through written communication, such as love letters and notes
   Expressions of love that have stood the test of time include love letters and handwritten notes. In this day and age of technology, it can be quite meaningful to take the time to put your thoughts and feelings down on paper. Whether it's a letter written from the heart that's tucked away in a lunchbox or a note written out of the blue that's stuck to the mirror in the bathroom, these seemingly insignificant acts have the power to provoke profound feelings and keep the connection alive.
   A Pleasant Awakening Surprise: Breakfast in Bed
   A simple yet meaningful act would be to wake up your sweetheart with breakfast in bed as a pleasant surprise. It demonstrates thoughtfulness, care, and the desire to spoil the person you care about. The aroma of freshly brewed coffee, the sight of warm croissants, and a message written by hand can put a grin on your partner's face first thing in the morning.
   At-Home Date Nights with a Romantic Twist: Tips for Creating an Intimate Atmosphere
   A night out on the town with your significant other doesn't have to include a meal at a fancy restaurant for it to be romantic. Dinners with candles lit, quiet music playing in the background, and home-cooked food all contribute to the creation of a warm and inviting ambiance at home. It is the ideal chance to get back in touch with one another and spend some quality time together without any interruptions.
   Verbal Affection Complements and Expressions of Appreciation
   A sincere praise or some kind words of thanks can go a long way toward helping your partner experience feelings of love and admiration from you. The emotional connection between you and your partner can be strengthened when you make it a habit to regularly express your admiration for the traits that they possess, such as their intelligence, sense of humor, or kindness.
3. Excursions and Uncharted Territory

Weekend Getaways: An Opportunity to Break from the Normal
An wonderful method for adding excitement to your relationship is to take it on the road for a few days, either to an unfamiliar location or to one of your all-time favorites. The flame of passion can be rekindled

by venturing into unfamiliar territory, participating in novel pursuits, and exchanging novel experiences with one another.

Road trips on the spur of the moment: making the most of the trip

There is something inherently romantic about putting together a suitcase, getting on the open road, and exploring new locations with the person you care about. It's possible for a couple to have just as much fun on a road trip as they do at their final destination, thanks to the ability to make spontaneous pit stops, take in breathtaking scenery, and listen to music together.

A Cosmic Connection Can Be Made Through Stargazing

An wonderfully beautiful moment can be had by simply dozing off beneath a clear night sky and taking in the view of the night sky's constellations. It is an opportunity to contemplate the immensity of the cosmos while basking in the comforting presence of your significant other.

You may perform stargazing from the comfort of your own backyard or from a remote location in the woods.

Exciting Experiences Outside Bring People Closer Together

Exciting and adventurous new experiences can be introduced into your relationship by participating in outdoor activities such as hiking, kayaking, or zip-lining. The connection between partners can be strengthened when they share the excitement of completing difficult tasks and witnessing the beauty of nature together.

VI. Love is Expressed Through Creative Acts

Art Classes for Couples: Letting Your Creative Side Shine

It is possible that taking art classes together, whether they be in pottery, sculpting, or painting, can be a great opportunity to express your creativity and connect with one another on a deeper level. It is an excellent opportunity to acquire new knowledge, encourage one another in their artistic aspirations, and produce works of art that will be remembered for a long time.

Creating Original Works of Art Through Songwriting or Poetry

An act of love that is both intensely intimate and artistically expressive is to compose a song or poetry for one's lover. It is a means to memorialize your emotions in a form that is both singular and enduring. You do not need to be an expert artist; what matters is the amount of thought and effort that you put into it.

Memory Book: Recording Your Travels and Memories

Putting together a memory book as a group activity is a heartwarming way to reflect on the times you've spent together in the past. Include images, souvenirs, and notes about the journeys you've taken together as a pair as well as the important milestones you've reached. It is a great keepsake, and throughout the years, you may keep adding to it to make it even more special.

Mystery and Thrills Await You on Your Unexpected Date Night

An wonderful method to bring a sense of intrigue and excitement into your relationship is to surprise your partner with a date night that you have planned in advance. Keep the specifics a mystery from your travel companion, and take them on an exciting and unplanned journey.

V. Reestablishing a Connection with Nature

Getaways to Beaches: Peace and Quiet by the Sea

The calm atmosphere that is created by the sound of the waves, the warmth of the sun, and the sensation of the sand beneath your feet makes it possible to relax and interact with others. Getaways to the beach give the ideal setting for romance with opportunities for long strolls along the water's edge, picnics at sunset, and other water-based activities.

Retreats in the Woods: Finding Calm in Nature

Couples have the opportunity to completely submerge themselves in the calming presence of nature when they take a trip to the woods and stay in a cottage or cabin. A profound sense of connection can be fostered by activities such as going on hikes through the woods, spending time together in front of a crackling fire, and taking in the beauty of the natural world.

Unplugging and letting go of stress during camping trips

Couples who go camping in the great outdoors are more likely to interact with one another and less likely to be distracted by their digital devices. Building a campfire, going stargazing, and telling stories to one another beside the tent offer a chance to get away from the hustle and bustle of everyday life and find the pleasure in the basics.

Rides in Hot Air Balloons: Taking Flight Together

A journey in a hot air balloon gives you and your companion a one-of-a-kind vantage point of the world below, as well as a sensation of excitement as you ascend above the countryside. The mix of awe-inspiring scenery and the thrill of doing something exciting together makes for an experience that is difficult to forget.

VI. Dining and the Pleasures of the Table

Creating a Common Bond Through the Art of Cooking

An activity that may be both pleasurable and intimate for two people is preparing a dinner together. Find a new recipe, go shopping for fresh ingredients, and then cook together while appreciating the tastes that you and your partner have crafted together. It is an opportunity to spend quality time together while indulging in a wonderful meal that was prepared at home.

Foodie Adventures: An Exploration of the Gastronomic World

Sharing the joys of good food is a wonderful way to bring people together, so it's a great idea to try out some new eateries, food markets, and other kinds of culinary experiences. Exploring a new place through its cuisine can be an adventure that leaves your mouth watering, whether you choose to indulge in fine dining or explore dishes from throughout the world.

A Sensory Experience Through the Tasting of Wine

Couples can engage their senses and expand their knowledge of wine production and appreciation through activities such as touring wineries and taking part in wine tastings. The flavors, fragrances, and enticing ambiance of vineyards can all be enjoyed to the fullest on this excursion.

Picnics are a form of outdoor dining.

A simple yet romantic way to spend a meal together in the great outdoors is to plan a picnic in a park, by the river, or in the countryside. This is a terrific opportunity to get to know each other better. Bring over some of your favorite dishes, a warm blanket, and a bottle of wine, and enjoy the scenery while you dine outside in the fresh air.

In a relationship, the cultivation of love and a sense of connection is greatly aided by the use of romantic gestures and activities. The possibilities for romance are endless; it can take the form of simple acts of affection, thrilling experiences that bring thrills and passion, creative expressions of love that celebrate individuality, reuniting with nature to find calm and peace, savoring culinary delights that indulge the senses, or any combination of these.

It is critical to make a consistent investment in the development of important and unforgettable moments with your partner, regardless of where you are in the progression of your relationship. The precise romantic gestures and activities that a couple chooses to engage in may vary from one another, but the aim behind them should always be the same: to honor the love that exists between two people and to strengthen the bond that exists between them. Remember that the actual essence of romance lies in the work, thoughtfulness, and genuine love that you bring to each moment you enjoy with your partner, whether it's a handwritten love letter, an impromptu road trip, a shared artistic project, or a picnic by the beach. Whether it's an artistic endeavor, a collaborative artistic endeavor, or a seaside picnic.

10.4 Packing for Tuscany: Essentials and Wardrobe Tips

Cotton shirts, skirts, and shorts are great examples of the types of lightweight, breathable apparel you should bring to Tuscany because of the region's hot summers. If you want to stay cool during the day, using lighter colors that reflect the sun is a good idea.

Footwear that is comfortable is recommended because you will be doing a lot of walking while touring the cities and countryside of Tuscany. Bring a pair of walking shoes or sandals that are comfortable for strolling around cobblestone streets and vineyard tours. For evenings out, you might think about purchasing a pair of shoes that are stylish but also sturdy.

Essentials for Layering: Bring a thin sweater or cardigan that you can easily wear over your clothing in case the temperature drops in the evening or if the weather takes an unexpected turn. In addition, you should bring a jacket that can be worn in a variety of ways as well as a windbreaker that is waterproof, particularly if you intend to travel during the fall or spring months.

Sun Protection: To protect yourself from the harsh sunlight of the Mediterranean, especially during the warm months of the year, be sure to bring along some necessary sun protection goods with you on your trip. These include sunglasses, a hat with a broad brim, and sunscreen.

Accessories That Can Serve Multiple Purposes Remember to bring along accessories that can perform multiple functions, such as a scarf or shawl, in the event that the weather takes a turn for the worse. When going out and about in the cities and towns, you might want to think about bringing along a crossbody bag or a small backpack to carry your essentials in.

Evening Attire If you want to experience the lively nightlife that Tuscany has to offer, make sure to pack a few sophisticated outfits that are appropriate for attending cultural events or having supper at luxury restaurants. A night out in Tuscany may call for something as simple as a smart casual dress or as sophisticated as a pair of dressy trousers paired with a fashionable top.

When going to places of worship or religious significance, it is important to wear clothing that shows respect by covering your shoulders and knees. This is especially important if you are going to a church. Bring along a lightweight shawl or scarf in your bag in case you need to cover your shoulders.

It is important to remember to pack in accordance with the activities you have planned as well as the season in which you will be traveling. You can ensure that your vacation to the stunning region of Tuscany will be one of the most pleasurable and memorable of your life by packing clothes that are adaptable, comfortable, and contain all of the necessary accessories.

www.ingramcontent.com/pod-product-compliance
Lightning Source LLC
LaVergne TN
LVHW011937070526
838202LV00054B/4683